BERTHE MORISOT
The Correspondence

BERTHE MORISOT:

*The Correspondence
with her family and her friends*
MANET, PUVIS de CHAVANNES, DEGAS,
MONET, RENOIR and MALLARMÉ

Compiled and edited by
DENIS ROUART

Translated by
Betty W. Hubbard

With a new introduction and notes by
KATHLEEN ADLER and TAMAR GARB

MOYER BELL LIMITED

Published in 1987 by Moyer Bell Limited

Preface and correspondence © 1957 Percy Lund, Humphries and Co. Ltd.

Introduction and Notes © 1986 Kathleen Adler and Tamar Garb

This edition published by arrangement with
Camden Press Ltd. London, England

Library of Congress Cataloging-in-Publication Data

Morisot, Berthe, 1841–1895.
Berthe Morisot, The correspondence
with her family and friends

Translation of: Correspondance de Berthe Morisot
avec sa famille et ses amis

Bibliography: p.237 Includes index
1. Morisot, Berthe, 1841–1895 — Correspondence.
2. Painters — France — Correspondence. I. Rouart, Denis.
II. Title.
ND 553.M88A3 1987   759.4 [B]   86–28626
ISBN 0–918825–50–4 (HB)
0–918825–62–8 (PB)

Set in 10pt. Imprint
by Inforum Ltd, Portsmouth
Printed by A. Wheaton and Co. Ltd
Exeter, Devon, United Kingdom

CONTENTS

List of Illustrations   vii

Berthe Morisot: Principal Dates   ix

Introduction
by Kathleen Adler and Tamar Garb   1

Preface
by Denis Rouart   13

THE CORRESPONDENCE
compiled by Denis Rouart

The Family. Early Stages in the Life of an Artist   15

Edouard Manet. Edma's Marriage   30

The War of 1870 and the Commune   53

After the War: Cherbourg, Saint-Jean-de-Luz, Madrid,
Maurecourt   75

Death of Morisot Père. First Impressionist Exhibition.
Berthe's Marriage   91

Great Auction. Trip to England. Second Impressionist
Exhibition   99

Death of Madame Morisot. Impressionist Exhibitions.
Birth of Julie Manet. Bougival. Nice   113

Death of Edouard Manet. Death of Eva Gonzalèz.
Impressionist Exhibition in London. The House
in the Rue de Villejust. The Manet Sale   130

Trip to Holland. The Circle of Friends of the Rue de
Villejust. Jersey. Valvins   142

The Villa Ratti at Cimiez   159

The Subscription for the Olympia. Mallarmé's Lecture on
Villiers de L'Isle Adam. Mézy   170

Death of Eugène Manet. Exhibition at Joyants. The Rue
Wéber   188

Valvins. The Duret Auction. Summer at Portrieux.
Death of Berthe Morisot   201

Notes
by Kathleen Adler and Tamar Garb   213

Further reading   237

Index   238

LIST OF ILLUSTRATIONS

All the reproductions at head and foot of chapters are of drawings by Berthe Morisot

BERTHE MORISOT, sanguine 12
BERTHE MORISOT, crayon 17
EDGAR DEGAS, *'Yves Gobillard'*, crayon 42
EDOUARD MANET, *'Eva Gonzalès'*, lithograph 50
BERTHE MORISOT, crayon 59
EDOUARD MANET, *'La Guerre Civile'*, lithograph 68
BERTHE MORISOT, water-colour 77
EDGAR DEGAS, *'Edouard Manet'*, crayon 86
BERTHE MORISOT, crayon 103
BERTHE MORISOT, crayon 112
EDGAR DEGAS, *'Edouard Manet'*, crayon 129
AUGUSTE RENOIR, *'Julie Manet'*, charcoal 150
BERTHE MORISOT, crayon 158
BERTHE MORISOT, sanguine 167
BERTHE MORISOT, crayon 178
BERTHE MORISOT, water-colour 193
BERTHE MORISOT, sanguine 211

The original quarto 1957 edition contained an additional 11 plates

BERTHE MORISOT: PRINCIPAL DATES

1841   Born 14 January in Bourges, the third daughter of Edmé Tiburce Morisot and Marie-Josephine-Cornélie Thomas.

1855   Family moved to Rue des Moulins (now Rue Scheffer) in Passy, Paris.

1857   Morisot sisters had first drawing lessons with Geoffroy-Alphonse Chocarne.

1858   Berthe and Edma continued lessons with Joseph-Benoît Guichard. Morisot registered as copyist at the Louvre.

c.1860   Family moved to Rue Franklin, Passy.

c.1862   Berthe and Edma had lessons from Camille Corot.

1863   On Corot's recommendation, they commenced lessons with Achille-Francois Oudinot. Summer at Le Chou, Auvers.

1864   Berthe and Edma exhibited at the Paris Salon. They exhibited again in the Salons of 1865–8. Summer at Beuzeval.

1866   Visit to Quimperlé and Ros-Bras.

1867   Through Henri Fantin-Latour, met Edouard Manet. Visit to Petites Dalles.

1869   Edma married Adolphe Pontillon and gave up painting. Visit to Lorient.

1870-1   Morisot showed in 1870 Salon. Remained in Paris during the Siege and Commune. Visited Saint-Germain-en-Laye and Cherbourg.

1872   Exhibited at the Salon. Visited Saint-Jean-de-Luz and Spain.

1873   Exhibited for the last time at the Salon. Visited Petites Dalles and Fécamp.

1874   Participated in the co-operative juryless exhibition entitled *Première exposition de société anonyme des artistes peintres, sculpteurs, graveurs, etc*, now known as the first Impressionist exhibition. Visited Fécamp.
22 December – married Eugène Manet. Moved to Rue Guichard, Passy.

1875   Participated in auction at the Hôtel Drouot in Paris with Claude Monet, Pierre-Auguste Renoir and Alfred Sisley.
At Gennevilliers. Travelled to London and the Isle of Wight; visited Cambrai.

1876   Participated in second Impressionist exhibition. Moved to 9 Avénue d'Eylau, Passy.
1877   Participated in the third Impressionist exhibition.
1878   *14 November* – birth of Julie Manet.
1879   Visited Beuzeval.
1880   Participated in fifth Impressionist exhibition.
1881   Participated in sixth Impressionist exhibition. Purchased land in Rue de Villejust (now Rue Paul Valéry), Passy. Summer at Bougival, 4 Rue de la Princesse. Winter in Nice, Hotel de Richmond.
1882   Participated in seventh Impressionist exhibition. Summer at Bougival.
1883   Moved to Rue de Villejust.
1884   With Suzanne Leenhoff Manet, Gustave and Eugène Manet, organized posthumous retrospective exhibition and auction of work of Edouard Manet. Summer at Bougival.
1885   Worked in Bois de Boulogne. Visited Vieux-Moulin, near Compiègne; Belgium and Holland.
1886   Participated in eighth Impressionist exhibition. Visited Jersey and Gorey.
1887   Showed at Georges Petit's International Exhibition; exhibited with Les XX in Brussels; included in Durand-Ruel's New York Impressionist exhibition. Visited Plâtrèries, near Touraine.
1888   Stayed at Cimiez, Villa Ratti.
1889   At Cimiez until May. Visited Vassé.
1890   Stayed at Mézy, Maison Blotière.
1981   At Mézy.
1892   *13 April* – death of Eugène Manet. First one-person exhibition at Boussod and Valadon, Paris. Visited Mesnil and Vassé.
1893   Moved to 10 Rue Wéber, Passy.
1894   Exhibited with *Le Libre Esthétique*, Brussels. First State purchase of one of her works, *Jeune femme en toilette de bal* (Musée d'Orsay). Visited Brussels; Brittany.
1895   *2 March* – death of Berthe Morisot.

INTRODUCTION

In 1904 Wynford Dewhurst wrote in *Impressionist Painting* of the women painters associated with Impressionism, Berthe Morisot, Mary Cassatt, Marie Bracquemond and Eva Gonzalès: 'For future historians they will prove an interesting study'. It has taken some eighty years for a political and social climate to emerge in which such a study is seen to be relevant. It is not a coincidence that a book of *Women Impressionists*, a monograph on Berthe Morisot, and the republishing of the Morisot correspondence, long out of print, should appear within a year of one another, or that books on Cassatt have proliferated in the last few years.

The source of this new interest in women artists, and specifically women associated with Impressionism, is twofold. The last decade and a half has seen a revolution in the understanding of the political nature of knowledge, especially its often unstated sexist assumptions. Emerging from the women's movement in the early 1970s, a growing number of women concerned with the history of visual images, and particularly those produced within that range of cultural practices called 'art', have sought to question the received wisdom of standard academic accounts of their history. The Modernist assumptions which coloured the historicizing narratives produced during the 1930s, 40s and 50s, were thrown into crisis by the political events of the late 1960s. These also have been opened to question, being both tenaciously defended and virulently opposed. Impressionism, too, has been subjected in recent years to some rigorous revision. The paradigm of Impressionism constructed by John Rewald in *The History of Impressionism*, first published in 1946, with its emphasis on a group of artists united in their opposition to academic conventions, marginalized the role played in Impressionism by women like Morisot and Cassatt, and presented a falsely homogenous view of a movement which recent research has shown to be varied and disparate in its aims and practices.

The nineteenth century artist Berthe Morisot occupies an interesting position in this conjunction. With the recent interest in women's art, a new awareness of her work has emerged.[1] At the same time, through the revision of the traditional construction of Impressionism, a theoretical space into which Morisot can be slotted has been opened out. She, and artists like Caillebotte, Bazille and others, are being reassessed in terms of a new expanded canon, while the old 'core' group (John Rewald's 'gang of four' consisting of Pissarro, Degas, Renoir and Monet) is subjected to rigorous analysis, with differences and dissimilarities emphasized to represent the lack of cohesion and order which in fact characterized the Independent exhibitions of the 1870s and 1880s.[2]

Feminist art history is central to the re-evaluation of previously ignored or undermined women artists. It has set out to 'question the litany' – that tradition of 'great' artists that art history has constructed – and the criteria by which it is formulated and evaluated. The 'woman artist' has been one of the primary sites for feminist interventions into academic discourses.

Early feminist writings sought to establish and proclaim the very existence of women artists and a number of important exhibitions in the 1970s set out to discover the extent of women's involvement in art and to make available through the exhibitions and the catalogues which accompanied them the range and quality of women's achievements. As part of the project of feminist art history, it became necessary to examine the language in which art history is written in order to uncover the hidden assumptions about creativity and gender which it encodes. One of the earliest of such 'recuperative' exhibitions, *Old Mistresses*, held at the Walters Art Gallery, Baltimore, in 1972, used this title to refer to the 'unspoken assumption in our language that art is created by men. The reverential term "Old Master" has no meaningful equivalent; when cast in its feminine form . . . the connotation is altogether different, to say the least'.[3] The use of the word 'woman' as the adjective preceding 'artist' implies that the latter is an exclusively male term. The necessary use of the term 'woman artist' when referring to a female practitioner exposes the implicit contradiction of this juxtaposition. Woman as artist is constructed through her difference to 'artist' as a generic, normative and exclusively male term.

It was Linda Nochlin who first challenged the institutional discourses of art history from a feminist perspective in her seminal essay 'Why Have There Been No Great Women Artists?' in 1971. She framed the question in the language of standard academic art history in order to expose its misguidedness and asserted that such a formulation took no account of the historical, sociological and institutional frameworks within which women's practice has functioned.[4] Later feminist accounts have distanced themselves from the notion of 'greatness' completely, uncovering and analyzing the ideology of

Introduction

'genius' as it emerged in the nineteenth century. This coincided with a circumscribing of women's roles to the domestic.[5] Examinations of how dominant definitions of culture have misrecognised women's position, undervaluing their achievements and discriminating against their forms of cultural expression, have formed some of the most crucial feminist interventions of the past few years.[6] In the context of this new atmosphere of discovery, and the thirst for knowledge on the part of the female reading and viewing public, the women's presses and publishing houses have flourished and even mainstream publishing houses have begun to include women's issues and histories in their lists.

Berthe Morisot and her female predecessors and contemporaries have been accorded new attention in accounts of women's history. All of the publications of the recent past which have sought to chart the history of women's production in art have included a re-evaluation of her work. But the new consciousness which has bequeathed this attention has not been without its ideological differences, even from within feminism. While some historians have sought to celebrate women's work within a self-enclosed, linear, and often spurious historicist tradition of women's achievements, others have rejected such a construction as essentialist and unhistorical, arguing that it is only in relation to institutions, wider artistic and political debates and discourses around sexuality that women's work can be assessed. With Morisot the problem is to some extent exacerbated by her easy recuperation into Modernist culture. As a member of an *avant garde* art group which has been heroicized in the Modernist art canon, she can, with some perfunctory apologies for years of neglect, be reinstated without any need to question the mechanism of her and many others' exclusion from visible history. Indeed, it is because of her involvement with *avant garde* circles and her adherence to the conventions of picturing inscribed in these circles that she has remained relatively visible as an artist, even when most women artists, some extremely successful in their own time, have been all but forgotten. She poses few problems for traditional art history and is easily reincorporated into a tradition whose criteria for assessments of 'quality' and 'significance' remain unchanged, and whose writing remains unproblematically framed within what Derrida has called phallogocentric language. The crucial problem that faces all feminist art historians is, of course, one of language with all its significations. In what language can one speak of women's art production when the language available, that of art history, is precisely that through which women's production has traditionally been undermined? Most women's work cannot be assessed in terms of the

3

criteria of quality which modernist art history has erected for itself without being found wanting, or insignificant, and it is here that Morisot's work is an interesting exception. Few people balk when one declares that one is working on Morisot. Most have a generous word or two to say about how she has been undervalued, how beautiful her work is, how central she was to the Impressionist enterprise. To succumb to this sort of flattery, although tempting, is dangerous. For in accepting these criteria in the assessment of Morisot, one is unwittingly collaborating in the dismissal of all other forms of creative activity in which women have participated in the last hundred years, whether these be flower painting, tapestry, needlework, suffrage banners, illustration or watercolour. The fact that most educated, western art audiences have little difficulty in accepting a re-inscribing of Morisot into an unproblematic tradition whilst the work of Rosa Bonheur, Louise Abbema, Louise Breslau, (to name only a few painters widely acclaimed in their own lifetime) continues to be regarded as at best an historical curiosity, at worst 'bad art', is little cause for celebration.

What needs to be confronted is Modernism itself and the ways in which its discourses institutionalize sexism. Modernism's foregrounding of certain technical qualities, (flatness, self-conscious assertion of surface, painterliness, all invoked within the interests of artistic autonomy) can and should be challenged from a feminist perspective. We have to resist succumbing to the temptation of unquestioningly ascribing value to certain women's work in terms of these criteria, for to do this is to allow only a few women artists into the exclusive (male-constructed) 'great canon'. With Morisot the temptation is great. But it is salutary to remember that where women have been admitted into the privileged canon of 'great art', their work has both been explained and explained away by virtue of its 'femininity'.

It is the very way in which Morisot is positioned in texts on Impressionism, that fecund moment for Modernist art history, which is interesting. One such important text is the compilation by Denis Rouart (Morisot's grandson) of the *Correspondence of Berthe Morisot with her Family and Friends*, a document which constitutes a particular representation of a nineteenth century woman artist and has formed an important element in the formulation of a now tenacious and repeatedly reproduced construct or image of Berthe Morisot, artist, woman and intuitive modernist. It would be an error to see this collected correspondence as a neutral document, providing empirical evidence for the events and concerns of Morisot's life. Of course it must partially fulfil such a function and it does provide a useful chronological framework around which her 'life' can be mapped. (The dates are not always to be trusted, however, as the footnotes accompanying the text demonstrate, and it is often difficult to work out the chronology from Rouart's ordering. Included in this edition, therefore, is a separate list of significant dates and events plus newly marginated dates accompanying the letters). But it must be remembered that the process of arranging letters to construct a sequential narrative which ostensibly documents a 'real life' and reads as biography presents a fortuitous arrangement of 'facts' relying on the availability of material, the censorship of the collator and the physical circumstances which made communication by letter necessary. It is difficult to know what Rouart chose not to publish and it is certain that letters, unpublished here, exist. The Morisot correspondence was not written with a view to publication and its collation and chronological structuring presents an artificial ordering and a selective view. Rouart's own prejudices are revealed early on: 'Her letters almost never touch on fundamental questions . . . They deal with accounts of exhibitions and Salons, events in Paris during the siege and Commune, travel impressions, invitations to dinner or to the country', he declares in a statement which all too clearly reveals his adherence to a view of art which perceives of the social as outside its domain, and in these terms renders irrelevant some of the most important political events of Morisot's time. It is a function of the questioning of the adequacy of such a model for artistic practice and historical inquiry that it is precisely those areas which Rouart disclaims as significant that appear to the art historian of the 1980s to be crucial. As such, the letters are both more important than Rouart suggests and more frustrating. For example, they give us only a tantalising hint of Morisot's contacts with art dealers, and we must assume that even if relevant documents existed in the 1940s when Rouart was engaged in compiling the publication, these would have been deemed irrelevant to proper art historical concern and therefore omitted.

The republishing here of Denis Rouart's compilation of the *Correspondence of Berthe Morisot with her Family and Friends* constitutes an interesting document: useful not only because it will make available some of the primary texts (the letters themselves) around which the image of Berthe Morisot has been historically constructed, but because we are provided with the edited, mediated version of her life with its linking passages. The drawings at the head and foot of chapters were originally included with no explanation for their presence and operate as if they were a 'natural' extension of the artist's personality. As such,

5

this publication provides the writings and selected graphic works produced by a nineteenth-century woman and her circle as mediated by her grandson in the 1940s and 50s. It is Rouart's Morisot which this document presents and it is, significantly, Rouart's Morisot which has determined much of the writing on this artist in the last thirty years. In addition to the compilation of the letters, he has been the author of a number of exhibition catalogues produced on the artist's work and, together with other members of the family, has been the major source of 'information' on Morisot's person and practice.

Rouart's image of his grandmother (his mother was Julie Manet) was itself produced through a number of French accounts, some of them eye witness accounts, of the artist by friends and acquaintances, and has in turn contributed to the perpetuation of a particular and highly selective view of the artist. While English language treatments of the art of the period in which she lived have repeatedly minimized her contribution, most often mentioning her in relation to various male artists, and regularly referring to her as a pupil of Corot or Manet, in French accounts Morisot has been consistently visible. But this visibility has been of a particular and astonishingly tenacious kind. From the first writing on her in the late 1860s to the most recent account of her production written in 1982, her work is repeatedly interpreted through a series of assertions on the nature of women and their relationship to art and its history. Impressionism, in turn, has readily been explained as a 'naturally' feminine style.

One of the first and most frequently repeated strategies used to cope with her position as a female member of a 'radical' art group and as an *haute bourgeoise* participating in what is perceived as an exclusively man's world, has been to construct her as exceptional. Unlike other women artists, both before and during her own time, she, it is claimed, does not fall into the inevitable traps which beset women artists. Her contemporary Théodore Duret claimed of one of her works that 'The impression is that of a work feminine in its delicacy, but never falling into that dryness and affectation which usually characterize a woman's workmanship'.[7] George Moore, writing in 1898, stated that Morisot's pictures 'are the only pictures painted by a woman that could not be destroyed without creating a blank, a hiatus in the history of art'.[8] As late as 1982, Jean Dominique Rey expressed the view that Morisot outstripped her contemporaries in 'femininity' when he stated that 'in comparison with the other two artists of her day or shortly afterward – Mary Cassatt and Suzanne Valadon – she has the advantage of never having fallen into the trap of excessive muscularity or falsely masculine toughness'.[9] The quality which differentiates

Morisot from her female colleagues is repeatedly seen to reside in her 'femininity'.

In turn, her painting 'style', Impressionism, is produced as a method which is suited to and the natural expression of an appropriately feminine temperament. 'Impressionism' is offered as the answer to the problematic of Morisot's 'femininity', the problem posed by a skilled and prolific professional woman painter in a world which deemed such activities to be 'unfeminine'. From as early as the 1870s Morisot's manner of working was seen to reflect a naturally feminine sensibility; it was repeatedly called 'charming', 'feminine', 'delicate' in a way which transposed onto the paintings those characteristics most favoured in the middle class woman of the time. In the texts of the 1890s, the decade which saw her first one-person show, the purchasing of one of her paintings by the French state for the Musée du Luxembourg, her death in 1895 and a large retrospective exhibition mounted in 1896, the claim that her work was a true expression of femininity and that Impressionism was an appropriately feminine style was so often repeated as to achieve the status of a cliché. The overriding view of Impressionism, both in Academic and Symbolist circles, was that it involved the apprehension and recording of surface appearances only. Women, as George Moore wrote, were believed to have a nature 'more facile and fluent than man's'. They, he believed, 'do things more easily than men, but they do not penetrate below the surface. . .'[10] Morisot's merits, according to the Symbolist writer Teodore de Wyzewa, writing in 1891, lay in not attempting to assume a masculine vision, but in being content to see things with her own (woman's) eyes. He explained how the very marks made by Impressionist painters are expressive of the qualities intrinsic to women, for example, the exclusive use of bright and clear tones parallel the lightness, the fresh clarity and superficial elegance which make up a woman's vision. It was appropriate, in his view, that women should not be concerned with the deep and intimate relationships of things, but that they should see the 'universe like a gracious and mobile surface, infinitely nuanced. Only a woman', he declared, 'has the right to rigorously practice the Impressionist system, she alone can limit her effort to the translation of impressions'.[11] In keeping with ideas about women's innate superficiality and intuitive working processes, it was widely held that it was in the painting of still lifes and genre scenes that women could most excel. As little scholarly background was required for the successful exploration of these genres, women were thought to be ideally suited to them. The Impressionist subject matter, with its elevation of the everyday and its scrutiny of ordinary objects, could be seen to be suited to the limitations of the female mind, and the Impressionist method to the limitations of female skill.

What representations of Morisot as the intuitive feminine painter do not take into account is the fact that she was one of many women working as professional artists at the period and that these women represented in their working methods the full range of artistic practices. Few used the painterly brushmarks and sketchy surfaces that are characteristic of much of Impressionist painting and most were unaware of Morisot's existence, preferring to define their context as that of the Paris Salons or alternatively the women's Salon which emerged in the early 1880s as a significant forum for the display of women's work. If Morisot shared any technical qualities with her contemporaries, it was with male artists like Renoir and Monet. They, like her, were committed to an aesthetic of apparent spontaneity, using separated brushmarks, revealing the light ground of the canvas, eliminating the use of the tar-based pigment bitumen, and striving to approximate the effect of natural light. The resulting 'delicacy of touch', present particularly in the work of Monet, Renoir, Sisley, occasionally Pissarro, and Manet, was part of a conscious strategy to free painting from the academic emphasis on finish, *le fini*, the highly polished surface with no traces of individual brushmarks, characteristic of French nineteenth century Salon painting, and can in no way be attributed to the outpouring of an essential femininity.

Accompanying the idea that Impressionism was a naturally feminine style of painting was the notion that Morisot's working methods flowed intuitively from her inner self without conscious intervention or mediation. As Paul Valéry was to put it: 'the peculiarity of Berthe Morisot . . . was to live her painting and to paint her life, as if the interchange between seeing and rendering, between the light and her creative will, were to her a natural function, a necessary part of her daily life'. Rouart himself declared: 'She allowed no ideology or spirit of any system to diminish the spontaneity of her art . . . she could not help painting the people and things she loved because painting to her was a form of loving', and, on another occasion, 'to paint for her was as vital as to breathe'. But the letters themselves do not allow this view to be sustained. If anything they represent her often painful and intense involvement with painting, described once as a 'pitched battle with her canvasses'. Several letters give a glimpse of her as a *pleinairiste* striving to record fugitive effects of light and movement and articulating this as an artistic aim which presents problems. In 1875 she wrote to her sister Edma Pontillion from Cowes on the Isle of Wight: '. . . it is the prettiest place for painting – if

8

one had any talent. I have already made a start, but it is difficult. People come and go on the jetty, and it is impossible to catch them. . . . There is extraordinary life and movement, but how is one to render it?' Equally, the letters represent a woman who is absolutely aware of the ways in which she and her colleagues are received in the press, and is mindful of the reception of her own work and that of her associates. Rouart's linking text, therefore, gives no real account of the extent of Morisot's involvement with the members of the Impressionist group although the letters themselves evidence her close relationship with many of them. As a woman she could not be part of the free exchange of ideas which took place in the cafés of Paris but through her close friends Manet and Degas, her husband Eugène Manet, her friend Puvis de Chavannes and her colleagues Monet, Pissarro, Renoir and Cassatt, with all of whom she shared varying degrees of intimacy, she must have been both privy to and involved in the artistic debates of her time. While the letters do not provide a systematic account of her painting procedures, nor much technical information about her palette, materials or working methods, they do enable us to anchor Morisot firmly within a specific artistic context and testify to her involvement with the thinking of the group of artists with whom she identified. Indeed her exhibition strategy (she exhibited in seven out of the eight 'Impressionist' exhibitions) is itself sufficient testimony to her commitment to the idea of independent exhibiting forums, and the agony of anticipating response and perusing the newspapers for reviews as revealed in the letters is ample evidence of the seriousness with which she regarded her enterprise. The letters do not *explain* her continued participation in the organisation and perpetuation of the independent shows but they hint at the sense of community felt by Morisot and her colleagues which helped to buttress them against the hostility which their work generated in some quarters. For instance, Morisot wrote to an aunt in 1876: 'If you read any Paris newspapers, among others the *Figaro*, which is so popular with the respectable public, you must know that I am one of a group of artists who are holding a show of their own, and you must also have seen how little favour this exhibition enjoys in the eyes of the gentlemen of the press. On the other hand, we have been praised in the radical papers, but these you do not read. Anyway, we are being discussed, and we are so proud of it that we are all very happy'.

But if the image of Morisot as an intuitive, unreflective artist, living out her natural femininity through her painting, cannot be sustained, neither can she be accommodated by today's feminist art historians in the role of the lofty female ancestor, politicized about her gender and willing to confront the institutionalized sexism of her time. The French Third Republic saw an unprecedented and prolonged intensification of feminist struggle which surfaced in the art world through the campaigns to open the Ecole des Beaux-Arts to women and in the critiques of the sexism of the exclusively male Salon juries which emerged in the press. Morisot played no part in the separate women's art world that centred on the *Union des Femmes Artistes* and its regular *Salon des Femmes*. This does not mean that she was unaware of the debates around women's position, or the restrictions, social and psychic, which were placed on women's lives, but that her responses are not unified and worked out. They are often confused, ambiguous, and tellingly self denigrating. On one occasion she sought to comfort her sister Edma, who on marrying was forced to give up her rich artistic life for the role of wife and mother. In consoling her, though, Morisot succeeded in belittling her own choices: 'Men incline to believe that they fill all of one's life, but as for me, I think that no matter how much affection a woman has for her husband, it is not easy for her to break with a life of work. Affection is a very fine thing, on condition that there is something besides with which to fill one's days. This something I see for you in motherhood. Do not grieve about painting, I do not think it is worth a single regret'. Years later, she was unable to overcome her inhibitions and attend one of her close friend Mallarmé's all-male (except for the presence of his wife and daughter who provided refreshments) Tuesday 'evenings'. She had often joked that she and her daughter would 'dress as men' and attend one of these gatherings, but she declined his invitation saying that 'the schoolbench would intimidate us too much'.

The 'evidence' provided in the letters is fragmentary and suggestive. It presents a woman, often confused, filled with self doubt, frequently discontent, berated by her mother for her stubborness and selfishness, envied and admired by her sister, a loving parent, an exacting partner in need of reassurance, a devoted friend and above all, a committed artist. The texts of the letters themselves, many of them by Morisot's family and friends, which emphasize her stubbornness and self absorption, provide a telling contrast to the idealized mythic representation of the enigmatic, even muse-like figure, which so many accounts of Morisot construct. It is the tension between Rouart's seamless introduction on the one hand, and the glimpses of the lived experience of a nineteenth-century woman with all its confusions and attendant problems on the other, which constitute part of the interest of this publication. As documents, the letters cannot sustain a mythic reading of the personality of Berthe Morisot from any point of view. But as pieces of factual evidence which allow us to map out some of the events of her life and work, or as fragments which in their juxtaposition with Rouart's assertions reveal the operation of historical misreading, the collected correspondence is interesting in itself and in the uses to which it has been and might yet be put.

Kathleen Adler
Tamar Garb
London, 1986

NOTES

1. The National Gallery of Art, Washington D.C., is to stage the first substantial one-person exhibition of Morisot's work outside France in 1987.
2. An example of such a revision is the exhibition shown in Washington D.C. and San Francisco, *The New Painting: Impressionism 1874–1886*, and its accompanying catalogue by Charles S. Moffett *et al*, Oxford 1986.
3. A. Gabhart and E. Broun, *Walters Art Gallery Bulletin*, vol. 24, no. 7, 1972, quoted in R. Parker and G. Pollock, *Old Mistresses: Women, Art and Ideology*, London 1981, p. 6.
4. L. Nochlin, 'Why Have There Been No Great Women Artists?', in E. Baker and T. Hess (eds.), *Art and Sexual Politics*, New York 1973, pp. 1–43.
5. There are a number of feminist histories which analyze women's position in the nineteenth century. Important analyses of the implications for women of the notion of genius appear in C. Duncan, 'Virility and Male Domination in Early Twentieth Century Vanguard Art', *Art Forum*, vol. 12, no. 4, 1974, reprinted in *Feminism and Art History*, N. Broude and Mary D. Garrard (eds.), New York 1982; and R. Parker and G. Pollock, *Old Mistresses: Women, Art and Ideology*, London 1982.
6. Important here is the wealth of feminist material which seeks to re-evaluate women's participation in 'craft' and traditionally female art forms. See, for example, R. Parker, *The Subversive Stitch*, London 1984.
7. Théodore Duret, *Manet and the French Impressionists*, London 1910, p. 173.
8. George Moore, 'Sex in Art', *Modern Painting*, London and New York 1898, p. 234.
9. Jean Dominique Rey, *Berthe Morisot*, Naefels 1982, p. 80.
10. George Moore, ibid., p. 226.
11. Teodor de Wyzewa, *Peintres de jadis et d'aujourd'hui*, Paris 1903, p. 216.

PREFACE

BERTHE MORISOT was above all else a painter. The whole of her message is contained in her paintings; it is not to be sought elsewhere. Her letters almost never touch on fundamental questions; intimate confessions or ideas on art are not found in them. They deal with accounts of exhibitions and Salons, events in Paris during the siege and the Commune, travel impressions, invitations to dinner or to the country. Many of them are addressed to famous contemporaries, including Mallarmé, Berthe Morisot's faithful friend who kept her regularly posted on life in Valvins and its inhabitants.

These letters of Mallarmé to Berthe Morisot will certainly not be the least of the attractions of this collection – these letters in which he manages to say the most trivial things in a way that proves once again that poetry has no specific subject matter, but can be found anywhere provided one is able to discern it. They reveal a distinct affinity between Mallarmé and Berthe Morisot, whose work characteristically reflects her ability to extract and express the poetry inherent in seemingly commonplace objects. In her paintings she made use of no elements other than those of everyday life. Her models were persons of her immediate entourage – her daughter, her nieces, her maid, the daughter of the concierge or of the corner grocer – all caught in their most habitual postures. The objects she painted are the things she used every day, and within the reach of her hands. The setting is that in which she lived; as Paul Valéry said, "she lived at the approaches of the Bois de Boulogne, which supplied her with all the landscape she required". But her brush divested prosaic objects of their ordinary appearance and meaning, and endowed them with a new and luminous magical quality.

This capacity for perceiving the poetry inherent in the everyday world, and of communicating it to others, is the gift of only a few beings – persons with a special grace that makes them authentic artists or poets. Both Mallarmé and Berthe Morisot were such specially favoured beings, although they did not use the same medium. For Berthe there could be no question of using any medium other than painting; to paint was for her as vital as to breathe. If it ever occurred to her to express herself in any other medium, the idea could have been only an early fantasy, which her first experience dispelled. She became aware of her potentialities only in struggling with problems of pictorial realization.

Since she was in no sense a writer, she could not communicate in her letters the poetry with which she endowed all things in her paintings. Therefore these letters are valuable chiefly as documentary sidelights. We have brought together the communications of Berthe Morisot preserved by the recipients and their descendants; to these we have added all letters addressed to her, which she thought it advisable not to destroy, and which have thus come down to us. The collection is sufficiently complete to re-evoke the atmosphere in which she lived. Her parental home, the artists she knew, and finally the small but choice circle of friends that formed about her, come to life in these letters, which constitute an intimate testament that is sometimes noble in its simplicity, and sometimes moving in its discretion and reserve.

D.R.

THE FAMILY
EARLY STAGES IN THE LIFE OF AN ARTIST

THE milieu in which the life of the Morisots evolved was quite bourgeois, but they were regarded as a somewhat original family. Although they were essentially middle-class as regards property, status, occupations, domicile, acquaintances, and many of their habits, they displayed traits of character and behaviour that contrasted with this background.

Monsieur Morisot had originally planned to become an architect like his father, but eventually gave up this idea in order to enter the Government service. He served as prefect in a number of French cities, and subsequently held the offices of *conseiller référendaire* (chief clerk of the commercial court), and that of *conseiller-maître* of the Cour des Comptes (chief councillor of the Audit Office).

In Madame Morisot's family, whose name was Thomas, a male member was usually a chief treasurer and paymaster, this office being passed on from father to son. Of her grandmother and mother, Berthe Morisot tells us in her notes:

"Marie-Caroline Mayniel, my grandmother . . . Great wit, straightforward like a boy, a very clear, very keen intelligence; her education at Saint-Denis, which was at that time regarded as superior, had given her, besides facility in French, which she wrote most correctly, scattered notions of ancient history and some rudiments of science. But her mind went no further; she firmly believed that this was the apogee of female intellectual development, and she would bewilder me with questions concerning Arabia Petraea or other similarly interesting topics.

"Marie-Cornélie Thomas, my mother, married very young to Tiburce Morisot, very much in love with him, delighted in social life, and was intoxicated with her success; however, she was safeguarded from the constant attentions of what became something like a little court by her devotion to her husband. She had wit, grace, and kindness, and wrote with great freedom and charm. Although she had not received much schooling (because of her sensitive nature, her mother had kept her at home and taught her only spelling, often boxing her ears in the process), she was well read and sociable, and an agreeable companion; she had the gift of pleasing people, and an amiable disposition.

"There were in Limoges two old bachelors, the brothers Lajeunesse, who were employed in the offices of the prefecture. We used to make fun of their name – it was in such comical contrast with their age. One of them, who suffered from some ailment, said to Louisa one day when she inquired about his health: 'I was quite ill this morning, but I saw *Madame la préfète* pass by, and I felt better at once'.

"And the fact is that my mother was at that time the picture of youth and happiness."

Marie-Cornélie Thomas was sixteen when she left the boarding school to marry Edme-Tiburce Morisot. Three years later she bore him a first daughter, Yves, who was soon followed by Edma and Berthe. She was mother of three children when she was only twenty-two. Her son, Tiburce, came into the world a few years later.

In the course of Monsieur Morisot's progression from one administrative post to another, his family lived successively in Valenciennes, Bourges (where,

in 1841, Berthe was born), Limoges, Caen, and Rennes, and finally settled in Paris in 1851.

In 1857 – Morisot was then councillor of the Cour des Comptes – Madame Morisot took her daughters to the painter Chocarne. Tiburce, their brother, describes their initiation into the world of art:

"Père Chocarne gave his lessons in a low-ceilinged room, darkened by curtains, on the third floor of a house in the Rue de Lille. On an easel, in a sumptuous frame, was displayed the portrait of a young woman. Her coiffure was so *comme il faut* and her hair was so carefully waved that it was surprising to see her nude to the waist; she was sitting on a patch of grass dotted with daisies, of which one could count the petals. A drapery in the classical mode enfolded her legs, her arms were raised in a gesture of supplication, and her gaze was fixed tearfully on a superlatively blue sky dotted with superlatively white clouds. This work was called *Invocation* and the serial number under which it was entered at the Salon was still pasted under the title plate at the bottom of the frame. Père Chocarne held Delacroix and, as he called it, the perverted romantic taste responsible for the fact that his masterpiece, though accepted by the Salon, had come back to him without having found a buyer.

"His teaching began with lessons of crosshatch. Crosshatch with straight strokes for plane surfaces, or with curved strokes for convex or concave surfaces, very compact crosshatch for shadows, less close for half shadows, and very loose for chiaroscuro. The result called to mind the dreadful landscapes in the showcases of shops that sell funerary articles.

"Oh, those wretched homecomings, those trips from the Rue de Lille to Passy! Silent, irritable, Monsieur Morisot would lead the three small girls in cloaks, long skirts, and bonnets tied under the chin, a little flock reduced to a stupor by the Chocarne instruction. They would walk to the Place de la Concorde, and board a horse-drawn omnibus that ran on rails, a service recently inaugurated to connect Paris with Saint Cloud. On leaving this conveyance at the barrière des Bonshommes, at the foot of the Trocadéro, they climbed that slope, with its trees planted in quincunxes, and reached the Rue des Moulins, the present Rue Scheffer, at the corner of the Rue Vineuse."

The three sisters soon had their fill of these dull lessons. Yves declared that she would rather be a dressmaker if that was drawing. But Berthe knew that it was not, and despite her disgust at this wretched teaching, she still wanted to become a painter – on condition that her teacher was changed.

Her mother took her and Edma to the painter Guichard, a native of Lyons,   *3*
whose wife kept a boarding school for girls in the Rue des Moulins. The
first lesson, an oral one, was devoted to values; then Guichard asked each
girl to prepare for the next lesson a sketch containing a white accent. Berthe
painted a landscape that included a flock of sheep, proving that she had
understood the lesson perfectly. In the course of his subsequent teaching,
Guichard found confirming evidence of talent in his pupils.

According to Tiburce: "Guichard was almost frightened by his discovery.
Taking my mother aside, he asked her whether she had given careful thought
to the matter. 'Considering the character of your daughters', he said, 'my
teaching will not endow them with minor drawing room accomplishments;
they will become painters. Do you realize what this means? In the upper-
class milieu to which you belong, this will be revolutionary, I might almost
say catastrophic. Are you sure that you will not come to curse the day when
art, having gained admission to your home, now so respectable and peaceful, will become the sole arbiter of the fate of two of your children?'

"My mother smiled, and declared herself ready to face these chimerical
dangers.

" 'In that case, Madam,' said Guichard, 'the first thing to do is to apply
for permission for them to work in the Louvre, where I shall give them
lessons before the masters'."

The copying sessions in the Louvre began in the spring of 1858. There   *4*
the girls met Bracquemond and Fantin-Latour, pupils and friends of   *5*
Guichard. After another two years Berthe, realizing that she had got all she
could from this teaching, voiced her determination to follow her compelling
desire to work in direct contact with nature. Sick at heart, Guichard, who
regarded outdoor painting as the negation of art, saw himself compelled to
yield his place to Corot.

Completely won over by Corot, Berthe and Edma soon established a   *6*
close friendship with him. They persuaded their parents to spend the
summer of 1861 at Ville d'Avray, in order to be near him. In Paris, Corot
became a habitual guest of the Morisots, who now occupied a house in the
Rue Franklin, near the Trocadéro. He dined there every Tuesday – having
obtained permission to smoke his pipe after dinner. He liked the cultured
atmosphere of this home, where he was received with simple and affectionate hospitality.

In the summer of 1862 Edma and Berthe went to the Pyrenees where
they travelled about on horseback and on mules. In one of her letters Yves

wrote: "Last night father said that we shall never be apprised of all the incidents of your trip, but that you will be telling them to each other for the next six months in the solitude and secrecy of your rooms. Anyone curious to know your impressions will have to listen at the keyhole."

Immediately on their return to Paris, they resumed work with Corot, and painting occupied them unremittingly in the year that followed. In the summer of 1863, Corot, planning to go on a journey and realizing what a void his absence would cause, asked a fellow painter, Oudinot, to take his place with his pupils and to accompany them in their outdoor studies. A very handsome young man proud of his broad shoulders and his athletic physique but a good companion – such is the picture of him as drawn by Tiburce who describes this period in Berthe's life:

"Oudinot was invited to Le Chou, a little village on the bank of the Oise, on the towpath between Pontoise and Auvers, where the Morisots had rented a little farm house. There the *études de bord de l'eau* were pursued with ardour. At that time Daubigny was living with his son Charlot at Auvers; he was working on a formidable imperial commission – a painting of the chateau and park of Saint-Cloud, a project that seemed to bore him greatly. He invited the Morisots to lunch in his home. A delightful old couple – Daumier and his wife – together with Oudinot and Guillemet, Edma, Berthe, and their mother, were the guests at table. In the foyer of the house there was a large decorative panel representing Don Quixote bent over the carcass of the dead Rosinante, a fresco brushed in by Daumier in his own furious style."

Ever more in love with their outdoor studies, Edma and Berthe persuaded their parents to spend the following summer (1864) in Normandy. The Morisots found a delightful windmill for rent at Beuzeval. They were charmed by the courteous welcome accorded them by the landlords, who were none other than Léon Riesener, descendant of the great cabinet-makers and cousin of Delacroix, and his wife. Of this couple and their home Tiburce writes:

"This charming old man, so young, so fresh, so spruce despite his white hair, was simple and yet had a sophisticated urbanity. He was a passionate rose grower. In February 1848 he was trimming his rose bushes in the little garden in front of his little house at Cours-la-Reine, when an echo of gunfire led him to inquire what was going on – he had been completely unaware of the advent of the Second Republic . . .

"At Beuzeval, Berthe devoted herself with feverish zest to her work; with her knapsack on her shoulders, her pointed stick in her hand, and laden with all the apparatus of the landscapist, she would vanish for entire days among the cliffs, pursuing one motif after another, according to the hour and the slant of the sun. One night she reported that she had met an interesting old peasant who had kept her company, watched her paint, and voiced opinions that were not at all stupid. 'It's strange', she said, 'how persons like this are misjudged; they are more sensible than many men of the world!'

"She continued to meet this man every day, until she learned that her good friend was a former inmate of the Toulon penitentiary. 'Now I understand', she said, 'why he keeps saying all the time, I don't like the south, I don't like it.' "

A letter from Corot roused in her a hope – though it proved vain – that he would come to Beuzeval:

"Madam, thank you for your letter; I am very busy this season, but I shall have a talk with Oudinot about finding a moment for paying you a little visit at Beuzeval. A thousand compliments to Monsieur Morisot and to your dear children. They should work hard and perseveringly, and should not think too much about Papa Corot. Nature itself is the best of counsellors."

At Cours-la-Reine, the Rieseners had as a tenant the Duchess Colonna, a sculptress known under the name of Marcello. She and Berthe became close friends when Berthe was studying sculpture under Aimé Millet during the winter of 1863-1864. Millet was then at work on a series of medallions representing the Muses, which were later to ornament the façade of an apartment house, at 14 Quai de la Mégisserie; he used Berthe as his model for the plaque placed above the portal. There is a touching letter of his to Edma and Berthe:

"I am writing these few lines to you in the house of your teacher Oudinot, unable as I am to resist the pleasure of letting you know what is being said in this room. Oudinot is showing your studies, your paintings to Monsieur Busson, a colleague of his, and my pen is too slow and too awkward to reproduce the latter's exclamations. He is absolutely overwhelmed. Three times he has asked your age, he refuses to believe that young ladies of nineteen and twenty can paint with such force and truth.

"Why are you not here, in some corner! Then you could form some estimate of the sincerity of those who urge you to persevere. Oudinot mentioned that you are reproached for painting like Corot. In the first place, it is not true in the absolute sense, and, further, I regard this kind of reproach as praise.

"Monsieur Busson is entirely of our opinion. How and why can they, at their age, wish to be no one's children? Was not Raphael the son of Perugino? Strong men have always been the sons of their masters until years, work, and experience enabled them suddenly to blossom and to become themselves; I shall go further and say that this is both inevitable and good . . .

"Bear in mind that I am giving myself the pleasure of telling you all this without anyone here suspecting to whom I am writing. I am sitting behind the draperies; I assure you that it is a deep joy for me to see thus that Oudinot's pains are so well rewarded by a colleague whose sincerity is beyond any doubt. I repeat, my pen is too slow, and I have to omit the best of what they are saying. I have no other New Year's gift that I can send you, but if you two find in these indiscreet lines a bit of encouragement to make you continue in the path you are following, it will make me very happy."

In 1864, Monsieur Morisot was appointed chief councillor of the Cour des Comptes, and moved to the other side of the Rue Franklin. The principal building of this block is still preserved; it is occupied by the Collège Saint-Louis de Gonzague. Tiburce thus describes the family home:

"This very simple house, standing in a beautiful garden with large shade trees, to which doors on the ground floor gave direct access, was attractive in itself. My mother was a born hostess: she received her visitors simply, without the slightest ostentation. The cordial welcome she gave her guests put them all at their ease; she not only had wit, without in the least claiming to have it, she also stimulated wit in those with whom she talked. And the intimates invited to the Tuesday dinners knew that they need have no fear of meeting tiresome or boring people.

"The two Ferrys frequented this house assiduously for a long time. They were determined climbers, then at the beginning of their careers. Jules was full of political ambition, and Charles was eager to make money. Jules was the brilliant intellectual, Charles the man about town. At the time they were inseparable; they lived together, chiefly on the money provided by Charles, who had no definite profession, but earned enough here and there to supplement their meagre private means, whereas Jules, a lawyer without clients and a writer who managed only with difficulty to publish a few occasional articles in *Le Temps*, certainly did not earn the modest cost of his personal subsistence. The two brothers stood by each other firmly, at the same time they were flawlessly correct. They were too polite, both of them, not to display some interest in the two young ladies of the house, who were neither ugly nor stupid, but Charles' politely fervid attentions to Edma and Jules' to Berthe met merely with aloof response, manifested even more politely. And this is not surprising, since these two strapping and somewhat burly fellows were completely lacking in elegance, in a period that carried social refinement to an extreme.

"It was from my father's candid talk – he was at that time an official of the Cour des Comptes – that Jules Ferry, not too discreetly, took the material for his pamphlet, *Les Comptes Fantastiques d'Haussmann*. The success of this facile play on words for the first time revealed to the public at large the existence of a Ferry other than the fashionable bootmaker . . .

"Little Charles Durant, a long-haired, romantic native of Lille, who had assumed the name of Carolus Duran, who wrapped himself Spanish-style in a red-lined *capa*, and who was always ready to draw an imaginary sword, was introduced in the Rue Franklin by a mutual friend, under the pretext that he could give advice to the young painters. His paintings were only halfway liked, his coxcomb poses were thoroughly disliked.

"Alfred Stevens and his wife, a young couple of striking beauty, radiant with happiness and *joie de vivre*, became close and dear friends. My father, under the amused eye of my mother, displayed a somewhat old-fashioned gallantry toward the delightful Madame Stevens, who – without being affected by it, of course – received not without pleasure the delicate and discreet homage of a still elegant sexagenarian. As for Stevens, he had a dazzling cleverness, without ever stooping to the vulgarity of a drawing-room wag."

Although Morisot was only a tenant of the place, he had a studio built in the garden for his daughters. There they copied the Italian studies they had borrowed from Corot who found Edma a more disciplined pupil than Berthe; the latter took liberties of which he disapproved. On one occasion he forced her to do over again a copy in which a step of a staircase was missing; on the other hand, he made an exchange of pictures with Edma. This may have been the reason why Berthe destroyed her copies of Corot. Only her canvas showing the terrace of the Villa d'Este at Tivoli has survived, having been salvaged by Pissarro.

In 1865 Edma and Berthe decided to send their paintings to the Salon. While they were staying with their uncle Octave Thomas at Chartres, their mother, in a letter to the eldest sister, gave them an account of her visit to the Salon:

"And so I walked out of the show. I had to go to a great deal of trouble to find Berthe's and Edma's pictures, the ones listed as second exhibits. Berthe's *Chaudron* is all the less conspicuous because it is not hung in the hall of the M's. Edma's *Pot de fleurs* can barely be detected in one of the square rooms at the end, next to Guillemet's landscape. It cuts a sorry figure – it has proved to me once again that the taste of the vulgar is not to be despised.

"Berthe's *Femme* is well lighted, at least in the mornings, and does not look bad at all; I saw people pointing it out to one another, and Monsieur Ducasse, whom I met there, gave it his full endorsement. Edma's *Paysage* has the honour of being on the line, Monsieur Belly is in the Salon Carré. Mademoiselle Riesener's exhibit is perched high above her father's, which I did not like. As for Fantin, he seemed to me just bad; two of the Daubignys' paintings are very good, but it must be said that the father's official picture of Saint Cloud is not much appreciated by anyone . . . Monsieur Oudinot is unfair in his estimate of Monsieur Flahaut; I thought his landscape there was charming. I did not find his second entry. As for Monsieur Oudinot, I did not fail to notice his large canvas, which does not look bad, but I was unable to discover his *Fontainebleau*, which, it is said, is lost in the vaulting."

On May 8 she wrote to Edma:

"This morning I received a letter of apology from Monsieur Oudinot whom I expected to lunch or to dinner yesterday. He had been in the country for a few days, and thus did not meet your uncle. I have not seen him again since your departure, consequently I have not talked with him about the exhibition. All in all, Monsieur de Tasia showed but scant interest in your affairs, since your *Vase* is lost somewhere at the end of the rooms, and Berthe's *Femme* is not marked with its serial number. It also looks as though your paintings, particularly the flowers, are not varnished; this is being too careless of the appearance of a painting when the aim is to please untrained eyes susceptible to a first impression. I think that next time you should show less contempt for ordinary people, even if they can make themselves heard only through your father or mother."

While she was making her plans for the summer, Madame Morisot wrote to Berthe:

"Dear Berthe, I know that your correspondence means about as little to you as your own flesh and blood, and so I am far from asking you for a letter. If I could only know that you are in good spirits and never tired, it seems to me that I would lack nothing for my happiness . . . My Bagnoles scheme is thus on the verge of succeeding . . . Does this project appeal to you? Yesterday morning we thought of something else – namely, of giving your father and you the diversion of a long trip to Italy during September and October. He decided that he could not afford it this year because of the studio; moreover, the prospect of such a tête-à-tête would dismay you more than it would please you."

The Morisot family stayed at the Petites Dalles in Fécamp, and then again at Beuzeval, where Berthe became more friendly with Rosalie Riesener who also painted.

In the years that followed, Berthe and Edma continued to send their works to the Salon. Berthe exhibited views of Paris and studies made in Normandy and in Brittany, where they went in 1866 and 1867. They painted at Rosbras on the Pont-Aven River, and then, on their mother's advice, they went to Douarnenez. There, each day on awakening, Berthe was enchanted to see from her window hundreds of barges with blue nets stretched on glistening masts that were impregnated with morning light – a sight she was to remember all her life. On September 10, Edma received a letter from her mother containing the following passage:

"We have more or less promised Oudinot that we will spend Thursday at Noisy. Corot is to be there. He is saying to us now that we should not have sent anything important to Versailles – that nothing sold there for more than 150 or 200 francs. He went to the studio to see what would in his opinion be most suitable for this exhibition, and he found nothing of Berthe's but this *Falaise du Desert*, and of your things, *Dives*, and the *Pot de fleurs de Fontainebleau*. He did not find the Dinard canvas that Berthe worked on to send to the last exhibition."

In 1867 the eldest Morisot sister, Yves, became engaged, and she referred to this event in the following letter addressed to Berthe:

"That day Monsieur Gobillard and I went for a walk, as I told you we had intended, at Ville d'Avray. On the bank of the pond we found Papa Corot set up under his landscapist's umbrella. I read in his subtle eyes that he sensed the situation at once, and it was no doubt to express his interest that he pressed my hand more cordially than usual."

Yves' husband, who had lost an arm while serving as a commissioned officer in the Mexican war, held the post of tax collector at Quimperlé; that was why her sisters returned to Brittany that year. Once again they went to Rosbras. The letters addressed to them by their mother at this time show the interest she took in their painting. One of these letters, written to Edma, contains an amusing reference to Manet whom the Morisots were to meet only the following year:

"I am frightened by what I have done. I have hung the canvases in the studio. Your father says that you will undo my work the moment you come back, and your brother says that you will be justified in doing so, because I ought not to meddle in other people's business. For my part I think that it is even less the proper business of Louis to pile up helter-skelter all those luckless canvases, some of which are torn, and to efface drawings by crowding them in among the paintings; yet he has to clean the place, and it is somebody's business to put a little order into this great mess. It breaks my heart to see all the works of each season thrown into corners; some of them bring back to me impressions of the moments when you were doing them – all your efforts, your labours, a part of yourselves. Now I need your directions in order to know what is to replace the canvas that is now at Cadart's. There are the *Effet de neige*, the *Etude de Fontainebleau, Dives*, the *Pot de fleurs*, and *Trousseauville*. May I also send Berthe's *Italienne* and all the paintings that have been exhibited so far? It would be a pity to have all these canvases unmounted just to economize on stretchers. The cost of labour would be perhaps the same . . .

"La Loubens has returned on Sunday . . . She told us that she had spent the evening at Manet's, that there was a great deal of talk about you, that Fantin expressed his admiration of your beauty, saying that he had never seen a creature as ravishing as you were a few years ago. So it is emotion that keeps his hat on his head! His friend Manet then told him that he should have proposed to you, but he answered that he had always heard that you did not want to marry. There was less talk about your painting, it seemed to me, than about your person. However, Manet mentioned the offer he had made to an art dealer when he saw something of yours that charmed him. Since painting is the thing that interests Madame Loubens least, she doubtless did not feel obliged to discuss this subject at length. She was asked what artists you are seeing, and at the mention of Carolus, everybody protested and found fault with him. Their disparagement was expressed chiefly in one remark: 'You don't call yourself Carolus if you were born in Lille.' They ridiculed Chatillon's painting, they made computations proving that Manet is losing about 150 francs a month with his exhibition. And that is approximately the substance of what may interest you of that conversation . . .

"Tiburce is a little better; I don't know what he is doing at his Ministry of Finance. He never leaves before a quarter to ten at the earliest, he takes an hour and a half for lunch, and he also has plenty of time to himself until four o'clock when the attendance list is circulated. Is all this quite proper? You know that one cannot venture a remark – or at least that it would be futile to do so: his answer is that he is not out of order, and that he has no intention of making a show of zeal."

On Tuesday, July 23, Madame Morisot wrote:

"I began to be full of hope, dear Bijou. The sky was clearing, but now it is again dark and rainy. What can be done about it? You do not tell me whether you have decided to return to Quimperlé. Yet this would be preferable, if life at Rosbras gets complicated because of the motion of that unfortunate boat. Why not look for something on your beach? I imagine that even if you were on the other side of the water, you would still have to cross it. I have never seen you choose something that is within your reach. Imagination is all very well, but not when it makes things more difficult. The true science of life, in little as well as in great things, consists always in removing difficulties, in facilitating things, in adjusting yourself to them rather than in trying to make them adjust to you. However, in this instance I am arguing without knowledge. Still it seems to me that even if you had only sandy moors with a horizon, some children or some animals that you could pose in your own way at the cost of a few pennies, this would be enough to arrange a picture. If it gave the sad and wild aspect of the region, it would be all the better. And the boat – why don't you, since it is so heavy, moor it at the shore and install yourself in it? You have both said that the view from a boat is charming. I know that you are shrugging your shoulders, and I can see Berthe's sneering and annoyed expression as she says to me: 'Why don't you take the brush yourself?' So this will be enough – indeed it is enough.

"Now I must tell you that Monsieur J. Ferry has asked me to let you know that your paintings are attracting much attention at Cadart's. He was looking at the pictures that were displayed in the window, in the company of a friend who is a connoisseur or an artist, I don't know which, who stopped in front of the pictures saying: 'Look, this is odd (in other words, this is something). By whom is this?' They could not read the name, and decided it must be that of some Englishman – Morz, or Monse. Finally, as they went by again, and again were attracted by the picture, they looked more closely, and Jules read your name at the very moment when people inside the gallery were turning the picture around in order to see it better. This seemed to him to be a good omen; however, the picture has not been sold, and I am still wondering how artists who depend on selling their work manage to live. The successful ones are surely not those who, like you, want to pursue art solely for art's sake. And this poor *Trousseauville* – why is it doomed not to see the light of day? Rosalie seemed to me more sensible when she said: 'Some works are made to be exhibited, others to remain in the studio; one must follow the public taste if one wants to be successful'. If this is true at all, it applies in regard to selling. Detrimont meant the same thing when he said to us: 'Why place at a *dealer's* only things that will not sell? The idea is to exhibit a little of everything – with some works one makes one's reputation among artists, with others one does business, if possible' . . .

"Carolus Duran came last night, apologizing a thousand times for not having come sooner. Your father despite his illness received him cordially and made an effort to stay up considerably beyond his bedtime. He talked mostly about himself, about his studio which is almost ready, and about his left wrist, which he sprained in a fall.

"He looked a little embarrassed or absentminded, for he came back continually to the subject of his recent difficulties with his workmen. He is to leave soon for Hyères, to spend some time with that very rich English friend about whom he has already taken occasion to tell you. He feels very sorry for you because I am venturing to clean the studio, and advises you to have a little patience and not to look for anything except what you find readily before you. I told him that this advice had already been given you, to be sure with less authority, but that it was otherwise exactly identical. For the rest, he is very nice, though too full of himself. Is it that he seeks to inspire confidence by flaunting an unassailable faith in his own future and great satisfaction with his present situation? Or is it a defect of character? I do not know. He accuses himself of having too much pride. He asked me very naïvely to console you in his behalf for not having seen *Hernani* – it is turgid, it does not bear scrutiny, etc. etc. . . . He says that he has more than two hundred canvases to disclose to the public eye, some of which he would call masterpieces if he had a quarter of Manet's cocksureness. As a matter of fact, I like him and don't like him, he pleases and displeases me. I have always had a horror of anything that is not absolutely simple, and if he were not so pretentious, I think I would find him very appealing.

"He promised me to introduce us to François. We parted the best of friends, without, however, saying anything about meeting again."

On August 19, she wrote to Berthe:

"Saturday I went to see Carolus without Madame Chatillon because she had left. It was quite daring on my part to give myself thus the airs of a connoisseur; it would be even more so to give you my impressions; however, I would not let a little thing like that stop me. I thought that he was using sombre, raw tones that are not quite true to life, that his portraits of men have much force and vitality, but that his female figures are lacking in grace. His compositions are broad and poetic, but there are only three, and they are to see the light of day only if he finds the right place for them and raises sufficient funds – conditions that he will find it difficult to achieve. I detest the backgrounds of his landscapes; I find them harsh and artificial, and then it is a scenery I am not familiar with, that of Italy and Spain. I pretended to look at everything, making a few excuses on the score of my ignorance, but without concealing my opinions. If I had told him that I thought all this was very ugly, he would not have cared a bit – he is certainly not lacking in self-confidence . . . He was lost in admiration of a head he had sketched the day before; he advises you not to give in to your fits of discouragement, for he himself is sometimes discouraged. He seemed greatly pleased with my visit, and thanked me effusively for it. I do not think that he has been very extravagant; the place is painted in red distemper, he has a green sofa and a few matching chairs, and curtains of the same shade concealing very dirty doors. But it's clean and tidy – quite unlike your studio. I can even understand the pleasure of working in an orderly place; above all one probably wastes much less time. Incidentally, I think that it would be difficult to find people more careless than you all are; you surely waste more, and always lack all sorts of things . . . It is a pity that your cousins are not making their tour in Brittany; you might have joined them. If you are comfortable at Rosbras, couldn't you arrange to spend the first fortnight of September there? Do whatever pleases you, and manage as best you can. If your health is good, that is a great point. Yesterday Tiburce went to bathe at Bougival, despite the doctor's orders, and he ran into Jules Ferry; they merely met and passed on, a little embarrassed no doubt at finding themselves at that place. It is said to be a very rustic little place used for rendez-vous by a very frivolous society, and that if a man goes there alone, he returns in company of at least one other person. So this great man at times relaxes from the cares of politics! Men indeed have all the advantages, and make life comfortable for themselves; I am not spiteful, but I hope there will be a compensation."

28

EDOUARD MANET
EDMA'S MARRIAGE

BERTHE continued her work at the Louvre. While her companion,
Rosalie Riesener, copied the figure of Marie de Medici in Rubens'
Capture of Juliers, Berthe undertook to do the *Exchange of the Two
Princesses*, of the same series, devoting special care to the figure of the naiad.

It was at this time that she made the acquaintance of Edouard Manet
whose work she greatly admired for its freedom and sincerity, and whom
she had long wished to meet. The introduction was made by Fantin-Latour,
and Manet asked Berthe to pose, with Mademoiselle Clauss and Antonin
Guillemet, for *Le Balcon*.

The Manets and the Morisots soon became intimate friends. Madame
Morisot and her daughters attended Madame Auguste Manet's Thursday

soirées, where they would find Manet with his wife Suzanne, and his brothers Eugène and Gustave. Other visitors included Baudelaire, Degas, Charles Cros, Zola, Astruc, and Stevens in whose home Berthe later met Puvis de Chavannes. There was singing by Bosc, to his own guitar accompaniment; Emanuel Chabrier would play Saint-Saëns' *Danse macabre* with great gusto; Madame Edouard Manet would give her unique interpretations of Chopin, her small fingers barely touching the keys of the piano; Cros would recite *Le Hareng sec, sec, sec*, and there was always a great deal of conversation.

In a letter dating from this period Baudelaire wrote to Madame Auguste Manet in reference to her son:

"Madame, I am very grateful to you for your gracious invitations. As for my feelings toward your son, you know that no particular credit is due me, and your words to me in this regard are much too gracious, since it seems difficult not to love his character just as much as his talents."

In 1869 a notable change occurred in Berthe's life. Early in that year her sister Edma, so long her working companion, was married to Adolphe Pontillon, a naval officer. Madame Morisot wrote to the young bride:

"You are in my thoughts and in my heart, dear children. I want you to enjoy the beauty of this first day of your married life, and I want it to bring to both of you my love, my need to know that you are happy. We have just spent the evening at the Stevenses, the two of us trying to look cheerful, but they had contrived an entertainment that our philosophy could not hold out against for long: they wanted to dance! After one quadrille we slipped away, and in less than an hour we were back at home. Except for Fantin, no friend was absent. Puvis seems to have renounced his prejudice against me. On the other hand he did not pay much attention to Berthe, although he whispered inaudible things in her ear. What she did make out, however, was that one must not go to see him, that he is losing his mind over his work, and that it will be ready only at the last minute. Monsieur Degas has asked Berthe to convey his apologies and regrets to you. He had a sitting at the time designated and could not postpone it. There are a great many things I could tell you."

The letters exchanged between the two sisters after Edma's marriage dwell on the fact that they had never before been separated for any length of time. On one occasion Edma wrote:

"I have never once in my life written to you, my dear Berthe. It is therefore not too surprising that I was very sad when we were separated for the first time. I am beginning to recover a little, and I hope that my husband is not aware of the void that I feel without you. He is very sweet, full of attentions and solicitude for me, something which I neglected to tell you yesterday. On learning that I had not mentioned him, he cried out: 'But they will think that I am making you very unhappy!'

"Now he proposes to write a few lines to my mother to make up for my omission."

Another of Edma's letters, dated March 15, reads:

"I thought that I should have a letter from you today, my dear Berthe, but the postman brought me only a *billet-doux* from Robert. The snow came down in big flakes all morning. The mountains have disappeared in the mist, and we remain by the fire. You thought it useless to bring any books, and I might not have needed books if there had been any walking to vary our pleasures, so I bought *Adolphe* which I had no difficulty in finding here, and I read a few pages of it when I am tired of doing nothing. This book grows on you, just as Monsieur Degas told me it would . . . Would you believe that I have been to see the exhibition of the *Société des Amis des Arts*, and that the sight of certain pictures gave me pleasure as though I hadn't seen any painting for a long time? We dine at the *table d'hôte* with a collection of Britishers; some of them are friendly, and occasionally we exchange a few words . . .

"I am often with you, my dear Berthe. In my thoughts I follow you about in your studio, and wish that I could escape, were it only for a quarter of an hour, to breathe that air in which we lived for many long years.

"Adolphe is always talking, and he asked me several times while I have been writing this to give you a thousand compliments. He wants you to know that no one can live near you without appreciating the charm of your mind, and I don't know what else, but this is of little interest to you, I presume."

Berthe, in reply, described one of the Wednesday soirées at the Stevenses:

"Monsieur Degas seems greatly pleased with his portrait. It is the only thing he has done for the exhibition. He talked about you to me last night: he finds you very strange. From several things he said about you, I judge him to be very observing. He laughed on hearing that you are reading *Adolphe*. He came and sat beside me, pretending that he was going to court me, but this courting was confined to a long commentary on Solomon's proverb, 'Woman is the desolation of the righteous'."

And on March 19 she wrote:

"If we go on in this way, my dear Edma, we shall no longer be good for anything. You cry on receiving my letters, and I did just the same thing this morning. Your letters so affectionate, but so melancholy, and your husband's kind words made me burst into tears. But, I repeat, this sort of thing is unhealthy. It is making us lose whatever remains of our youth and beauty. For me this is of no importance, but for you it is different.

"Yes, I find you are childish: this painting, this work that you mourn for, is the cause of many griefs and many troubles. You know it as well as I do, and yet, child that you are, you are already lamenting that which was depressing you only a little while ago.

"Come now, the lot you have chosen is not the worst one. You have a serious attachment, and a man's heart utterly devoted to you. Do not revile your fate. Remember that it is sad to be alone; despite anything that may be said or done, a woman has an immense need of affection. For her to withdraw into herself is to attempt the impossible.

"Oh, how I am lecturing you! I don't mean to. I am saying simply what I think, what seems to be true."

For her part Madame Morisot wrote to Edma:

"I have just found Berthe so touched by Adolphe's letter that she is crying over it with her nose pressed against the wall, refusing to show it to me. She will nevertheless try to get up. We have made our round of the artists. This sort of people have no brains. They are weathercocks, and use you for their sport. On Wednesday, while Stevens was giving me a letter from Puvis, politely inviting me, just as he was inviting Stevens, to visit him the next day, Manet took Berthe into a corner and said to her, 'Don't be constrained. Tell him all the worst things that you can think of about his painting!' "

Edma replied from Pau on March 21:

"You are right, my dear Berthe, in all that you say to me. It is disheartening that one cannot depend on artists. My infatuation for Manet is over; as for Monsieur Degas, that is a different matter. For one thing, I am curious to know what he could have to say about me, and what he finds strange in my person. The commentary on the proverb must have been pretty and piquant. You may call me crazy if you like, but when I think of any of these artists, I tell myself that a quarter hour of their conversation is worth as much as many sterling qualities.

"I know how you leave your letters lying about; so, once again, burn this one, and continue to write me your gossip, as you call it. I have nothing better to do than to decipher it.

"Life here is always the same. The fireside, and the rain pouring down.

"Adolphe is greatly touched by your letter. He gave it to me to read, saying that you are charming."

Somewhat earlier Madame Morisot had written to Edma about *Le Balcon*, the painting on which Manet was then at work:

"Tomorrow we are going to see Manet's paintings. Antonin says that he made him pose fifteen times to no effect and that Mademoiselle Clauss is atrocious. But both of them, tired of posing on their feet, say to him: 'It's perfect – there is nothing more to be done over'.

"All these people are amusing, but not really very responsible. Manet looks like a madman: he hopes that his picture will be a success, then all of a sudden he is filled with doubts that cast him down.

"He has reproduced his wife. I think it was high time."

And on March 25 Madame Morisot reported:

"I spend my days, or almost all of them, in the studio. Berthe says she is waiting for you, to know whether what she is doing is good or bad. After you leave, she will never dare show anything to anyone."

After a brief stay in Paris, Edma returned to Lorient, and the sisters resumed their correspondence. On April 23 Berthe wrote:

"I am not any more cheerful than you are, my dear Edma, and probably much less so. Here I am, trapped because of my eyes. I was not expecting this, and my patience is very limited. I count the days passed in inaction, and foresee many a calamity, as for example that I shall be spending May Day here with poultices on my eyes. But let us talk about you. I am happy to think that your wish may be fulfilled. I have no knowledge of these matters, but I believe in your premonitions. In any case, I desire it with all my heart, for I understand that one does not readily accustom oneself to life in the country and to domesticity. For that, one must have something to look forward to. Adolphe would certainly be surprised to hear me talking in this way. Men incline to believe that they fill all of one's life, but as for me, I think that no matter how much affection a woman has for her husband, it is not easy for her to break with a life of work. Affection is a very fine thing, on condition that there is something besides with which to fill one's days. This something I see for you in motherhood.

"Do not grieve about painting. I do not think it is worth a single regret."

In a subsequent letter she said:

"I am remorseful having written in such a worried and discouraged tone. Today my eye is beginning to open again; I am recovering some slight taste for life, and I reproach myself for having given in to my mania for lamentation.

"I see from your letter that you are enjoying the same sunshine as we are, and that you know how to benefit from it. Spring is a lovely thing; it makes itself felt charmingly even in a little restricted corner of the earth like the garden. The lilacs are in bloom. The chestnut trees are almost so. I was admiring them a little while ago; my father listened to me, then put an end to my enthusiasm by immediately forecasting the end of all these splendours. I am wondering what I shall do with my summer. I should be glad to come to you on condition, first, that it will not inconvenience you, and second, that I shall find opportunity to work. My inaction is beginning to weigh upon me. I am eager to do something at least fairly good. There is one worry that you are rid of. Since you left, I have not seen a single painter: I live as far from Paris as you do. Tomorrow is the opening of the exhibition of the circle. I wanted to write a note to Manet to ask him to send me an admission card. I hesitated to do so, and as it turns out, my application would have been perfectly useless, because on account of my eyes I cannot yet go out. I often imagine myself in your little home and wonder whether you are gay or sad: It seems to me that you are both. Am I wrong?"

In a letter dated May 2, 1869, Berthe described to Edma the opening of the Salon:

"The first thing we beheld as we went up the big staircase was Puvis' painting. It looked well. Jacquemard was standing in front of it and seemed to admire it greatly. What he seemed to admire less was my person. There is nothing worse than a former admirer. Consequently he forsook me very quickly. However, we next met Carolus Duran, who was with his wife, and who on seeing us blushed violently. I shook hands with him, but he did not have a word to say to me. His wife is a tall and handsome woman. He is showing a portrait of her, which, I think, is going to be a success, although it is quite vulgar. It isn't absolutely bad, but I find it mannered and flat. I don't have to tell you that one of the first things I did was to go to Room M. There I found Manet, with his hat on in bright sunlight, looking dazed. He begged me to go and see his painting, as he did not dare move a step.

"I have never seen such an expressive face as his; he was laughing, then

35

had a worried look, assuring everybody that his picture was very bad, and adding in the same breath that it would be a great success. I think he has a decidedly charming temperament, I like it very much.

"His paintings, as they always do, produce the impression of a wild or even a somewhat unripe fruit. I do not in the least dislike them, but I prefer his portrait of Zola."

In referring to *Le Balcon*, Berthe wrote:

"I am more strange than ugly. It seems that the epithet of *femme fatale* has been circulating among the curious, but I realize that if I tell you about everything at once, the people and the paintings, I will use up all my writing paper, and so I think I had better tell you another time about my impressions of the paintings, all the more so because I could scarcely see them. However, I did look for our friend Fantin. His insignificant little sketch was hung incredibly high, and looked extremely forlorn. I finally found him, but he disappeared before I could say a word about his exhibit. I do not know whether he was avoiding me, or whether he was conscious of the worthlessness of his work.

"I certainly think that his excessive visits to the Louvre and to Mademoiselle Dubourg bring him no luck. Monsieur Degas seemed happy, but guess for whom he forsook me – for Mademoiselle Lille and Madame Loubens. I must admit that I was a little annoyed when a man whom I consider to be very intelligent deserted me to pay compliments to two silly women.

"I was beginning to find all this rather dull. For about an hour Manet, in high spirits, was leading his wife, his mother, and me all over the place, when I bumped headlong into Puvis de Chavannes. He seemed delighted to see me, told me that he had come largely on my account as he was beginning to lose hope of seeing me again at the Stevenses, and he asked if he might accompany me for a few minutes. I wanted to see the pictures, but he implored me so eagerly: 'I beg of you, let us just talk. We have plenty of time for looking at paintings'. Such conversation might have appealed to me had I not found myself confronted at every step by familiar faces. What is more, I had completely lost sight of Manet and his wife, which further increased my embarrassment. I did not think it proper to walk around all alone. When I finally found Manet again, I reproached him for his behaviour; he answered that I could count on all his devotion, but nevertheless he would never risk playing the part of a child's nurse.

"You will ask what has become of my mother during all this time. She was afraid of getting a headache, and sat on a sofa, where I would join her from time to time. I brought Puvis to her while she was already engaged in conversation with *petit père* Riesener. We all went again to see Manet's picture, and there we found Monsieur Oudinot, orating. He pretended not to see us, but don't you think this encounter was rather strange? I've talked about everything now except paintings; but be patient, I shall review the Salon for you in my own way. I must go back Monday. I almost assented to a rendez-vous there with Puvis. We shook hands, and he promised to come to see me."

On May 5, 1869, Berthe wrote:

"On Monday I met Carolus Duran. It seemed silly not to compliment him on his painting, which appears to be having a certain success, but he seemed surprised by my kindness and responded with an endless stream of compliments for Manet's painting. Monsieur Degas has a very pretty little portrait of a very ugly woman in black, with a hat and a cashmere falling from her shoulders. The background is that of a very light interior, showing a corner of a mantelpiece in half tones; it is very subtle and distinguished. Antonin's entries look well, despite the fact that he is horribly placed; but landscapes bore me, although I did see one by Lépine that I find charming. *34* It is, as always, a view of the banks of the Seine near Bercy. I didn't see any of Oudinot's paintings. Those of Daubigny, father and son, tire me and seem common and heavy, etc., etc. . . Corot is poetic, as usual. I think he spoiled the etude we admired so much when we saw it at his home, by re-doing it in the studio.

"The tall Bazille has painted something that I find very good. It is a *35* little girl in a light dress seated in the shade of a tree, with a glimpse of a village in the background. There is much light and sun in it. He has tried to do what we have so often attempted – a figure in the outdoor light – and this time he seems to have been successful.

"Here I stop to laugh at myself passing this judgment. It seems to me that our friends would laugh even more if they could hear me dealing out censure and praise. I met Bracquemond, who was very amiable, paid me compliments on my exhibits of last year, and reproached me for not showing this year. It seems that he has a painting in the exhibition. I shall look for it and give you my opinion of it.

"The Fantin is decidedly weak. It is reminiscent of Veronese, and must have a certain charm of colour when seen at close range. Because it is placed so high, one can only perceive the insignificance of the composition. It is a

woman surrounded by others in fancy costumes à la Titian or à la Veronese.
36 It is called *Le Lever*. The Tissots seem to have become quite Chinese, and
one cannot bear to look at the Toulmouches."

Edma replied to Berthe on May 8:

"The little glimpse that you give me of the Salon does not lack a certain
merit in my eyes. I see it just as you describe it to me, probably because we
look at things in much the same way. On the whole, it seems to me that
there is nothing very remarkable there. Yves tells me that this is her impression too. I pity Monsieur Degas with his latest fancy, and Fantin like-
wise, judging by what you tell me. The latter has certainly fallen even
lower since his intimacy with Mademoiselle Dubourg. I cannot believe that
he is the person we admired so much last year."

On May 11, after being introduced to a possible suitor for her hand,
Berthe wrote to Edma:

"I have missed my chance, dear Edma, and you may congratulate me on
having got rid so quickly of all my agitations. I think that I should have
fallen ill, if at that moment I had had to decide in favour of Monsieur D-.
Fortunately this gentleman turned out to be completely ludicrous. I had
not expected this, and was quite surprised, but by no means disappointed!
Now that I am free of all anxiety, and am taking up again my plans for travel,
which in truth I had never given up, I am counting definitely on my stay
in Lorient to do something worthwhile. I have done absolutely nothing
since you left, and this is beginning to distress me. My painting never
seemed to me as bad as it has in recent days. I sit on my sofa, and the sight
of all these daubs nauseates me. I am going to do my mother and Yves in
the garden; you see I am reduced to doing the same things over and over
again. Yesterday I arranged a bouquet of poppies and snowballs, and could
not find the courage to begin it. On Wednesday we went to the Stevenses.
Yves has certainly made a conquest of Monsieur Degas. He asked her to
permit him to paint a portrait of her. He is always talking about you, asking
about you, and is indignant at my keeping you posted about his new in-
fatuations. If you think that I have given you a review of the exhibition,
that is only kindness on your part. I see it so badly that it is difficult for me to
37 judge it. Friday I looked with great interest at Mademoiselle Callart's two
pictures. They did not seem as good as those of last year, though the subjects are about the same.

"I have never once been to the Salon without meeting Oudinot in Room

38

M. The other day, as we were passing him, Puvis asked me with astonishment if that was not my former teacher. I think he has heard some gossip
in that connection. You are right in thinking that there is nothing remarkable in the Salon; personally I can see in it only mediocre work – or am I
too severe? Every now and then I hear some praises that I cannot join in,
nor even comprehend. Did you read Charles Blanc's long article on Chen-
avard? For myself, I shall forbear to give you a description of his picture. *38*
It is certainly the work of an intelligent man, but much too classical for my
taste. Monsieur Riesener admires greatly certain aspects of it. I am the only
one at our house who likes Puvis' paintings. They are thought to be un-
interesting, cold. Well, anyway, you will see them at Marseilles, and you will
give me your opinion. What makes me think my taste is not entirely perverted is that I recall Fantin's admiring them a lot. I do not meet him anywhere, this dear Fantin! Yet I need to talk with him a little to recover my
zest for life.

"You are very fortunate to have seen Rosbras again, my dear Mamie!
The only thing I see again is rain coming down in torrents. I drag myself
about aimlessly, and I say twenty times a day that I am tired of everything.
That is how my life goes. I am ashamed of being so weak-minded, but what
can I do? I have just finished arranging some papers, and re-reading a batch
of letters from Monsieur Oudinot. There are some that are screamingly
funny. I would not have believed that he could ever seem so likeable. I
wish I had my replies to them. The complete collection would be too funny
for words. These are diversions that unfortunately cannot be enjoyed over
again every day, but they cost me many a tear in bygone days. Now I think
that I was very foolish, very silly to have cried so much for so little. There
are expressions of despair that are simply ridiculous, and that I took quite
seriously. My God, how stupid women are, but I think that I go beyond all
bounds in this respect. Did the trip to Rosbras tire you? I regret not having
been there with you. I adore that part of the country, but I would have
missed Corentin. I am surprised to hear that our paintings are not too bad;
this was one of the things that have been bothering me. Is the amateur at
Pont-Aven the one who comes to the Stevenses? You do not speak of the
weather; we are having terrible storms here; it is as though one were at the
seashore, and one hears of nothing but disasters."

To this Edma replied:

"I quite understand that the Oudinot correspondence can only make
you laugh now. To anyone but ourselves it would have seemed ridiculous

far sooner. I also have saved a packet of letters that I shall reread some day to amuse myself. I still feel too much hate for that man to go back to the time when we lived so closely together."

Madame Morisot gave her own version of the opening of the Salon in a letter dated May 23:

"Manet was laughing heartily. This made him feel better, poor boy, because his lack of success saddens him. He tells you with the most natural air that he meets people who avoid him in order not to have to talk about his painting, and as a result he no longer has the courage to ask anyone to pose for him. He has made indirect overtures to the Gonzalès; as for Madame Stevens, that prospect seems to have fallen through. However, he told me that he had been asked the price of *Le Balcon*; it must be someone who wants to make fun of him or perhaps to satisfy his curiosity. He said naïvely that Berthe was bringing him luck. He seems to me very nice because he is interested in Berthe; he also spoke of Tiburce in a tone that shows he likes us.

"Do you know that Monsieur Degas is mad about Yves' face, and that he is doing a sketch of her? He is going to transfer on to the canvas the drawing that he is doing in his sketchbook. A peculiar way of doing a portrait!"

Berthe referred to these sittings:

"As for your friend Degas, I certainly do not find his personality attractive; he has wit, but nothing more. Manet said to me very comically yesterday, 'He lacks spontaneity, he isn't capable of loving a woman, much less of telling her that he does or of doing anything about it'. Poor Manet, he is sad; his exhibition, as usual, does not appeal to the public, which is for him always a source of wonder. Nevertheless he said that I had brought him luck and he had had an offer for *Le Balcon*. I wish for his sake that this were true, but I have grave fears that his hopes will once again be disappointed.

"Monsieur Degas has made a sketch of Yves, that I find indifferent; he chattered all the time he was doing it, he made fun of his friend Fantin, saying that the latter would do well to seek new strength in the arms of love, because at present painting no longer suffices him. He was in a highly satirical mood; he talked to me about Puvis, and compared him to the condor in the Jardin des Plantes."

At this time Yves was temporarily residing in Paris, her husband having been transferred from Quimperlé to Mirande. Edma wrote to Berthe:

"Your life must be charming at this moment. To have Bichette in one's bed every morning, to talk with Monsieur Degas while watching him draw, to laugh with Manet, to philosophize with Puvis – each of these experiences seems to me enviable. You would feel the same way if you were far off as I am . . ."

But Berthe went off to join Edma even before Yves left Paris. On June 26 Yves wrote from Limoges:

"As mother must have told you, my dear Berthe, Monsieur Degas took up all of my time during the final days of my stay in Paris, with the result that I have neglected my correspondence . . . The drawing that Monsieur Degas made of me in the last two days is really very pretty, both true to life and delicate, and it is no wonder that he could not detach himself from his work. I doubt if he can transfer it onto the canvas without spoiling it. He announced to mother that he would come back one of these days to draw a corner of the garden, and to tell her shocking stories, for he is absolutely amazed at her guilelessness . . ."

Madame Morisot described the last sitting:

"Yves asked me to tell you that she would write from Limoges. Monsieur Degas took up her last moments here. That original came on Tuesday; this time he took a big sheet of paper and set to work on the head in pastel. He seemed to be doing a very pretty thing, and drew with great skill. He asked me to give him an hour or two during the day yesterday; he came to lunch and stayed the whole day. He seemed to like what he had done, and was annoyed to tear himself away from it. He really works with ease, for all this took place amidst the visits and the farewells that never ceased during those two days."

After a short trip to the environs of Brest, Berthe rejoined Edma at Lorient, where she received the following lines from her mother:

"Your father seemed to be deeply touched, my dear Bijou, by the letter you wrote to him. He appears to have discovered in you unsuspected treasures of the heart, and an unusual tenderness toward him in particular . . . In consequence he often says that he misses you. But I wonder why. You hardly ever talk to each other, you are never together. Does he miss you then, as one misses a piece of furniture or a pet bird? I am trying to convince him on the contrary that it is a more complete rest for him not to see your poor little face bewildered and dissatisfied over a fate about which we can do nothing. It is a relief; this is what we have come to think, and we conclude that it is much better for you to be with Edma, that you two should remain together for a while.

"I have taken the books back to Manet, whom I found in greater ecstasies

than ever in front of his model Gonzalès. His mother made me touch her daughter-in-law's hands, saying that she was feverish; the latter forced a smile and reminded me that you had promised to write to her. As for Manet, he did not move from his stool. He asked how you were, and I answered that I was going to report to you how unfeeling he is. He has forgotten about you for the time being. Mademoiselle G. has all the virtues, all the charms, she is an accomplished woman – that is what the poor girl whispered into my ear as she showed me to the door. Last Wednesday there was nobody at the Stevenses except Monsieur Degas."

Somewhat earlier, on June 22, Madame Morisot had written to Edma expressing her concern regarding Berthe's future; her letters frequently referred to her wish to see her third daughter married. Madame Léouzon-Leduc, née Louise Riesener, relates that according to her mother a disconcerting incident occurred at one time when the latter arranged an introduction for Berthe. Madame Morisot had told Berthe to go upstairs to her room to dress a bit for the expected visit. Berthe was slow in coming down to the drawing room; suddenly her mother appeared before her saying: "How long are you going to leave me face to face with that idiot?"   *40*

Although she had no daughters to accompany her, Madame Morisot attended the Stevens soirées and sent accounts of them to Edma and Berthe, mentioning the absence of Degas. On her younger daughter's return, she wrote to Edma in a letter dated August 7:

"The great joy we have had in seeing each other again is more imaginary than real. It is cruel to admit this, nevertheless it is easy to explain. Berthe does not find me as communicative as I was before her departure; she also claims that I looked at her with surprise, as though I were thinking that she has grown decidedly plainer, which in fact I do – a little.

"I think the two paintings she has brought back are pretty; they look very well in the studio, and I shall be pleased to hang the sketch of you, though she will not let me put it in any spot where it can be seen."

The sketch referred to was the full-length portrait of Edma in a white dress. It was exhibited in the Salon of 1870. The other painting was that of   *41* the port of Lorient, which is mentioned in another letter dated August 14:

"Berthe asks me to tell you that it is very wrong of you not to take up your pen. She has made a present of her painting to Manet; thus nothing will remain at home. This souvenir of Lorient would have been nice to have. She thinks that you will find good excuses for your laziness. As for her, she has not done anything with the little Delaroches. After two sittings out-doors, and one in the studio because the sun had bothered them, they left for Houlgate. Thus this little project seems to be going to rack and ruin. What she did in the studio spoiled a little what she had done outdoors. Berthe is not satisfied with her work, and I encourage her just enough to keep her occupied, for I don't think that to replace idleness with frenzy will improve her health . . ."

In the meantime Berthe had resumed her correspondence with her sister. On August 13, she wrote to Edma:

"Manet lectures me, and holds up that eternal Mademoiselle Gonzalès as an example; she has poise, perseverance, she is able to carry an under-taking to a successful issue, whereas I am not capable of anything. In the meantime he has begun her portrait over again for the twenty-fifth time. She poses every day, and every night the head is washed out with soft soap. This will scarcely encourage anyone to pose for him!"

Edma wrote in reply:

"I made an attempt to work during the day, and I completely ruined a still life on a white canvas, and this tired me so that after dinner I lay down on my couch and almost fell asleep. Following your advice, on Saturday I went to the boat, just to get the view. There was a mist in the air, and the scene was pretty. Since then the weather has not been propitious, and all the charm of this place is in the effect. If your landscape does not look good at home, I am even less inclined to try. What is the good of tiring yourself over something that satisfies you so little?

"The thought of Mademoiselle Gonzalès irritates me, I do not know why. I imagine that Manet greatly overestimates her, and that we, or rather you, have as much talent as she . . . To have seen Manet again is already something, it must have helped you recover from the family visits of the day before."

In a subsequent letter Edma wrote:

"Like you, I found *Madame Bovary* a very remarkable work from an artistic point of view, and very interesting as a realistic study. Decidedly this is where the superiority of contemporary art lies, and sooner or later its value will be generally recognized."

On September 10 she wrote:

"It is a pity, my dear Berthe, that you could not make up your mind to follow the Manets or go elsewhere, for a change of air. And what is happen-ing to you in this unsettled weather? It must be impossible to work in the garden, if you are carrying out your project of painting the little Delaroches.

"As for myself, yesterday I came home in a bad temper after a third try at the boats. This unique spot is most exasperating, because of the movement of the boats, which hide the whole landscape for hours on end. Moreover my canvas has been damaged, so that my attempts at working outdoors are probably going to end here. However, I reproach myself for having done nothing this season. My passion for painting has not yet left me."

Berthe reported in turn:

"I wanted to write yesterday, day before yesterday, in fact I have wanted to write all of these past days: painting alone is the reason for my silence. Roused by your example, I too wanted to do my plums and my flowers, the whole thing on a white napkin. This gave me an awful lot of trouble, with insignificant results. This mode of exercise annoys me deeply . . .

"I saw your friend Fantin, who inquired about you. He has become more ill-natured and unattractive than ever. While listening to his disparagements of everyone, I thought of what Degas says of him, and I concluded that he is not wrong in maintaining that Fantin is becoming as sour as an old maid. . . . We spent Thursday evening at Manet's. He was bubbling over with good spirits, spinning a hundred nonsensical yarns, one funnier than another. As of now, all his admiration is concentrated on Mademoiselle Gonzalès, but her portrait does not progress; he says that he is at the fortieth sitting and that the head is again effaced. He is the first to laugh about it . . ."

In a later letter she wrote:

"During the day I received a visit from Puvis de Chavannes. He saw what I had done at Lorient and seemed to find it not too bad. Tell Adolphe that when we examined the pier he complimented me on my knowledge of perspective, and that naturally I gave full credit where it was due . . .

"The Manets came to see us Tuesday evening, and we all went into the studio. To my great surprise and satisfaction, I received the highest praise; it seems that what I do is decidedly better than Eva Gonzalès. Manet is too candid, and there can be no mistake about it. I am sure that he liked these things a great deal; however, I remember what Fantin says, namely, that Manet always approves of the painting of people whom he likes. Then he talked to me about finishing my work, and I must confess that I do not see what I can do . . . As he exaggerates everything, he predicted success for me in the next exhibition, though he has said many unpleasant things to me . . . Since I have been told that without knowing it I produced masterpieces at Lorient, I have stood gaping before them, and I feel myself no longer capable of anything. The little Delaroches came three times to pose. It is a nightmare. I have not heard anything more about them, hence I hope that they are at Houlgate, and that my attempt may end at this point. Decidedly, I am too nervous to make anyone sit for me, and then the opinions of this one and that one worry me, and make me disgusted with things before they are in place . . .

"Manet exhorted me so strongly to do a little retouching on my painting of you, that when you come here I shall ask you to let me draw the head again and add some touches at the bottom of the dress, and that is all. He says that the success of my exhibition is assured and that I do not need to worry; the next instant he adds that I shall be rejected. I wish I were not concerned with all this."

Writing on September 28, Berthe says:

"I have wanted to write to you, my dear Edma, but then I feel myself overcome by an insurmountable laziness. I am reproached by everybody and I do not have the strength to react. And I understand perfectly the difficulties you have in painting; I have reached the point of wondering how I have ever in my life been able to do anything . . .

"Didn't you try to work by the river in that place at the water's edge that we thought was so pretty? It seems to me that the season ought to be most favourable, particularly if you have sun . . .

"Yves writes that she continues to be bored; as for me, I am sad, and what is worse, everyone is deserting me; I feel alone, disillusioned, and old into the bargain . . ."

In the winter of 1869-1870 Edma came to her parents' home in Passy for her confinement, and it was during the week preceding the birth of her first daughter that Berthe painted the portrait showing her sister in a white dress, sitting beside her mother who was reading to her. In regard to this painting Edma wrote to her sister:

45

"I do not know what P. can have found wrong with the figure of mother; it seemed to me good. I hope that your latest endeavour will be to the liking of these gentlemen. I shall regret very much if this picture is not finished for the exhibition . . ."

In a letter announcing the return of her brother Tiburce from America, Berthe recounts the vicissitudes of this painting:

"Tiburce arrived yesterday morning, my dear Edma. He is absolutely mardi

Mademoiselle Berthe,

Je vous prierai de remettre à plutard la visite que vous m'aviez promis de me faire jeudi à l'atelier, je ne suis pas encore assez avancé pour risquer votre fin jugement; je tiens à ne me montrer devant vous que dans à mon avantage.

Veuillez agréer mademoiselle l'assurance de mon amitié et de mon dévouement

Ed. Manet

the same as he was before his departure; I think he is even a little more scatterbrained, this between ourselves. But aside from that I do not see any transformation; he is full of confidence, sure that people are going to take an interest in him, enchanted with his life abroad. He tells me the funniest, most unbelievable stories about America, stories not exactly for the ears of young ladies, as my father said; anyway he makes a great commotion here, and finds us all stuffy. Nevertheless I wish I were even more so; and while I am on the subject of myself, I shall at once tell you about my misfortunes, and then we shall speak of them no more.

"Mother wrote to you at the time Puvis told me that the head was not done and could not be done; whereupon great emotion; I took it out, I did it over again. Friday night I wrote him a note asking him to come to see me; he answered immediately that this was impossible for him and complimented me a great deal on all the rest of the picture, advising me only to put some accents on mother's head. So far no great misfortune. Tired, unnerved, I went to Manet's studio on Saturday. He asked me how I was getting on, and seeing that I felt dubious, he said to me enthusiastically: 'Tomorrow, after I have sent off my pictures, I shall come to see yours, and you may put yourself in my hands. I shall tell you what needs to be done'.

"The next day, which was yesterday, he came at about one o'clock; he found it very good, except for the lower part of the dress. He took the brushes and put in a few accents that looked very well; mother was in ecstasies. That is where my misfortunes began. Once started, nothing could stop him; from the skirt he went to the bust, from the bust to the head, from the head to the background. He cracked a thousand jokes, laughed like a madman, handed me the palette, took it back; finally by five o'clock in the afternoon we had made the prettiest caricature that was ever seen. The carter was waiting to take it away; he made me put it on the hand-cart, willy-nilly. And now I am left confounded. My only hope is that I shall be rejected. My mother thinks this episode funny, but I find it agonizing.

"I put in with it the painting I did of you at Lorient. I hope they take only that.

"Pity me, and now let us return to something else, that is more interesting. That day tired me more than a long journey would. In the evening Tiburce, who had slept during the day, felt no inclination to go to bed; he kept me up until one o'clock in the morning. He had travelled by way of Liverpool, and was late in arriving because he had lost his baggage. Since I understand nothing about his affairs – moreover he does not talk about them to me – I cannot tell you about them. I see that he is confident without being able to say whether this confidence has a solid basis.

"I am talking about myself, about him, and not about you, my dear Edma. Although I understand quite well the difficulties you have in your situation, I think that you are particularly upset. I think that for all our stuffiness, we take a lot of trouble about things. In spite of myself, I am always returning to the subject of myself; I feel a great weight on my stomach, and I am disgusted for all time with painters and with friendship. I hear that Fantin was sick over our visit. Another silly trick of that madman Manet!

"Manet has never done anything as good as his portrait of Mademoiselle Gonzalès; it is perhaps even more charming now than when you saw it. As for our friend Chavannes, everybody agrees that his picture is very good: this proves that I was right and mother wrong.

"Good-bye – I embrace you, write to me, and tell me as much about yourself as I tell you about myself."

The sequel to these tribulations is related by Madame Morisot who wrote on March 22, 1870:

"Berthe must have told you about all the mishaps. Except for your sake she certainly would not have set pen to paper. Yesterday she looked like a person about to faint; she grieves and worries me; her despair and discontent were so great that they could be ascribed only to a morbid condition; moreover she tells me every minute that she is going to fall ill. She overworked herself to such a point on the last day that she really could not see any more, and it seems that I made matters worse by telling her that the improvements Manet had made on my head seemed to me atrocious. When I saw her in this state, and when she kept telling me that she would rather be at the bottom of the river than learn that her picture had been accepted, I thought I was doing the right thing to ask for its return. I have got it back, but now we are in a new predicament: won't Manet be offended? He spent all Sunday afternoon making this pretty mess, and took charge himself of consigning it to the carter. It is impossible to tell him that the entry did not get there in time, since the little sketch of Lorient went with it. It would be puerile to tell this to anyone except you; but you know how the smallest thing here takes on the proportions of a tragedy because of our nervous and febrile dispositions, and God knows I have endured the consequences. It is these constant ups and downs that make it impossible to compose oneself.

"I do not think that Berthe has eaten half a pound of bread since you

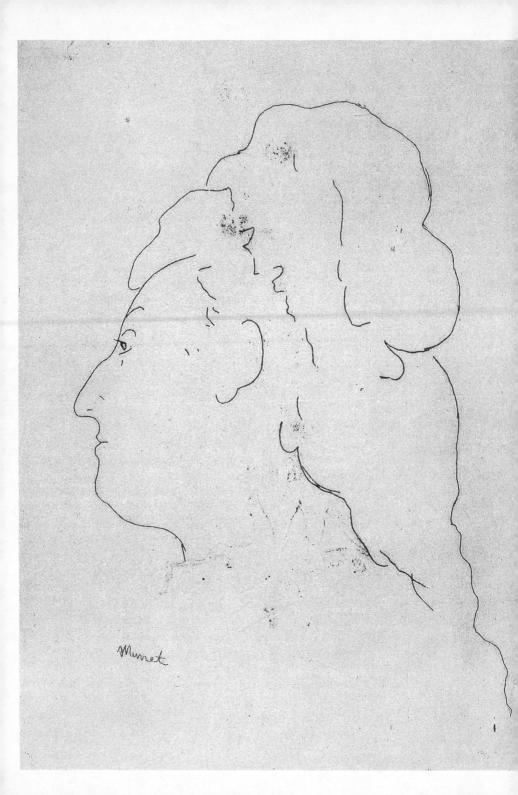

left; it disgusts her to swallow anything. I have meat juice made for her every day. Oh, well ! . . ."

On May 5 Madame Morisot reported:
"Berthe was somewhat revived by the exhibition; yesterday she took Mademoiselle Carré, who seemed to be much appreciated by the artists . . ." *46*
This was followed by a fuller account dated May 8:
"Berthe is receiving quite a number of compliments on her exhibits: her spirits fall and rise again but there is no doubt that the activities of this week have diverted her a little. I fear that this will serve only to plunge her into greater gloom."

After the opening of the Salon Berthe wrote:
"Your friend Fantin is having a real success; the portrait of the two Dubourg sisters is a real gem. I met him Saturday morning, and he was very friendly to me; because he had criticized me, I accepted his praise as genuine and it has given me a little courage again. All in all, since I am talking about myself, I do not make as absurd an impression as I feared; the little portrait of you I did at Lorient is hung so high that it is impossible to judge it.
"Manet is in despair about where he is placed. However, his two paintings look well; as usual, they attract much attention. Monsieur Degas has sent a very pretty painting, but his masterpiece is the portrait of Yves in pastel. I am sorry that you did not see it during your stay here.
"Mademoiselle Gonzalès is passable, but nothing more. Puvis de Chavannes is having a great success with the famous picture that my mother thought was awful. I am a little disconcerted this morning at the thought *47* that I allowed him to accompany me all day yesterday. I wanted to be dignified, but that decidedly is impossible; I have nothing of what is required to inspire people with respect; I do not know at all how to hold a grudge, even when I have a right to, and God knows that in his case I have a right."

To this Edma replied on May 8:
"There is nothing that could surprise me less than to learn that Fantin has produced a masterpiece; he is at his best in studies from nature and in the *genre intime*; I am sure that I should prefer this picture to the one I know. Your enthusiasm for Manet does not seem to be at the same pitch, and this makes me think that he has spoiled *Mademoiselle Gonzalès* and *Leçon de guitare*.
"Do you know that I am not yet clear as to whether you did exhibit your picture or not? You write that you 'do not make as absurd an impression as

you feared'. This sentence obviously cannot refer to the study you did of me at Lorient. I am sure that you receive compliments, and refrain from mentioning them."

Berthe in turn replied:

"The garden has become pretty again; the chestnut trees are in flower, and for the first time this year we are enjoying spring; the pleasure is somewhat diminished by the thought that we shall soon be deprived of it. Do you know that I am very sorry that I did not go to Cherbourg? First because of you two (I should say three), and then because I might have done something there. I am still engrossed in this wretched painting. I certainly did show my two pictures; it is my principle never to try to rectify a blunder, and that is the main reason why I did not profit from my mother's intervention. Now I am thankful: having got over my first emotion, I find that one always derives benefit from exhibiting one's work, however mediocre it may be. On the other hand I am not receiving a great many compliments, as you think, but everyone is sufficiently kind enough not to make me feel any regrets, except of course Degas, who has a supreme contempt for anything I do . . ."

"One day when I was walking in the salon with that fat Valentine Carré, Manet had a glimpse of her and has been lost in admiration of her ever since. He is pressing me to let him come and do a study of her in the studio. I have only half a mind to do it, but when he takes it into his head to want something, he is like Tiburce – he must have it at once. The best part of it is that this project annoys Puvis, who makes his feelings about it very plain to me.

"I cannot say that Manet has spoiled his paintings. Indeed I saw them in his studio the day before the exhibition, and they enchanted me, but I do not know how to account for the washed-out effect of the portrait of Mademoiselle Gonzalès: the proximity of the other paintings, although execrable, is enormously detrimental. The delicacies of tone, the subtleties that charmed me in the studio, disappear in this full daylight. The head remains weak and is not pretty at all."

At Berthe's suggestion, Manet had Valentine Carré pose for him not in the studio but in the garden of the Rue Franklin, on the grass, with Tiburce reclining behind her. Because this offended Madame Carré, her daughter was replaced by Edma who posed during a visit she made to her parents. As a result the head that Manet painted is more or less a failure; it is neither that of Valentine nor that of Edma.

THE WAR OF 1870 *AND THE COMMUNE*

AT this point the war broke out, interrupting all normal activities. The Morisots constantly referred to it in their letters posted to Mirande, where Edma had joined her sister Yves. Most of these letters were sent by balloon.

On September 18, 1870, Berthe wrote: "I am writing to you, my dear Edma, though I do not think that my letter will reach you. I received your letter only this morning, and have received nothing from Yves since you left.

"I have made up my mind to stay, because neither father nor mother told me firmly to leave; they want me to leave in the way anyone here wants anything – weakly, and by fits and starts. For my own part I would much

53

rather not leave them, not because I believe that there is any real danger, but because my place is with them, and if by ill luck anything did happen, I should have eternal remorse. I will not presume to say that they take great pleasure in my presence; I feel very sad, and am completely silent. I have heard so much about the perils ahead that I have had nightmares for several nights, in which I lived through all the horrors of war. To tell the truth, I do not believe all these things. I feel perfectly calm, and I have the firm conviction that everything will come out better than expected. The house is dreary, empty, stripped bare; and as a finishing touch father makes inexplicable and interminable removals. He seems to be very much occupied with the preservation of some old pieces of furniture of the First Empire. On the other hand he smiles pityingly when I tell him that the cabinet, the mirror, and the console in the studio are not absolutely worthless. To avoid argument, I refrain from interfering in anything, and to tell the truth all this interests me very little. Since it is possible to work where you are, why don't you do so? The militia are quartered in the studio, hence there is no way of using it. I do not read the newspapers much any more; one a day is enough for me. The Prussian atrocities upset me, and I want to retain my composure.

"I am stupefied by this silence. I certainly wish I had news of you – though I dare not hope for an answer to this letter – and of poor Tiburce, from whom we still have not heard. Perhaps you will hear from him before we do; there are moments when I think of him with a terrible tightening of my heart. I embrace you, my dear Edma . . . If you are cut off from Paris, do not worry on our account. Mother is better, and father is in as good health as can be expected. Adieu."

In another letter she says:
"You do not spoil either of us very much, my dear Edma, but I am writing you anyway, because we do not know whether in another few days we shall still be able to correspond. Paris has changed still more since your departure. I think of that day of September 4, and it seems to me that it is not the same city. I see no one, absolutely no one. I received a note from Puvis de Chavannes, who writes as if our last hour had come (keep this to yourself). Moreover, I see that the National Guard is very restive. Manet's brother (Eugène) told me very calmly that he did not expect to come out of it alive.

"My good Papa pins all his hopes on the success of Monsieur Thiers' mission – as for me, I think that this great man is manœuvering in such a way that he will not be able to enter Paris.

54

"Adieu, dear friend. Do enjoy the peace of Mirande. It is better than the agitation here.

"Kisses for Bibi and Bijou. Father continues to be in good health and is driving us all crazy."

On September 25 Berthe wrote to Edma:

"We write to you every day, hoping that out of all of these letters some will reach you, but we have nothing new to tell you. The victory of Friday has raised the morale of many. Would you believe that I am becoming accustomed to the sound of the cannon? It seems to me that I am now absolutely inured to war and capable of enduring anything.

"We saw M. Millet yesterday; he very insistently offered us an apartment, and I think we shall take advantage of his offer if the bombs hit Passy. We should be very safe there – and protected by the National Guard.

"Father and mother are well. We are also having wonderful weather, which helps us to endure a lot of things. I think often of Adolphe. I wonder what is happening to his squadron. The total ignorance in which we live is very distressing. I embrace all four of you."

And on September 30 she wrote again:

"I hope, my dear Edma, that this note will reach you, because I imagine that you are worried, and, truthfully, there is no reason for you to be so. We are still in Passy, perfectly well, but very unhappy, very sad because we have not heard from you, nor from poor Tiburce.

"After looking over all the apartments of our acquaintances, we are resolved to rent a little *garde-meuble* in the Rue Argensen; we shall put part of our furniture there, and our persons if need be. Grandfather would take possession of the Mayniel apartment, and thus we should all be reunited.

"We have heard the cannon again all morning, but so far it is impossible to know the outcome. We are very well situated for hearing the cannon, but very badly for obtaining any news. You must surely be without news-papers. Aren't you trying to get some from England?"

The first of a series of letters from Madame Morisot to her daughters at this time is dated September 12:

"I am sorry that Berthe is not with you. The tales that the Manet brothers have told us about all the horrors that we are liable to experience are almost enough to discourage the most stout-hearted. You know how they always exaggerate, and at present they see everything in the blackest possible light. Their visit has had a bad effect on your father, who is again taking up his favourite theme, trying to persuade us to go away without him. His over-wrought nerves are very trying; he would drive an entire regiment crazy, and at present he is exasperated by my calm. I am accused every minute of being a real doubting Thomas. The fact is, things never turn out as well or as badly as one anticipates. I am not worried, and I think that we shall survive. The Manets said to Berthe: 'You will be in a fine way when you are wounded in the legs or disfigured'. Then Berthe took me to task for refusing to believe such things possible. Nevertheless she does not want to go away."

On October 18 Madame Morisot wrote:
"Each day we hear the cannonading – and a great deal of it. All the fighting is taking place near us – so far without any important results. It is impossible to keep still; Berthe and I got as wet as water spaniels when we went to see where the fighting was taking place, and we almost fainted when we saw a body on a stretcher, the victim of a fire near the viaduct. There are often disasters of this kind. For instance, two chemical plants across the river blew up only a short time ago.

"Monsieur Degas was so affected by the death of one of his friends, the sculptor Cuvelier, that he was impossible. He and Manet almost came to blows arguing over the methods of defence and the use of the National Guard, although each of them was ready to die to save the country. Stevens had an attack of rheumatism; he did not come. The doctor flirts with Berthe. If the situation were not so serious, these goings-on would be fairly comical. M. Degas has joined the artillery, and by his own account has not yet heard a cannon go off. He is looking for an opportunity to hear that sound because he wants to know whether he can endure the detonation of his guns.

"The poor little Delaroches are no longer able to speak without bursting into tears. Their brothers are at the fort of Vanves, which is likely to remain the hottest spot. Issy and Vanves will obviously be defended. If these forts are taken we shall move away, but not before. The stormy weather adds still more gloom to the situation. We have not yet suffered in any way. Ferry has joined the volunteers; it is noble of him, and he deserves to be commended for it. I hear that his brother is an active and intelligent member of the government."

On December 15 she described the situation as follows:

"We see no reason why this should end; Paris will not yield as long as it is possible to hold out. The people are beginning to suffer, but are so courageous, and those who advocate capitulation are but a small minority. The general opinion is that we could indeed go on in this way for another two months. Obviously, if the defence is maintained for that length of time, we shall all suffer . . . It is more than two weeks now that we have been without news from Tours. Monsieur de Moltke has let us know that we were defeated on the Loire – official letter. Three pigeons arrived carrying the most sinister reports. They were identified as birds belonging to a balloon captured by the Prussians, hence the whole thing is regarded as a ruse and a hoax. The answer to Moltke's communication was a proud gesture: the dispatches brought by the carrier pigeons were made public without any comment, except in regard to their origin. We are very much on edge, very sad. Berthe worries me a great deal. She seems to be getting consumption. She fainted last week. For almost two months she ate enough and looked fairly well; now all that is wiped out. We see no one; at rare intervals we see Manet, M. Dally, and Riesener, and that is all."

In another of her letters, dated January 8, 1871, she wrote:
"My dear Yves, my dear Edma, I have not had the courage to take up my pen for a week. We celebrated the birth of the new year in sadness and tears. Berthe's health is visibly affected. I sent for the Neutorts' doctor, who, from what they themselves say, takes good care of them and accomplishes the miracle of keeping them on their feet. I was pleased with his attention, and with his questions; I have the impression that her frail health will improve under his care . . .

"The bombardment never stops. It is a sound that reverberates in your head night and day; it would make you feverish if you were not already in that state. This is not my complaint, but Berthe's. Yet the bombs do not do much harm – all told there are not many dead and but few wounded, and so far there is little destruction. The Panthéon and the Grenelle quarter receive most of the bombs. However, some did hit Auteuil and the Point du Jour. It is even said that Passy was hit – the Rue de Ranelagh. The force of the detonations was such that it is quite possible. It could be supposed that we would be afraid, but we are not all frightened; it is curious how much of its force an evil loses when faced at close quarters.

"Paris does not lose courage. I find it superb, and yet what suffering, what dire need. It is heart-rending."

57

On January 20 Madame Morisot wrote:

"We are very happy today, my dear Edma, thanks to you, or rather to Juliette! At last we have news! A long letter from her has reached us. She says that all of you, big and little ones, are in good health, that Adolphe is at sea, and that Tiburce has escaped from Mayence, and is a lieutenant! That is an unexpected joy!

"We are preparing a great sortie here. Each time this happens, we take the honours the first day, then the Prussians come at us in overwhelming numbers, and we are compelled to fall back. To be victorious, Paris would have to be capable of holding out for a very long time, and we would have to receive substantial aid. I doubt that either will happen.

"Your father wept on hearing that all of you are well; he has been less concerned about his son than about you.

"Take care of yourself, and do not worry. The bombs have not done us any harm; only one reached the Rue de l'Eglise. We do not see yet that it is urgent to move. Berthe is a little better. I think that the doctor is giving her the right kind of treatment. When she was under the care of M. Rafinesque, she kept to her bed, and could not get up . . ."

And on February 4 she wrote to her daughters:

"I don't understand very well why your letters are so slow in coming, any more than I understand why Tiburce has to go by way of Bordeaux, Tarascon, and Périgueux, to fight against the Prussian army. Now I am sure that we have arrived at the armistice without his having received a scratch – something to be thankful for. Provisions are not coming in very quickly; we have been living on biscuits for about twelve days, for the bread is impossible and makes us all sick.

"Berthe has grown thinner; she has hollows in her cheeks, this morning she is in bed with stomach cramps. We have a great wish to escape from this confinement. We are in a way planning to do so, because we are told that it would be bad to return to Paris soon and that the air there is unhealthy, and because I have a great need to hold you in my arms."

The privations of the siege of Paris shattered Berthe's health. She suffered ever afterward from a weak stomach, and could take only small amounts of nourishment at a time.

The correspondence between the sisters continued. On February 9 Berthe wrote to Edma, who was still at Mirande:

"Do you know that mother and I have a great wish to join you? The thought of spending a couple of weeks away from Paris, and with you, revives us. If you knew how sad this poor Paris is! And how sad everything is!

"I have come out of this siege absolutely disgusted with my fellow men, even with my best friends. Selfishness, indifference, prejudice – that is what one finds in nearly everyone.

"I am eager to see you; it seems to me that we have so much to tell one another, so much to grieve about together.

"Father says that he has written you a long letter. He is far from sharing Yves' opinions; I do not quite share them either, nevertheless I still manage to disagree with father. We talk so little to each other that this does not make much difference. We are awaiting the result of the elections with the same impatience as you.

"I have not written to you for a long time, because I have been as much demoralized as sick. I am very well now. Mother is sometimes well, sometimes tired; I find that she has become very thin. She says that she has great need of a change of air, but the thought of leaving my father nevertheless troubles her a little. Adieu."

A letter of Edma's dated February 19 contains a reference to Tiburce, who had been taken prisoner, succeeded in making his escape by hiding in the hold of a ship that was carrying coal to the port of Hamburg, and returned to France and rejoined the army. It runs as follows:

"Tiburce truly arouses one's admiration for his bravery on the battle-field – indeed, also for his courage in face of the great hardships he endured after the capitulation of Metz. One would never believe that he had gone through such ordeals."

On February 23, Edma wrote again:
"When I left you neither of us anticipated such a long separation. I remember your packing my trunk and saying to me each time I handed you something: 'So you intend to spend the winter there'.

"I see that every one of us is upholding whichever government he saw in action in such a critical moment. We feel just as indignant as mother does when Gambetta is unjustly attacked. It was he who did most for the defence, and it is he who is most thoroughly denounced today. He is unanimously attacked in the provinces and held responsible for our defeat. In this world success is everything.

60

"This reactionary Chamber does not inspire me with great confidence. *53* Those who advocate caution and moderation do not seem to be the men of the hour. However that may be, the task is grave and difficult. We must wait to judge them.

"There is talk in the newspapers of the German army entering Paris. Perhaps you are now witnessing that sad spectacle. Nothing is to be spared us."

Berthe wrote in reply on February 27:

"You are right, my dear Edma, in believing that nothing will be spared us. The Prussians are to enter on Wednesday, and our arrondissement is explicitly mentioned among those to be occupied by them. This news was circulated in the afternoon; it was announced that they would arrive tonight; then the report was denied in the evening, but this only meant that the entry was being delayed. Our Passy, usually so quiet, was animated, the Place de la Mairie and the main street were filled with noisy crowds. The National Guard was against surrendering its arms, and protested loudly. All this is very sad, and the terms are so severe that one cannot bear to think about them.

"Each day brings us some new sorrow, some new humiliation. The French people are so frivolous that they will promptly forget these sad events, but I am brokenhearted.

"It appears from what you tell me that Garibaldi is as much detested in *54* the provinces as Favre, J. Trochu, and the others are detested here; it seems to me that the Parisians have more justification than the provincials. If I happen timidly to voice this opinion at home, father throws up his hands and says that I am a madwoman; he would approve the attitude of the people of the south . . .

"P.S. I have just been told that there was a great commotion yesterday. The National Guard contingent at Belleville declared that they intended to fire their guns when the Prussians enter. I think we are at the beginning of an emotional period.

"Do you know that all our acquaintances have come out of the war without a scratch, except for that poor Bazille, who was killed at Orléans, I think. The brilliant painter Régnault was killed at Buzenval. The others *55* made a great fuss about nothing. Manet spent his time during the siege changing his uniform. His brother writes us today that in Bordeaux he recounted a number of imaginary exploits.

56   "I am told that it is Puvis de Chavannes, and not his brother, as I had thought, who is a member of the assembly. I know him to be so reactionary that despite all my interest in him, I should prefer to see someone else in his place. Degas is always the same, a little mad, but his wit is delightful."

When Edma expressed a wish to rejoin her husband in Cherbourg, Madame Morisot, in a letter dated February 27, advised her to postpone her journey, adding:

"You know that we shall have the Prussians here on Wednesday, and for God knows how long! Our quarter is the only one so honoured. They will encamp between this side of the Seine and the Faubourg Saint-Honoré, up to the Place de la Concorde. This is really a bit of luck. On account of a false alarm indicating that they would enter tonight, all the militia were ordered to clear out. They all took up station on the other side of the water, with the bridges guarded by a compact line of sentries. Some rowdies, with a predilection for noise and rioting, even began to build a barricade in the Champs Elysées. Our poor Passy was in a great commotion. Feeling ran high everywhere. Some madmen seized this opportunity for perpetrating an act odious and revolting in the last degree. They drowned an officer of the peace or policeman, after subjecting him to two hours of torture, and not a soul among the millions who were there did anything to save the unfortunate man, who only begged for the mercy of having his brains blown out. What infamies! What a nation! When I hear accounts of such misdeeds, I begin to hate the Prussians less. No doubt we shall have to billet some of them. God knows what senile or childish idea has got hold of father; he says he will have his door broken in rather than open it, and that if they use force, he will sacrifice his life rather than yield."

Early in March, Madame Morisot wrote to Yves:
"My dear Yves, we have waited each day for a letter announcing Edma's arrival. We have also been saying among ourselves that we only hope she does not come while the Prussians are with us. Their presence has been merely like a bad nightmare that is soon forgotten. To my mind the blow that really strikes home is the realization of the causes of this situation. About these I feel as you do, with this reservation, however, that since there was no way of winning the war, it was better to negotiate than to be swallowed whole. I think this is what would have happened, according to what we have heard on all sides about the morale of the troops in the provinces. We had a

foreboding of it, alas, and M. Thiers has only been the spokesman for all people of common sense. Now the revolutionaries will take advantage of the state of things to plunge us into chaos. They themselves would not have acted any better or differently from the others, fighting against impossible odds as we were. But now it will be easy for them to pose as heroes, to manipulate the passions that have been aroused, and to incite the populace to bold deeds by flattering words in order to further their personal ambitions. It is shameful and painful to admit this, but I do not think that there is a single really honest feeling or conviction behind all this noble façade. Now our municipal administration has resigned en bloc, thus condemning the present policies. What is the purpose of it? Men who have never yet come forward except to criticize – and now all they want is to put themselves in a position advantageous for the future.

"Paris is far from peaceful; since you are getting newspapers again, you can read in them that the National Guard, under the pretext of salvaging the cannons that had been placed at certain points, kept these pieces, scarcely concealing their intention of using them if need arose. Paris does not want to be tricked out of its republic – it wants the real thing, the republic of the communists and of disorder. Yesterday M. Riesener said something that I think is very true, namely, that the most injurious thing we were able to do to the Prussians was to contaminate their troops, and that the war could not have gone on longer without damage to them in this respect. I think our poor country is rotten to the core. You who are in favour of resistance will admit that the people of the south are not in accord, nor do those of the west make a secret of the fact that they feel the same way. All those fire-eaters of the inland provinces who clamour so loudly for a war to the death took to their heels during our sorties. Nothing is more shameful than the conduct of the men of Belleville and Ménilmontant, who have the courage only to fight their own countrymen, hoping thus to find an opportunity for plunder and for gratifying all their passions. I am sending you in haste a clipping of an article we found in the last night's *Temps*; if what it says is true, Edma will not be coming to Paris, and will be spared a long and difficult journey."

But Edma had already left Mirande. She spent several days in Paris, and then went to Cherbourg. Berthe wrote to her:
"The day of your departure, after that sad walk on the boulevard that upset us so greatly, we had a visit from the fat M. Dally. I myself was still

disturbed, although my father and my mother had recovered on seeing Tiburce. The doctor was returning from the Place Vendôme, where he had been attending the wounded and helping to collect the dead. He told me their names, at least the names of those he knew; I was greatly worried, nervous, being troubled for fear of hearing bad news. This sad evening that the four of us spent together brought back the siege to me as if I had never come out of it. Life has been a terrible nightmare for six months, and I am surprised that I am strong enough to be able to bear it . . ."

After many discussions pro and con, the Morisots finally made up their minds to leave Paris for Saint-Germain, even before they were advised to do so by the reactionary Puvis de Chavannes, who wrote to Berthe from Versailles:

"Mademoiselle, please be so kind as to send me news of you and your family to Versailles, poste restante. I have been here for several days with my sister and brother-in-law, who is a member of the Assembly.

"No other place is more unlike Paris than this. That is why I should have chosen it in any case, in order to escape certain sights and certain contacts. I was happy to leave my awful quarter, where informing against one's neighbour is becoming a daily occurrence, and where one may at any moment be forced to join the rabble under penalty of being shot by the first escaped convict who wants the fun of doing it.

"I hope that your parents will not think that the place can hold out forever, and that they will leave Paris to await the denouement elsewhere. If Versailles were not overflowing with refugees, it would be the best place for you, but, short of Versailles, there are Cernay, Saint-Cyr, Marly, and many other places . . . One is truly bathed in a feeling of grandeur in this admirable and magnificent setting, the sight of which is reassuring, since it recalls a beautiful and noble France, and one can forget for a moment how false and corrupt she is today. Once again, I repeat my prayer to you: please let me know what is happening to you. I assure you of all my respectful devotion."

From Saint-Germain, Madame Morisot wrote to Yves and Edma – to the one at Mirande and to the other at Cherbourg – a number of letters relating the events of the Commune. On March 13, she said in a note to Edma:

"We have been here for a week, my dear loved one, and I have not received a word from either Yves or you. I hear that there is going to be a battle near Courbevoie tonight; there has been continual activity over in that direction since this morning . . ."

On March 23 she commented as follows:

"How overcome we were when we saw all the shops closed, people at the windows, the boulevards and the Rue Royale deserted, and all this part of the quarter dismal and dreary. The marchers had gone to the Place Vendôme to seize the post of the National Guard of the district. As on the preceding day, they carried no arms, and were met with gunfire. Twenty-five men were killed or wounded – the exact number is unknown. We did not dare to ask anyone, knowing well that although Tiburce did not intend to repeat his performance of the day before, he was in the front ranks. Realistic as usual, *ma foi* – he dropped in for a moment to reassure us, but he spent the night out. He sent us word this morning to let us know that they are assembling at the Grand Hôtel, which has become the rallying point of all decent people, and that they are awaiting reinforcements. Our servant, who has just taken some civilian clothes and some linen to him, says that they are a large contingent and well armed. This development gave some people confidence enough to venture into the street, but what are we going to do? My husband is free to go, as all the courts are closed: but how can one leave one's son in the thick of this fighting? We are hardly alive here, but a little farther away we should not be alive at all. No omnibuses today, nor even boats; there is general consternation. M. Dally dined with us yesterday. He picked up nine dead and nine wounded in the Rue des Capucines, where the battle or rather the slaughter took place."

And on the 24th she reported:

"Your father saw Tiburce yesterday. He is on Admiral Saisset's staff. He seems to have won considerable respect: his fellow officers come to take orders from him. Unfortunately people are not enrolling quickly enough; it is said publicly that there are two thousand of them, but Tiburce estimates their number at no more than five hundred. The greater part of the hotel is closed, some windows are padded with mattresses, others have cannon and barricades in front of them. Yesterday, when they were negotiating, Tiburce volunteered to conduct all communications or parleys with General Chiseret and Lullier, both of whom he knows. To put it simply, he has done his duty, while taking good care of himself – at least I hope so. It took a certain amount of courage to place himself in the front ranks of the demonstration in uniform, with the party ribbon in his buttonhole. He could not have done more to make himself a target; he must think he is invulnerable by this time, and I am inclined to share this confidence of his a little. At all events, danger or no danger, I find it good that he does not spare himself. This is my idea of the way men should behave in a time of peril."

Berthe too wrote to Edma from Saint-Germain:

"My dear Edma, you hardly ever write to me, but I am not reproaching you, for I understand, better than most people, that one has little inclination these days to talk or to write. However, the more I think about your life, the more favoured it appears to me to be. I wish you would tell me whether it is really possible to work in Cherbourg. This may seem an unfeeling question, but I hope that you can put yourself in my position, and understand that work is the sole purpose of my existence, and that indefinitely prolonged idleness would be fatal to me from every point of view.

"The countryside here is the prettiest in the world; there would be a lot of subject matter for someone who liked entirely bare landscape and who had the necessary equipment for work. Neither of these conditions exists in my case, and I no longer want to work just for the sake of working.

"I do not know whether I am indulging in illusions, but it seems to me that a painting like the one I gave Manet could perhaps sell, and that is all I care about.

"Since you understand perfectly well what I mean, answer me on this point, and now let us talk about more interesting things. Everyone is engrossed in this wretched business of politics. We can hear the cannon throughout the day; we can even see the smoke on Mont Valérien from the terrace. From time to time we meet people who have got out of Paris. Their accounts are very contradictory: according to some, people there are dying of starvation; according to others, the city is perfectly peaceful. The only thing certain is that everyone is fleeing from it, and this is sufficient proof that life there is not pleasant.

"Up to now the news we have had from Passy has been good. You know that of all our acquaintances in the Rue Franklin, the only one who is still there is Madame Heymonet. We were almost reassured about the fate of our house, but I see this morning that they tried to destroy the batteries of the Trocadéro from Mont Valérien; such an operation cannot be carried out without splattering the neighbourhood, and we are philosophically awaiting the outcome of all this . . ."

59

60

A little later Madame Morisot wrote to Edma to inform her that Berthe would shortly arrive in Cherbourg. In a note dated May 2 she said:

"I shall send Berthe to you soon, and the thought that you are going to be together again soothes my heart a little. Berthe will not fail to be bored in Cherbourg, that is certain, but since she will be working there, she will be less bored than she is here; moreover, the companionship between two sisters of like age who love each other is always more pleasant than association with parents who have become morose as a result of either illness or anxieties. Therefore do not worry if she is sad at times; sadness has become like a second nature to her, but you will notice it less than I do, since you have an interest closer to your heart and a constant occupation in little Minou."

Shortly after arriving in Cherbourg, Berthe received a letter from her mother, dated May 18, which conveyed the false report of the destruction of the Trocadéro.

"Here is some news, and it is sad news, my dear Bijou; we cannot complain that life is monotonous. We learned last night that the Trocadéro has been blown up. Edma has chosen a fine time to ask for painting materials! Everything has surely been pulverized. Your father, because he always expects the worst, is fairly stoical when it does come. Tiburce is mourning only for Pucq! He has just a word for Ludovic . . . And the paintings! You had better set to work! I should have liked to preserve all the memories of your youth and of your common hopes; now I am deprived of those things that were realized, and that might some day have had value in eyes other than mine. Incidentally, you will see in the newspapers that Achille Oudinot is now administrator of the Louvre. What a strange time! And the Column! To think that people could be found who would do such a thing, and others who would stand by and see it being done . . ."

61

Puvis de Chavannes wrote to Berthe from Versailles:

"Your letter gave me great pleasure, dear Mademoiselle, and I should like to prove this to you by my promptness in answering it. I wish, however, that it had been more detailed about several things, such as the welcome you received from your sister, who must have been happy to see you again, and also about the outcome of your journey. You know how much such things interest me, whether they pertain to your art or directly to your personal life – which I presume to be the case at present, for one hardly paints while

travelling in a railway carriage. You are enjoying fresh air in the company of your family who love you; you are seeing a place that is new to you, and you are no longer hearing the stupid cannon. Meanwhile you are as well informed as we are of every important event, and finally, you are always in your own company. Why then should one be sorry for you? You ask me what is being talked about and what is happening in Versailles. Well, it's always the same things. The Rue des Reservoirs has not become easier for Parisians to climb, and they mark time in their souls even more than on the street. As for me, I produce as much as I can, but these things remain in a latent state, so to speak – formless sketches or spots of colour that I expect nevertheless to turn to account some day. It is cold, sharp, unpleasant. The shade is frigid and the sun pitiless. Add to that some great dust squalls that blind you from time to time, and an absolutely artificial existence, and you will know as much about Versailles as if you were living there. It is really a relief to take refuge in certain intellectual circles that fortunately seem to want to resist the general disaster – without this, one would die of boredom, indignation, and disgust, and of other moral poisons. Thiers upbraided the Chamber at yesterday's meeting in very severe terms, to the acute displeasure of the great majority, despite appearances to the contrary, and despite the vote of absolute confidence that followed the lashing. But all that, I think, does not interest you very much. It is so far away. I have given up my trip to Nantes; so far as this goes, I am more prudent than you have been. But the idea of more than twenty hours in the train, with nothing to look forward to, discourages me. I am growing callous and shall soon rival M. Riesener in whiteness of hair. I am already imitating him in another way, for here I have written four pages addressed to you. May you find them agreeable, and may they quickly bring me a good reply. Above all, do not use too faint-coloured an ink, and tell me everything you are doing or thinking – you see that I am not doing things by halves, but that's the way it is. It is more than likely that we shall soon return to Paris. You must come to see what is left of my poor studio – perhaps I should say studios, for it is quite possible that the one in Paris is also wrecked.

"Ah, those cannon balls – brutal things, aren't they? I often think of those very pleasant hours I spent last year in that big bazaar that has become a dressing station, filled today with every sort of disease. Not so long ago it was full of strollers, paintings, sculptures, pastries, etc., etc. But you have told me that you don't want to hear about these things, so let us not talk about them; but the point is that time passed quickly there. All this is now strangely gone with the wind, and no sooner will the ruins be more or less restored than one will be oneself a ruin. If only ivy would grow around old men, as it does around the statues in Versailles! But we do not have even this final bit of luck – we must die as scarecrows.

"And so, you see, you must tell me in great detail what is happening to you, whether you are working, whether you are succeeding – in other words, everything. Boom!

"Adieu, dear Mademoiselle. Forgive me this outburst of garrulity. I forgot to tell you that I had a very funny dream, so funny that I woke up laughing. I was calling on some very charming people, I was exerting myself to be agreeable, while the master of the house, using his hand as a shield, and thinking that I could not see him, was making the most horrible faces at his wife and children, which he thought very amusing. I could see everything, and restrained myself only with the greatest difficulty – so much so that when I exploded, I woke up. You see that I am telling you everything that happens to me. Follow my example."

This dream perhaps related – without any suspicion of this on the part of Puvis himself – to his relations with the Morisot family, to which he refers in his next letter to Berthe. In the meantime, Edma received two letters from her mother. The first, dated May 21, reads:

"While we were at lunch we heard a terrible hubbub, a rumbling of carriages, at full speed, people running, cavalry squadrons galloping, and cries in the midst of it all. We flung down our napkins, and in no time we were in the street, and learned that it was Rochefort being escorted to Versailles. But this report remains rather vague; first we were told the opposite – that he had managed to escape and was being pursued."

On May 22 Madame Morisot wrote:

"It was yesterday about dinner-time, dear Mamie, that we heard the good news. Your father, who is always afraid to be happy, did not believe it, but I thought that since our troops have entered Paris, I should be in Passy in a few days. Tiburce left this morning; he does not want to miss any part of the affair. If he can make his way to the house, he will stay there. Otherwise he will bring us the news tonight. Louis has written that the explosion could be felt at Passy with such force that he thought the house was collapsing. All the window panes are broken, the little curtains are on the floor with the plaster. There are only three window panes intact in the studio;

all the pictures are down. However, no one was hurt. There was a shower of stones and dust over the whole neighbourhood. There is less damage at my father's house. Louis sleeps in the cellar.

"We have not much hope that the place will soon be cleared. What is going to happen? I tremble to think. It is said that M. Thiers, once Paris is taken, will resign, and without him there will be nothing to restrain the reactionaries. We shall advance to a full-fledged monarchy, new struggles, open or hidden, with no respite. I am afraid that such will be our lot. I have read something about the financial terms, which if true will please me greatly; this arrangement will deliver us from these odious Prussians. They regale the terrace with their music every day. They are deployed and concentrated nearer to Paris. Their arrogance is extreme. I don't like them any better since it has been decided that they are no longer our enemies."

To Berthe she wrote on May 23 as follows:

"Tiburce came back yesterday, dear Bijou. He gave us additional details, but did not confirm everything the newspapers are saying. Montmartre is taken, but the Place de la Concorde put up such a strong resistance that the shells rained all about our house. And did I tell you that the second and third stories of my father's house are gone? That is to say, Madame Heymonet's apartment was penetrated by a shell that exploded on the second floor, smashing everything to atoms. There was a rumour that the Scheffer house was gone, but only a part of the wall is damaged, and the furniture is still intact. The linen, some pictures, a clock, Lucien's wardrobe, and all of the wine cellar were stolen at Maria's. In Charles' house only the big pieces of furniture are said to be left, and the Communards scrawled disgusting arabesques on his embroidered coat. All these reports, however, are perhaps not too accurate. One thing that is certain is that the gunboat is firing upon us continually; the reason is that the headquarters are in the Rue Franklin, MacMahon is in the Guillemet house, Vincy is at the Cosnards', and the *intendant général* is in our house. Tiburce has invited these gentlemen to dinner. It seems that it is not easy for them to get provisions; all the butcher shops are closed, and one has to send to Sèvres to get meat. Yesterday morning they reciprocated by asking Tiburce to luncheon. He has put the cellar at their disposal, as well as the linen, the china, etc. However, they sleep on mattresses on the floor, and almost in the open, since not a windowpane is left. During the luncheon the shells did not stop whizzing, and fragments fell in the garden. The officers of the general staff thought they would have

63

to lift the siege. They did not feel inclined to let themselves be killed for no reason. By half past nine, when Tiburce left, the situation had not changed.

"You see that we are not yet sure as to what is happening to our neighbourhood. As for returning there, that will be impossible for several more days; also we must wait until those gentlemen clear out. General Vinay was very amiable to Tiburce, who was received cordially by everyone. While they were on the Cosnard terrace, a bullet struck the summer house; it was fired from an unseen point, and was destined no doubt for the general. It follows that Passy is not yet cleared of all Communards. It is impossible to venture anywhere. Tiburce tried to go as far as the Rond-Point, in order to cross the Pont d' Alma. Bullets were whistling, and the soldiers are in such a violent mood that they don't give you time to explain yourself. It was not easy to enter Paris. Lucien is amazed over Tiburce's coolness and daring. Turned back at one point, they went to another. Getting out of Paris was easier; they met J. Ferry in a cab and he brought them back to Versailles – of all places – and from there they got back without difficulty. It is a great coming and going . . .

"In short, it is over, yet not over. First of all, the important places are not taken, and then there is the danger of isolated attacks, betrayals, and surprises . . . I had got this far when there was a new excitement – a fire alarm – everyone ran to the terrace. Paris was burning, they said. The truth was that MacMahon had sent a dispatch to the Mairie calling out all firemen available in the suburbs, because the insurrectionists are trying to avenge their defeat by setting fire to everything. Rumours of all kinds are circulating – that the Louvre is burning, or the police headquarters, where all the hostages are being held, that ten different places are on fire, etc., etc. In truth we know nothing, but we may indeed suspect that the insurgents want to promote disorder, under cover of which they could escape.

"Do not regret that you are not witnessing this final stage of the struggle; we have no more light on what is happening than you others; moreover we feel helpless."

Madame Morisot wrote again to Berthe, on May 25:
"Paris on fire! This is beyond any description . . . Throughout the day the wind kept blowing in charred papers; some of them were still legible. A vast column of smoke covered Paris, and at night a luminous red cloud, horrible to behold, made it all look like a volcanic eruption. There were continual

explosions and detonations; we were spared nothing. They say the insurrection is crushed; but the shooting has not yet stopped. Hence this is not true. By ten o'clock, when we left the terrace, the fire seemed to have been put out, so that I hoped very much that everything had been grossly exaggerated, but the accounts in the newspapers this morning leave no room for doubt. Latest official dispatch: the insurrection is now driven back to a very small part of Paris, the Tuilleries is reduced to ashes, the Louvre survives, the part of the Finance Ministry building fronting on the Rue de Rivoli is on fire, the Cour des Comptes is burned down, twelve thousand prisoners, Paris strewn with dead . . . Now that the Cour des Comptes has been burned down, my husband has resumed his pet theme more insistently than ever, namely, that this gives good reason for abolishing it. In actual fact all the documents are being scattered to the winds, and this made me say right away that I thought it a good riddance . . . Should M. Degas have got a bit scorched, he will have well deserved it."

In a letter of June 5 she recounted further:
"I saw only the Hôtel-de-Ville the day after my arrival . . . What I saw was frightful. To think that this great massive building is ripped open from one end to the other! It was smoking in several places, and the firemen were still pouring water on it. It is a complete ruin. Your father would like all this debris to be preserved as a perpetual reminder of the horrors of popular revolution. It's unbelievable, a nation thus destroying itself! Going down by boat, I saw the remains of the Cour des Comptes, of the Hôtel de la Légion d'Honneur, of the Orsay barracks, of a part of the Tuilleries. The poor Louvre has been nicked by projectiles, and there are few streets that do not bear traces of the struggle. I also noticed that half the Rue Royale is demolished, and there are so many ruined houses, it is unbelievable – one rubs one's eyes, wondering whether one is really awake . . .
"Tiburce has met two Communards, at this moment when they are all being shot . . . Manet and Degas! Even at this stage they are condemning the drastic measures used to repress them. I think they are insane, don't you?"

On June 10 she sent Berthe the following item:
"Guillemet told me yesterday that the Manets have finally managed to return; it was Edouard whom Tiburce met, not his brother. Manet hardly shows much eagerness to come to see me; it is true, of course, that you are not here . . ."

The return of the Manets was confirmed by the following letter, addressed to Berthe by Edouard Manet from Paris on June 10:

"Dear Mademoiselle, we came back to Paris several days ago, and the ladies ask me to send their regards to you and to Madame Pointillon, with whom you are probably staying.

"What terrible events, and how are we going to come out of this? Each one lays the blame on his neighbour, but to tell the truth all of us are responsible for what has happened.

"I met Tiburce a few days ago, and I have been unable to go to see your mother as I had planned. But all of us are just about ruined; we shall have to put our shoulders to the wheel.

"Eugène went to see you at Saint-Germain, but you were out that day. I was pleased to hear that your house in Passy has been spared. Today I saw that poor Oudinot – he too has had his moment of power. What a fall! I hope, Mademoiselle, that you will not stay a long time in Cherbourg. Everybody is returning to Paris; besides, it's impossible to live anywhere else."

AFTER THE WAR : CHERBOURG
SAINT-JEAN-DE-LUZ, MADRID, MAURECOURT

BERTHE was now staying with Edma in Cherbourg, where she had gone to seek a bit of peace and quiet after the ordeal of the war. Now that this crisis was over, Madame Morisot returned to a preoccupation of another kind, which the recent events had caused her to put aside – the problem of marrying off her youngest daughter. A letter of hers to Edma, dated June 22, turns wholly on this concern.

"Yesterday I saw Papa Riesener. He is not any better; he is restless and nervous. He and his wife seem much concerned about Berthe; with great tact they show that they understand my anxiety, and we talk about the situation frankly as good friends. I am earnestly imploring Berthe not to be so disdainful. Everyone thinks that it is better to marry, even making some concessions, than to remain independent in a position that is not really one. We must consider that in a few more years she will be more alone, she will have fewer ties than now; her youth will fade, and of the friends she supposes herself to have now, only a few will remain. I think that Eugène Manet is crazy most of the time, and that the erratic behaviour of all these individuals augurs no assurance for happiness in life.

"I know that now the activity and artistic milieu of Paris are of great attraction for Berthe. She should take care not to yield to still another illusion, not to give up the substance for the shadow. Were you referring to the gentleman with the carriage? Money, however, certainly matters. Ah, how I wish the dear child had all this turmoil of feeling and phantasy behind her . . .

"To come back to Manet – I wonder whether he spoke so lightly only to be forgotten for his reluctance to do Berthe a favour. Perhaps he wants us to think that he acted from some special motive, while actually he hadn't any at all, and was thinking only of himself at the time of his departure. If his brother had any sort of serious intention, it would not require a chance opportunity or an impulsive moment for him to declare himself – for in that case he would only be committing a folly that he would regret the next day. It is only too obvious that this is not the way to go about marriage; for where there is mutual attraction, all practical difficulties are cleverly circumvented . . . Men fill me with disgust; I have a horror of them, and I am beginning to dislike everyone. La Loubens spent the evening being amiable to Monsieur Degas, and he, who is supposed to despise her, was charming to her. She has become much fatter, which does not make her any prettier in my eyes, though Tiburce says it does . . .

"Kiss my precious little Berthe for me. Tell her that I wish she would steer her ship wisely and cautiously, not like her daredevil of a brother. For when one has ruined one's own life beyond retrieve one is only too eager to put the blame upon others . . ."

This letter reveals that even at that time Eugène Manet and Berthe were interested in each other, although it was several years before they married.

On June 23, Puvis de Chavannes wrote to Berthe:
"I had intended to wait for good weather before replying to you, but that would mean putting it off indefinitely, so I hope that you won't hold my despairing, disgusted, dull prose against me. Everything conspires to make

my life unpleasant – even down to the glaziers, whose charges are exorbi-
tant. We have shot many persons who weren't such thieves and plunderers
as they are. And then this rain, this maddening rain, never stopping. Now,
because of the flooded fields and ruined crops, the country will not be able
to offset the losses and the disaster suffered by the city. Ah, if instead of
learning Greek when we were young, we had learned to make counterfeit
money, we might still manage in a pinch; it would be risky, I know, but in
this last year we have become somewhat hardened to dangers of all kinds.
And what one reads and hears – bad faith, dissension, ingratitude, are all
rampant and outdoing one another.

"You are right indeed in thinking of taking refuge outside of France –
even with that selfish, hypocritical, tiresome, and treacherous nation that is
protecting those assassins of ours. You say to me also that our relations will
never be simple or easy; I know this. I met your father, and although he
urged me to come to Passy, I took that as I was supposed to take it, that is,
as purely a polite gesture, for I know that your family does not like me, and
that their chief feeling toward me is a wish never to see me. That is more
than enough to put an end to friendship, for nothing in the world is more
horrible than a situation that is false and strained – which ours would be.
Therefore all we can do is to trust in God. I must add that the fault is not
mine, in that case things could be set right. The whole misfortune comes
from the fact that I arouse antipathy instead of love, as others do. There is
no remedy for that. Despite all my troubles, all my preoccupations, and
although I am beset by most depressing thoughts about my present and my
future, I am immersed more deeply than ever in work, and I am finding
such joy in it that I dare not admit it to myself, lest I bring my bad luck
down on myself and take a blow in this quarter too. Therefore, not a word!

"You have said something to which I have always forgotten to reply,
namely, that last winter I deserted you. But, good heavens, don't you remember that you yourself advised me to keep away, and that I withdrew,
taking your word for it that your parents were unfavourably disposed
toward me. At one time I hoped to be able to maintain a social relationship
with your family, with that nuance of intimacy, ease, and naturalness which
comes from a mutual liking, which I believed to exist. It existed, and still
exists, but only on my part – despite certain appearances by which I could
not, without presumption, let myself be deceived, as your mother will surely
agree. And since it is never too soon to do the right thing, the moment I
was enlightened as to your family's feelings I cleared out. What else could

I do? But let bygones be bygones, and let us not talk about it any longer. Or rather, let us proceed to another reproach. Why don't you tell me anything about your life? You write in such general terms that my mind has nothing to lay hold of. It is hard to find even a faint gleam of light, and I strain my eyes trying to find you in the fog . . ."

Madame Morisot wrote again to Edma on June 29:
"On Tuesday at last I saw our friend Manet . . . We were unable to say anything to each other, even in a casual way. And really that family is most unprepossessing. Manet told us that at lunch his two brothers had almost come to blows, and everywhere one hears talk about their quarrels. Incredible as it may seem, Fantin did not leave Paris. He never stuck his nose outside his house throughout the siege and the Commune – and he worked. What greater courage would it have taken to go to the ramparts? He lived without air, and for a good while in the cellar. I think he must be puffier and more unhealthy than ever.

"Manet irritates me with his railings against Monsieur Thiers, whom he calls a demented old man; he says that anyone else would be better, and that the only capable man we have is Gambetta. When you hear talk of that sort, you can scarcely have any hope for the future of this country.

"Today the long-awaited review was held. There were many rumours that should it be postponed, it would be because of a conspiracy. That is all we need – to mess things up again. France is split between madmen – such as the Manet clique and others – and fools, the party of Chambord and his following. I saw – I don't know why – Mademoiselle Bourbon Busset. These people gloat over the return of their prince, and flaunt all their old prejudices – it's pathetic! Poor France! It has fallen low indeed when such nonentities can display such effrontery. And yet the success of the loan made me proud and happy. I invested a thousand of our savings; their value had shrunk to seven hundred . . ."

66

Some time later, Puvis de Chavannes, at Berthe's request, called upon her parents and described his visit in the following letter:
"You end your letter with a question, which you could easily answer yourself if you stopped to think a little. Among many proofs, I shall offer only this one that shows my perfect docility; for, without losing a day, I went to see your parents, who had the good fortune not to be at home, or perhaps almost not . . . I saw your brother, and after a short talk with him I

walked on through that Bois de Boulogne, which is quite scorched . . . Your Passy studio was open but dark and sepulchral – the curtains three-quarters drawn. I looked for you in a white peignoir, but had to content myself with my own evocation. I did not cross the threshhold, however, postponing that until the return of the one animator of this solitude.

"At this moment I am scheming to obtain the release of an unfortunate boy who was taken to Cherbourg much against his will, and who is confined in the fort of Homet . . . Just think – I had considered using your influence, but at the last moment I thought better of it, and had recourse to a gentleman. It would have been far too indiscreet. Moreover, it is better for him not to see you for the sake of his composure and his peace of mind. A vision of you would not be good for a prisoner . . . I have embarked (as you put it) on this third sheet of paper, and so I continue prattling. This time it is your fault; you should not have encouraged me. And now, you are going to take a good pen and a big sheet of paper, and you are going to write me sweetly everything that passes through your brain, that brain which is set in such a strange and charming head."

In another letter, dated July 21, Puvis again touches on the feelings of the elder Morisots toward him:

"You must admit that you are pretty brazen, with your eight folded pages, and saying 'ouf' at the end of a page and a half! Lord, what impudence! If you have any heart at all, you will write me eight pages at once.

"A passage of your letter leads me to suppose that your parents do not care to see me at present, any more than they did in the past. Thus you will have to arrange matters as you see fit. I must leave it to you, and will simply do as you direct. You yourself are to determine the day and hour of your visit to me, and you are to let me know in advance, so that I may be ready to receive you – this will be a very, very great pleasure for me. And so it is agreed; I shall be waiting. You won't see many paintings in my studio, although I have worked assiduously, and I am very much afraid that you will not find that I have replaced quantity with quality. But you are, after all, indulgent.

"I hope to free my protegé from the clutches of the court martial; I have not mentioned him to you again only because I wish to be discreet. That too is one of my virtues. You will discover the others little by little and in due time . . . Good-bye, or better still, au revoir. Come now, let us have those eight pages."

In the same month, Madame Morisot wrote several letters to Berthe. On July 14 she reported:

"I found the Manet salon in just the same state as before; it is nauseating. If people were not interested in hearing individual accounts of public misfortunes, I think little would have been said. The heat was stifling, everybody was cooped up in the one drawing room, the drinks were warm. But Pagans sang, Madame Edouard played, and Monsieur Degas was there. *67* This is not to say that he flitted about; he looked very sleepy – your father seemed younger than he.

"Mademoiselle Eva has grown uglier. Madame Camus had a sugary manner, but Tiburce found her ravishing. Champfleury wore an air of *68* importance, occupied the best chair with his legs stretched out, not saying a word to anyone – you can see this ensemble from where you are . . . Eugène looked alert until ten o'clock. He asked me in a very amiable manner how you are, but after being with me for a moment, his eyelids fluttered, struggling against sleep. Edouard kept asking me whether you are coming back, or abandoning all your adorers because you have found others . . ."

In a note of July 15, she wrote:
"Just as Tiburce was putting on his hat we heard a loud explosion, and he rushed to Vincennes to find that the cartridge factory had just blown up. Stores of gunpowder had been brought there from Passy and other places. It was bound to happen, as you can see; we are not told the number of dead and wounded, but the rumour was that there was a clash between French and Prussians, and that the latter cut down our soldiers, who were unarmed. Hearing of these things, and of the way these people give orders in the occupied provinces, drives me wild with rage and indignation. We are told that this is a law of war, that it is we who should keep quiet . . ."

She wrote again on July 24:
"Manet is very nice; he has taken a liking to Tiburce. He made an appointment with him, in order to propose to him a position as dramatic critic for the newspaper *La Verité*, and now he is going to introduce him there. However, he credits himself with a longer arm than he really has; the plain fact is that no one is ever engaged merely on the recommendation of a friend. But Manet thinks that if his literary friends find out that he has proposed this to Tiburce, they will resent it; he asks us to keep silent about it – something he will never do himself . . .

"Your friend Manet took back the little canvas that he was to give me as a gift from his family. He wants to show this specimen to a buyer. Much good will it do him: if he builds his hopes of success on such works as this, he must be crazier than ever. He agrees with me that the Gonzalès have lost ground. He says that one should never drop out of society, for on returning one is always at a disadvantage. His wife is somewhat recovered, but he must have experienced a great shock at the sight of this bucolic blooming . . .

"All the cackle of these people seems very stupid and very boring after the upheavals we have just gone through. It shows how frivolous and at the same time habit-bound the Frenchman is. His little world, his little vanities, his little satisfactions – these are what survive. Everything else is apparently not worth the trouble of talking about. I think that France is still very sick . . ."

On returning to Passy after her stay in Cherbourg, Berthe wrote to Edma: "The water-colour looks very well now that it is framed. The dealer, who is, I am told, one of the most important in Paris, complimented me very highly, and said that it had attracted notice from all the artists who came to his establishment. I did not dare to ask him whether he would buy some of my work. I shall wait to do that until I have other pictures to offer him.

"I hear that Fantin is making a fortune in London. Tissot is earning a lot of money, and little Clauss is delighted with her stay there. All these people are stealing my idea. Write to me in all seriousness what you would do if you were in my place. Yesterday my mother told me politely that she has no faith in my talent, and that she thinks me incapable of ever doing anything worthwhile. I see that she thinks me raving mad when I tell her that I must certainly have as much talent as Mlle Jacquemard.

"I did not go to Manet's last Thursday . . . On the preceding Thursday he was very nice to me. Once more he thinks me not too unattractive, and wants to take me back as his model. Out of sheer boredom, I shall end by proposing this very thing myself. I should like very much to see what you are doing. I am sure it is very good. The atmosphere of Cherbourg is favourable for painting. It seems that the water-colour of you in gray is my masterpiece – not the other. I am sorry you have not attempted this medium, which is much easier, because one can be successful without being aware of it.

"I am doing Yves with Bichette. I am having great difficulty with them. The work is losing all its freshness. Moreover, as a composition it resembles a Manet. I realize this and am annoyed."

Madame Morisot in turn wrote to Edma as follows:

"Berthe is sorry to have left Cherbourg now that the weather is so beautiful and so warm. She could have worked as much as she liked, at least so she thinks. She's always sure she could do such wonderful things in any place where she is not at the moment, and hardly ever makes an effort to use the resources at hand. That is why I do not put any faith in your practical advice. She has perhaps the necessary talent – I shall be delighted if such is the case – but she has not the kind of talent that has commercial value or wins public recognition; she will never sell anything done in her present manner, and she is incapable of painting differently. Manet himself, even while heaping compliments on her, said: 'Mlle B. has not wanted to do anything up to now. She has not really tried; when she wants to, she will succeed.'

"But we know that she wants to, and that when she does something, she sets about it with the greatest ardour. But all she accomplishes is to make herself sick. If one must do bad work in order to please the public – for, really, you have made me feel that all my ideas of painting are wrong – she will never do the kind of work that dealers buy in the hope of reselling it. When a few artists compliment her, it goes to her head. Are they really sincere? Puvis has told her that her work has such subtlety and distinction that it makes others miserable, and that he was returning home disgusted with himself. Frankly, is it as good as all that? Would anyone give even twenty francs for these ravishing things?

"I have become sceptical – that's quite possible. But now much time has passed, enough to convince me that my family is fairly distinguished, fairly gifted, but incapable of the efforts needed to reach certain rungs of the ladder. That is how we are, and that is how we'll always be, because of physical obstacles and because our means are insufficient in all sorts of ways. I am therefore a bit disappointed to see that Berthe won't settle down like everybody else. It is like her painting – she will get compliments, since she seems to be eager to receive them, but she will be held at arm's length when it comes to a serious commitment."

In a subsequent letter she says:

"I hope for only one thing now – that you are right and that Berthe can become independent. I for my part do not believe so at all, but I shall do everything I can to help her reach this goal; it is at least an objective – after all, one has to do something in life. But what an arduous task it is! At present she is trying to do a study of Yves. Whenever she works she has an anxious, unhappy, almost fierce look. I cannot say how much of this comes from wounded pride, but I do know that this existence of hers is like the ordeal of a convict in chains, and I should like to enjoy greater peace of mind in my old age."

Another letter of Berthe's mother concludes as follows:

"M. Degas dropped in for a moment yesterday. He uttered some compliments, though he looked at nothing – he just had an impulse to be amiable for a change. To believe these great men, she has become an artist!

"Stevens wants to visit us, he says. He is buying a house for himself, with an enormous garden. He will make more than a hundred thousand francs this year. That is a blow to the others who think they are more talented. However, the marital life of the Stevenses is somewhat unsatisfactory at the moment. Madame is protracting her stay at Saint-Valéry, and Monsieur is bewailing in advance the approaching end of his celibacy. According to Manet, things might have gone further than that, and it was that little rascal C. who came between them."

At the end of 1871, Edma Pontillon came to Passy for the birth of her second daughter. It was at this time that Berthe executed the pastel portrait of her sister that is now in the Louvre. She exhibited it in the *Salon* of 1872. The following summer she stayed with her sister Yves in the southwest of France, but she did not like that region, which she seemed to find unsuitable for work. Her mother wrote to her:

"I ventured a visit to the Manets . . . Manet seemed very pleased to see me, and complained because we had not come to see him in the café. The Stevenses will hold their last soirée on Wednesday, but they did not even attend their last one. The Manets and M. Degas were playing host to one another. It seemed to me that they had patched things up. Everyone knows now with whom Tiburce is in love, and it is causing much astonishment. M. Degas admires his courage, Manet protests indignation, and says that in a few years Tiburce will be ashamed of his wife – he admits that she has a pretty face, but he cannot endure her figure. Tiburce would do much better to marry Mlle Gonzalès – there is a woman who is ravishing in every respect, and so intelligent and such good manners! All this does not prevent him from saying that he would be delighted to plan a little trip with us to the seashore. The talk is of Saint-Valéry-en-Caux. I said that this would not do for Manet. If he is allowed to go to the seashore to choose the place, there is the danger that he will not come back, or, at the very least, that the money for the trip will be used up in the search.

"Braquemond is marrying a Spaniard, a pretty woman, I hear." 70

Berthe wrote to her mother from Saint-Jean-de-Luz:

". . . I am not too disappointed, because I did not expect the countryside to be beautiful nor the accommodations too comfortable. Yesterday I went to the beach; the people you see there are elegant; I would not be up to them. However, I shall not see them! There is no place where everybody meets. Today I shall take an exploratory walk. Bayonne seemed very pretty; I regret very much not being nearer to it . . .

"The temperature has been somewhat more bearable for several days, dear mother, and thanks to this change I begin to find the country very lovely. I realize that what I disliked here was chiefly the sun . . . I am working a little, but not enough to tire myself. The place is ruined by the children. There is no way of setting up my easel anywhere without being surrounded by them, and I dread having them about – so much so that I have given up working in the streets or on the roads. I take walks in the morning, I work in the afternoon. I douse myself with salt-water. In the evening, Yves and I sit in the square or by the sea, and talk. Theodore either is not with us, or if he is, he is not there. That is our life; you would not find it amusing. The night is spent in struggling with the fleas; never in my life have I seen so many.

"I think we shall leave without having spoken to a single person. There are few Frenchmen here. The Spaniards are in the majority and do not seem to wish to associate with us . . . Heaven knows here I don't have to protect myself or be afraid of admirers. I am surprised at being as un-noticed as I am; it is the first time in my life that I am so completely ignored. The advantage of it is that since no one ever looks at me, I find it unnecessary to dress up . . ."

Puvis de Chavannes had asked her in a letter, before she had left Paris, to write to him from the seashore. She did so, and received from him the following reply:

"Dear Mademoiselle:

"In all sincerity, I pity you for having so much sun – a quarter of it would drive me insane. I hate nothing so much as that light which like a merciless spear pierces your eyes, your ears, in short everything; it is just like those flies that also always know where to attack you, where to sting you. Let us acknowledge that this essentially bourgeois and ill-bred heavenly body is a necessary evil and let us not talk about it any more.

"You will become accustomed, I think, to that beautiful country. I confess, however, that I have seen it only from the inside of a railway carriage, but from there it seemed to have real character, and to be paintable, which is rare for places reputed to be beautiful, such as that horrible Switzerland, with its glaciers and its artificial décor, in which man is crowded out.

"Though I do not know Saint-Jean-de-Luz itself, I lived for six weeks near there, and I can easily imagine your house. It must be white, with brown shutters. The staircase doesn't amount to much, and the rest is nondescript. You are wrong in saying that it is like Passy, you certainly have not the comfort of your studio there, with its red sofa, and the beautiful pouf in the centre. But imagination makes up for everything – and it is not for nothing that you are a thoroughbred artist, as our friend Stevens says.

"It is a long time since I have seen him; he has had trouble with his eyes, I hear. I am so busy that at night I collapse on my bed like a dog (a dog that has a bed, that is); the weather here is bad, dry and scorching, and cold. Figure that out if you can, but that is the way it is. The days are unbearable because of dust and sun; the Neuilly studio is suffocating, and I begin to breathe only after this frightful daylight is replaced by the lamp. Have you begun to work? . . ."

Berthe wrote to Edma from Saint-Jean-de-Luz:
"I have been at Saint-Jean-de-Luz, dear Mame, for an eternity. I do not like this place; I find it arid, dried up. The sea here is ugly. It is either all blue – I hate it that way – or dark and dull . . . Bayonne seemed lovely; I should like to spend a few days there . . . I have not yet found anything worth painting; everything is in the full sunlight, and on the whole nothing is very pretty . . ."

In another letter she said:
"We shall stay here only three or four more days. I am not sorry, for

frankly I am beginning to tire of being here. There is constant sun, good weather all the time, the ocean like a slab of slate – there is nothing less picturesque than this combination. We are going to Madrid, at least we think we are. I have written to Manet asking him for the address of Astruc who, I know, has been there for a fairly long time. He will be of great help to me, since he speaks Spanish and knows Madrid thoroughly, and he certainly will be able to point out to us the things worth seeing. He must feel about the Museum pretty much as I do. I am very sorry that you are not with us. I should enjoy the trip much more if you were in the party. We should give ourselves plenty of time to admire the Velasquez and the Goyas. That is for me about the only interest in going . . .

"Decidedly, I shall never return to the Midi, I only half like this region. Nevertheless, I shall go to Mirande. I haven't worked well; I am ashamed of what I shall be bringing back, as regards both quality and quantity. I assure you that Maurecourt is just as good for working, even better. I have not done even one water-colour. I wanted to do sketches in pastel but I only made one. The sea is usually so ugly that I have no desire to work. I recently started something that was supposed to be very pretty, but it is very poor; anyway, you will see."

In a subsequent letter she wrote:

"In reality I do not regret this sudden change, particularly if it should facilitate my trip to Madrid. This is our intention – to live frugally at Saint-Jean-de-Luz, then to send Theodore and the children back to Mirande, and go to Madrid for five or six days. Probably nothing will come of all these projects for lack of money. In any case, we shall stay here only until the fifteenth. You see that I have not much time left in which to work, and so far I have done almost nothing. Right now the place is much more pleasant than when I came; it is possible to go out during the day now – before this, it was real torture. And yet we have had extremely stormy weather for two days, heavy, threatening, and a scorching wind; we dress as lightly as possible, and we are drenched with perspiration at the slightest exertion.

"Nothing was ever as pretty as the sea was yesterday, yet I never thought of making a sketch; it is true that it threatened to rain at any moment, and then I am somewhat of the same mind as Fantin: I feel quite stupid setting my easel before something and fancying myself able in an hour's time to reproduce nature.

"You will be surprised by the meagreness of my output when I return, but I am very philosophical. I work when I can, and when I feel like it, without being much concerned about the result."

From Madrid Berthe wrote to her mother:
"So far we have seen only the museum, which is magnificent, as you know. The city has no character. But we don't know it very well; we are so stupid in the streets, unable as we are to speak or to understand ...
"I have found the handsome Astruc; he has put himself entirely at our disposal for visiting the city, which he knows well. We shall content ourselves with him; he has the advantage of speaking French, and he is no more commonplace than anyone else. I have no intention of exerting myself to see anything but paintings. Perhaps we'll go to Toledo, and come back here to see the bullfights, if we feel stouthearted enough."

After her trip to Spain, Berthe went to join Edma at Maurecourt. She returned there the two summers following. The garden and the light of Ile de France provided conditions conducive to painting, and her sister's children made interesting subjects. It was there that she painted, among other things, her *Chasse aux papillons*, now in the Louvre. In an interval between such visits to Maurecourt, she wrote to Edma from Paris:

"I saw our friend Manet yesterday; he left today with his fat Suzanne for Holland, and in such a bad humour that I do not know how they will get there. He wrote to me this morning to inform me about his departure, and to tell me that he had given my address to a very rich gentleman who wants to have portraits of his children done in pastel. He advises me to make him pay handsomely if I want him to respect me. This is an extraordinary opportunity that I must not let slip. If I were actually sure that this gentleman was coming to see me, I should be somewhat worried. I know my nerves, and the trouble I should have if I undertook such a thing. Suppose that by chance he does come: tell me what I can ask – 500 francs, that is to say, 1,000 francs for the two? That seems to me enormous!"
Referring to a painting she had made at Maurecourt, she wrote:
"What I did there seems less bad here than I thought. On the other hand, what I am doing in the garden is becoming quite bad . . ."
On another occasion she wrote:
"I sent my Cherbourg seascape to M—. He was to show it to Durand-Ruel. I have not heard anything about it since. I am eager to earn a little

73

money, and I am beginning to lose all hope. Have you worked this week? You are far more fortunate than I am: you work when you feel like it, and that is the only way in which one can do good work. As for me, I work hard without respite or rest, and it's pure waste . . .

"I am invited to go to the country, where I could ride horse-back, paint, etc., but all that scarcely tempts me. I am sad, sad as one can be . . . I am reading Darwin; it is scarcely reading for a woman, even less for a girl. What I see most clearly is that my situation is impossible from every point of view."

DEATH OF MORISOT PERE
FIRST IMPRESSIONIST EXHIBITION
BERTHE'S MARRIAGE

THE beginning of 1874 was darkened for Berthe by the death of her father. He died January 24, of a heart ailment from which he had been suffering for several years.

Some months later, in the spring, joining Monet, Pissarro, Sisley, Renoir, Degas, Cézanne, and Guillaumin, Berthe was working busily to organize the first exhibition of the Impressionists. It was held at Nadar's from April 15 to May 15. It was the first time that a group showing brought together the canvases of these painters, who until then had been working as isolated individuals. This made the exhibition an important event: it marked the

74
75

91

awakening of these artists to the realization of what they had in common, and the advent of Impressionism as a new school.

Forsaking the Salon, although it had always accepted her work, Berthe entered in this exhibition her *Berceau* and *Cachecache*, a seascape, a pastel of Maurecourt, and three water-colours. Commenting on the occasion, Guichard, who had been the former teacher of Berthe and Edma, wrote in a letter to Mme Morisot:

"Madam, the kind welcome you gave me this morning touched me deeply. I felt younger by fifteen years, for I was suddenly transported back to the time when I guided your delightful girls in the arts, as teacher and friend.

"I have seen the rooms at Nadar, and wish to tell you my frank opinion at once. When I entered, dear Madam, and saw your daughter's works in this pernicious milieu, my heart sank. I said to myself: 'One does not associate with madmen except at some peril; Manet was right in trying to dissuade her from exhibiting'.

"To be sure, contemplating and conscientiously analysing these paintings, one finds here and there some excellent things, but all of these people are more or less touched in the head. If Mlle Berthe must do something violent, she should, rather than burn everything she has done so far, pour some petrol on the new tendencies. How could she exhibit a work of art as exquisitely delicate as hers side by side with *Le Rêve du Célibataire*? The two canvases actually touch each other!

"That a young girl should destroy letters reminding her of a painful disappointment, I can understand; such ashes are justifiable. But to negate all the efforts, all the aspirations, all the past dreams that have filled one's life, is madness. Worse, it is almost a sacrilege.

"As painter, friend, and physician, this is my prescription: she is to go to the Louvre twice a week, stand before Correggio for three hours, and ask his forgiveness for having attempted to say in oil what can only be said in water-colour.

"To be the first water-colourist of one's time is a pretty enviable position.

"I hope, Madam, that you will be kind enough to answer this devoted communication, which comes straight from the heart, for I am greatly interested in this promising artist; she must absolutely break with this new school, this so-called school of the future.

"Please forgive my sincerity . . ."

The Morisot and Manet families became increasingly intimate. They spent part of the summer of 1874 together at Fécamp. It was at this time, on a day when Berthe and Eugène Manet, who also painted occasionally, were sketching some boats under construction in the harbour, that the young man cast aside his usual reserve and clearly revealed his feeling for her.

In one of the letters Eugène wrote to Berthe after his return to Paris he reported to her:

"Do you know that Durand-Ruel sold 180,000 francs worth of paintings? A word to the wise is enough. Also, I doff my hat to the beautiful artist, as you are called by a friend of my mother's whom I have mentioned to you, a crone who has gone apace, but who, in my opinion, is a good judge of women. 77

"How I miss Fécamp and the charming walks that we took! There at least we were always sure of meeting. I wandered through every street in Paris today, but nowhere did I catch a glimpse of the little shoe with a bow that I know so well.

"Paris is full of paintings, but paintings of the worst kind – many pictures of cows, not two-headed cows, but cows that one cannot make head or tail of. Your pictures would be quite a success. Nevertheless I wouldn't mind at all if you were to compliment me a bit on my painting. Some day I'll show you a few sketches that I hope will raise me in your estimation.

"Why don't you have habits, like Mlle Campbell? Imagine this: today I was walking along the Boulevard des Capucines, when I decided to return to the Rue de la Paix, where I had something to attend to. As I was retracing my steps, it occurred to me that I would meet Miss Claire; I always run into her at the corner of the Rue de la Paix, and, sure enough, after a few minutes there she was, at the very place.

"When shall I be permitted to see you again? Here I am on very short rations after having been spoiled. In the future I shall choose paper that will enable me to write to you at greater length, This small size is in no conformity at all to my feelings.

"*P.S.* Excuse this white-and-blue paper, but my own envelopes are marked with my initials, and I thought it unnecessary that my communication should be identified."

In another letter Eugène wrote:
"*Thonjoun*, you overwhelm me. A letter bearing compliments, without

periods or commas – that is indeed enough to cause even a stronger man than I to lose his breath.

"I can answer you only with a Turkish endearment – *Thonjoun,* which means 'my lamb', is the choicest epithet one can address to a woman in the language of those mutton eaters . . .

"I had begun to write to you in the tone of Jeremiah, when I received your dear little note. I was thinking that you were very tardy, and that in replying to me you were like Madame Holliot, who, so the Gonzalès girls say, wants a hair in return for each hair she gives you, and that having written to me twice, you were waiting for two letters from me before answering.

"How naïve I was – I imagined that you had reserved Sunday for me, and I expected a note from you on Saturday, inviting me to a little chat. Hence, what a sad Sunday was mine!

"To seal myself off hermetically from gloomy thoughts, I read all the Paris and London newspapers. What do you think of the Prince of Wales visiting the Duc de Mouchy – wearing the cross of the Legion of Honour and the *médaille militaire* adorned with a bouquet of violets?

"Would you believe that Englishmen are now talking only about us? *Punch,* once so British, is now appearing half in French, and makes atrocious puns in our language. What makes our country so fascinating? What a misfortune to be born without a grain of imagination, and not to be able to seize power and make France the leading nation in the world.

"A few days ago I read that Cardinal Richelieu once made a vow because he had been bothered by a headache for a week. The lucky man! Unfortunately I should be quite embarrassed if I had to make a vow. Oh no, I could make one in regard to you – a vow to make you the most adulated, most cherished woman in the world.

"Your letter has relieved me; I had begun to fear that *X, Y,* and *Z* had gained some ground. I know that I have a slight head start; I would not feel any assurance, however, if I did not have the considerable advantage of having seen you in a costume that I shall call Madame Pontillon's triumph.

"Last night we were talking about all of you, with the fondness that we have for all of you – and naturally the conversation was more guarded when we spoke about you. My mother, speaking of your sister, said: 'Madame Pontillon's triumph is her bathing suit'.

"*X, Y,* and *Z* may pay you compliments, but they will never pay homage to you with the delicate praise that is due to goddesses.

"Despite everything, how sad it is to be a suitor of the moon. I should gladly court you for one thousand, five hundred years, as the inhabitant of Sirius courted his wife (but don't read Voltaire's *Micromégas*) on condition that I might pay my respects at least once a week. You are secretive, for you do not tell me what you were looking at in that shop window last Wednesday."

In the course of that autumn Edouard Manet painted several portraits of Berthe Morisot. One shows her in a black gown, with a fan; another presents her in a half recumbent pose; the third was later acquired by Degas, and the fourth, in which her face is behind a fan, is in the Moreau-Nelaton collection.   *78*

Because she was in mourning for her father, she was married very quietly in a street dress, at the *mairie* and then in the church of Passy, on December 22, 1874.

Mme Morisot gave the young couple her apartment in the Rue Guichard,   *79* and went to Cambrai to stay with her daughter Yves. From there she wrote to Berthe in January, 1875:

"I am glad you wrote me, for I thought of you the day we had ice in the streets. You yourself seem to be as surefooted as a cat, but I was worried about Eugène. You know that in my opinion he is rather unsteady, and this made me wonder that day whether he could stand on his own two feet(!).

"Edma wrote me that he had been charming to her, that he had kissed her, and that she found his beard to be very soft. This amused Yves and me . . .

"Today is Tuesday: will you attend our little family party as usual? Poor Eugène will be yearning for it. I congratulate you upon your successes, and especially on the contentment that you seem to find in your new life . . ."

On February 2, she wrote:
"Why not go out if you have the occasion, dear little *Bétaud*? There are indeed enough unavoidable tears in life not to try to take advantage of the good moments. I mean that we must fight against that part of ourselves which disposes us to excessive sensibility and melancholy, and that you owe it to your husband to dress well for him and to please others in order to please him more – for he would take great pleasure in seeing you enjoy yourself. Without being heedless, one must be young while one is young. There is my prescription."

In a later letter she said to Berthe:

"All the ordeals we have endured together, my child, have considerably strengthened the bonds, naturally strong in themselves, that link mother and daughter. That is how I feel about you, and I assure you that this feeling fully includes your husband – for now he has become a part of you, and must come first in your affections . . ."

To her brother Tiburce, who had gone to seek his fortune in far-off lands, Berthe announced her marriage as follows, in a letter of January, 1875:

"My dear Tiburce: Eugène tells me that this is the day the mail goes off and for fear of missing another opportunity of writing to you, I am scribbling a few words in haste. The thought of you has obsessed me for several weeks, *mon pauvre ami*; where are you, what are you doing? I should give a great deal to know these things, and even more to be able to contribute in some way to your happiness. As for myself, I have been married a month now; it's strange, isn't it? I went through that great ceremony without the least pomp, in a dress and a hat, like the old woman that I am, and without guests.

"Since then I have been awaiting developments, but up to now luck has not favoured us much. The trip to Constantinople, so definite, so certain at first, is no longer so. I must not complain, however, since I have found an honest and excellent man, who I think loves me sincerely. I am facing the realities of life after living for quite a long time in chimeras that did not give me much happiness – and yet, thinking of my mother, I wonder if I have really done my duty. All these questions are complicated, and it is not easy, for me at least, to distinguish clearly between the right and the wrong.

"Mother is at Cambrai with Yves; she will have written to you, I think. She is there, poor woman, seeking a little peace of mind that she does not find. Her sorrows are not appeased by time, and you, my dear friend, you are a great cause of anxiety to her.

"How long it is since we heard from you! Today is January 24, a sad day, the anniversary of the death of poor father. How my heart tightens at the thought of these last years that were so agonizing, of his long suffering, and how I regret that I did not know how to ease his last moments!

"No, you see, my dear Tiburce, life is too short – we cannot afford to live so far from one another. Come back . . . unless you are getting rich, since that wretched thing, money, represents perfect happiness.

"Edma is still at Passy with her two babies and her husband; she has again been very ill; decidedly the state of her health has been very precarious since her last confinement.

"Do not take too many risks with your own health; you know that in the long run those climates are murderous. At times I have a kind of vague hope that you are on your way back home, and since I have never lost my faith in your future I can see you here, writing and making money, which is the ultimate goal of success . . . Where did you meet with Louis C—? Recently he has praised you to the Duchess Colonna in the most glowing terms: you are a genius . . . those are the words he used. It is a pity that such praise does not come from someone else; but never mind, it is the fools who run the world – one must not scorn them too much. Are you still interested in your country's politics?"

A little later she wrote to him again:

"My dear Tiburce: I am writing to you today for the last time – at least, that is my ardent wish. I should like to know that you are already en route, far from that dreadful climate, and ready to return to us. Mother has sent me your letter; I read it with much emotion, realizing how much you have suffered and how sick you still are. Take care of yourself, be prudent; the change of air will do the rest.

"How we are looking forward to seeing you again, to be talking with you about so many extraordinary adventures! We'll make you relate them in detail. Then you will replace me a little at the side of poor mother, whom I have deserted; she will even benefit a great deal from the change, for our tête-à-tête has not been gay. You will give her new life.

"I am just as confident of your future here; do not be distressed because you are returning empty-handed. Life is full of sudden changes; let us hope that this time they will be favourable for you."

At that time the chief concern of the family was to find a position for Eugène Manet, as appears from a letter Mme Morisot wrote on arriving in Grenoble, where she had gone to see her brother Octave, as well as from several other letters of that period.

The first of these letters came to Berthe from her mother and was dated May 16, 1875:

". . . I have been received with the hospitality that you know so well; everybody was at the station, the weather was beautiful. The house is very elegant, and it has a bed-sitting room in which are hung several of your works. A little Louis XVI dressing table conceals the incongruity of making one's toilette there, and I strongly suspect, since it was recently purchased, that it was acquired to some extent on my account.

"If I am writing to you first, though I was the last to embrace you, it is because Octave advises Eugène to apply for the position of tax collector in Grenoble. It pays 17,000 francs. He has been officially informed that the position has just been abolished. This burdens him with an additional function that he does not care for; he says that he is very much tempted to demand that the decision be reversed, and that this will readily be done if his superiors are willing, since Monsieur Thiers has acted similarly in many other instances. It is your uncle's influence with Gambetta that gave him this idea. And once you have gained a foothold, you find something else more easily. This would not be as far away as Constantinople; the place is superb – this is a prosperous city because it is full of tourists and foreigners throughout the summer."

GREAT AUCTION - TRIP TO ENGLAND
SECOND IMPRESSIONIST EXHIBITION

EARLY in 1875, Manet, Renoir, Berthe Morisot, and Sisley, hoping that an auction would bring them greater public success than an exhibition, organized a one-day sale at the Drouot. The auction took place on March 24, and was a sad failure: the four artists received a total of about ten thousand francs for seventy paintings. Berthe sent in twelve paintings, among them the *Chasse aux Papillons*, which was sold for 245 francs.

80

Le Charivari commented on the event as follows:
"Do you recall an exhibition held in the Boulevard des Capucines in the old premises of Nadar-le-Grand? At the time certain schismatic painters

99

erected their own temple there in competition with the Salon. Their efforts were not successful. Nevertheless four of these audacious individuals (one of whom is a lady) have organized an auction at the Hotel Drouot. This new group is called the school of the Impressionists, and yet it has made no impression on the public. This style of painting, which is both vague and brutal, strikes us as an affirmation of ignorance and a negation of the beautiful as well as of the true. We are too much harried by false eccentricities, and it is only too easy to attract attention by producing trashier works than anyone else dares."

Towards the end of the spring, the Eugène Manets stayed for some time at Gennevilliers, where the Manet family had owned land for several generations, and where one of their ancestors, Clément Manet, had earned the gratitude of the local population by his stand during the Revolution. While Berthe was there Edma wrote to her from Maurecourt in a letter dated June 9:

"How are you getting on, dear Berthe? Not a line from you, not a visit for almost two weeks now. You make me feel that you are strangely isolating yourself from me . . . I should like to know how you are, and what you are doing, and not to be living as though we were a hundred leagues' distance from each other.

"I saw Corot's exhibition. I attended the auction of some of his paintings at the Hotel Drouot, and went to the reopening of the Salon. There I met Fantin, who this time deigned to speak to me; and this was enough to put me again under the spell . . . Puvis de Chavannes fled before me from room to room; in the end, unfortunately for him, he found no way of escaping the hard necessity of saying 'how do you do' to me, and exchanging a few words. His painting, *Famille de pêcheurs*, has been moved. It makes a very good appearance; the eye is attracted to it as soon as one enters the hall. Edouard's painting has been hung a notch higher . . ."

During her stay at Gennevilliers, Berthe produced her painting called *L'enfant dans les blés*, now in the Personnaz Collection, and *Percher de la blanchisseuse* in the Donop de Monchy Collection. Mme Morisot, who was still trying to find a position for her son-in-law, wrote to him:

"You don't need to reassure me as to your ability to fill any position; it is not that which worries me, but the fear that no one will offer you one – dogged as we seem to be by such good luck . . .

81

"Reading the book by your Monsieur Zola had for me the frustrating   *82*
effect of obstructing my intelligence and putting a big stone on my stomach.
That is perhaps very good proof of his talent, but it is not at all to my taste.
His accumulations of objects, his colourful descriptions of all varieties of
foods, in which he indulges with so much love, give one an indigestion; that
is what happens to the painter Claude and the hero of the book, but they
arouse no more sympathy than the rest. And that style! Without doubt, he
does this in order to be true to life; yet it is so dull and diffuse, it is hard
work to get through a few pages. At first it interested me to find that there is
a parallel between this literature and the painting of the new school; I
intended to read it through to the end, but it was with delight that I opened
Topffer's *Le Presbytère* the other day, and found myself in an atmosphere of   *83*
lofty and touching sentiment, of that subtle gaiety and that graceful elo-
quence which make our French language so charming. How many compari-
sons I could make in favour of this literature to the detriment of the other!
No, decidedly, I am not yet of the new school!

"I am very happy about my little Bertat's success; the dear child is saved
by the very delicacy of her nature, and because she could not possibly be
vulgar. But I groan sometimes over some of her admirations that I am
absolutely unable to understand."

Some time later the Eugène Manets left for England. Berthe wrote to
Edma from Cowes:

"It is not too expensive here, and it is the prettiest place for painting – if
one had any talent. I have already made a start, but it is difficult. People
come and go on the jetty, and it is impossible to catch them. It is the same
with the boats. There is extraordinary life and movement, but how is one to
render it? I began something in the sitting room, of Eugène. The poor
man has taken your place. But he is a less obliging model; at once it becomes
too much for him . . .

"Nothing is nicer than the children in the streets, bare-armed, in their
English clothes. I should like to get some of them to pose for me, but all this is
very difficult. My English is so horribly bad, and Eugène's is even worse . . .

"The little river here is full of boats, a little like the river at Dartmouth
in the photographs Tiburce sent us. I am sure you would like all this very
much, and that it would even give you a desire to start working again. The
beach is like an English park plus the sea; I shall have to make a water-colour
of it, for I shall never have the courage to set up my easel to do it in oil.

"At Ryde, everything takes place on the pier, which is interminably long. It is the place for promenading, for bathing, and where the boats dock.

"I found a superb Reynolds there, for a little less than two francs. My black hat with the lace bow made the sailors in the port burst out laughing.

"You should really write me a little. Cowes is very pretty, but not gay; besides, we constantly miss our home life. Eugène is even more uncommunicative than I.

"I have worked a little, but what rain we have had for a week! Today we have been to Ryde. I set out with my sack and portfolio, determined to make a water-colour on the spot, but when we got there I found the wind was frightful, my hat blew off, my hair got in my eyes. Eugène was in a bad humour as he always is when my hair is in disorder – and three hours after leaving we were back again at Globe Cottage. I nevertheless took the time to take a little walk through the big town of Ryde, which I decidedly find even drearier than Cowes. There are more people in the streets but fewer boats on the water; and the pretty little river adds a lot of charm to the place. Anyway I am happy with our choice, which is a rare thing.

"At Ryde there are many shops, and even a picture dealer. I went in. He showed me water-colours by a painter who, I am told, is well known; they sell for no less than four hundred francs a piece – and they are frightful. No feeling for nature – these people who live on the water do not even see it. That has made me give up whatever illusions I had about the possibility of success in England. In the whole shop, the only thing that was possible and even pretty was by a Frenchman; but the dealer says that sort of thing does not sell."

In a subsequent letter she wrote:

"I regret very much, my dear Edma, that your wish should be a wish impossible of realization, and that you cannot come to join me here. It is actually no more difficult to get here than to go anywhere in France, but one makes a great to-do of this crossing. Cowes has become extremely animated; a few days ago the whole of the smart set landed from a yacht. The garden of the Yacht Club is full of ladies of fashion. At high tide there is an extraordinary bustle. But all that is not for us – we are only humble folk, too insignificant to mingle with this fashionable society. Moreover, I do not know how one would go about it, unless one had a fortune of several millions and a yacht, and were a member of the club. I am completely indifferent to all this; I do not care for new acquaintances, and this society,

from the little I have seen of it, seems to be as dull as it is wealthy. At the Goodwood races I was struck by the elegance and the bored air of the women. On the other hand, the populace seemed very gay – there was an animation that contradicts the notions we have about the people of the north.

"I am horribly depressed tonight, tired, on edge, out of sorts, having once more the proof that the joys of motherhood are not meant for me. That is a misfortune to which you would never resign yourself, and despite all my philosophy, there are days when I am inclined to complain bitterly over the injustice of fate.

"My work is going badly, and this is no consolation. It is always the same story: I don't know where to start. I made an attempt in a field, but the moment I had set up my easel more than fifty boys and girls were swarming about me, shouting and gesticulating. All this ended in a pitched battle, and the owner of the field came to tell me rudely that I should have asked for permission to work there, and that my presence attracted the village children who caused a great deal of damage.

"On a boat one has another kind of difficulty. Everything sways, there is an infernal lapping of water; one has the sun and the wind to cope with, the boats change position every minute, etc . . . The view from my window is pretty to look at, but not to paint. Views from above are almost always incomprehensible; as a result of all this I am not doing much, and the little I am doing seems dreadful to me . . . I miss the babies as models; one could make lovely pictures with them on the balcony. If Bébé Blanc were willing to come to see me with her Lize, I should gladly paint them.

"I am sending you an article on Goodwood to give you an idea of its splendours. I was enchanted by my day there, but it was rather costly – though I shall tell the *mamans* the opposite – and horribly fatiguing. Never in my life have I seen anything as picturesque as these outdoor luncheons. Gustave Doré was there with a group of women of fashion. Why doesn't he know how to profit from all this?

"Au revoir, a thousand *tendresses* for the darlings and for you; do not forget to remember us to your husband when you write to him. I always forget to tell you that Eugène has a great feeling for you; the brothers-in-law would gladly change places."

Another letter of Berthe's was addressed to Edma from London, at 51 Manchester Street:

"I have received your letter here, my dear Mame. It was forwarded from

Cowes. We left that little place very hurriedly; Eugène was depressed and I was in a bad temper, because I was doing only poor work. Here we have recovered our spirits a little. We walk a great deal, we look at many things, we even work. At least, for two successive days now we have made attempts to work on the Thames; the results are an unsuccessful water-colour and a pastel that according to Eugène is very good.

"You will be surprised that having so little time to spend in London we waste the hours on the water. But Eugène does not like to see the sights any more than I do. We live in London as Parisians live in Paris: we stroll about, we spend our days sometimes here, sometimes there.

"I visited the National Gallery, of course. I saw many Turners (Whistler, whom we liked so much, imitates him a great deal), Wilkies, Gainsboroughs, and Hogarths. Unfortunately the museum is small; but the things I saw gave me a great desire to become thoroughly acquainted with English painting. We went to see Tissot, who does very pretty things that he sells at high prices; he lives like a king. We dined there. He is very nice, a very good fellow, though a little vulgar. We are on the best of terms; I paid him many compliments, and he really deserves them.

"Today I shall hasten to that handsome Stanley, the bishop of Westminster Abbey, to whom I have a letter of introduction from the Duchess; he is in the country, in the vicinity of the Crystal Palace – all the others are away. Tissot tells me he is a very important personage, who can open all doors for us. If we should return to London, it might be interesting to know him.

"Curiously enough, Eugène who has asked me a hundred times to write to the Duchess, refuses to make use of her letters now that I have them in my hands. He would spend his life on the Thames, thinking of nothing. This Thames is really beautiful. I often think of how much pleasure you would have in seeing this forest of yellow masts, through which one can catch a glimpse of the dome of St. Paul's, the whole thing bathed in a golden haze. We should contrive to make this voyage *en famille* . . .

"Tissot tells me that during the regatta week at Cowes we saw the most fashionable society in England."

In reply to this letter of Berthe's, Edma wrote:
"I have seen only your first letter, my dear Berthe, and I was glad to hear that merely following your instinct you had gone to the Isle of Wight. My blockhead of an Englishwoman says that Cowes and Ryde have the reputation of being the prettiest places and that they are very fashionable.

Did you see distinguished people there? Everything you tell me makes me regret that I am unable to join you; I am beginning to find Maurecourt very drab. One must have children to be able to endure these six months in the country . . ."

During her stay in London Berthe wrote in a letter to her mother:
"I am reconciled with London, my dear little mother. I don't know what ill luck during the first days took me into the dreary streets of the city, including my own, which is terribly so. I am tired out. We race about like lost souls. We don't want to take cabs; we board the omnibus, the train; this city is a world in itself – a kind of fantastic Babylon, as one sees it from the Thames on a foggy day.

"It is frightfully hot, the clouds are low, the air is suffocating. It is like being in a room without ventilation. This morning I let Eugène rove about alone, and stayed peacefully in my bed, where I would still be if I had not been dragged out of it just now by a letter from Tissot – an invitation to dinner for tomorrow night. I had to get up and ransack everything to find a clean sheet of paper in order to reply . . . I don't mind seeing someone; it will be a change from the boarding-house routine. We went to see him yesterday. He is very well installed, and is turning out excellent pictures. He sells for as much as 300,000 francs at a time. What do you think of his success in London? He was very amiable, and complimented me although he has probably never seen any of my work. We went to see Deschamps, Durand-Ruel's man in London; he was out of town, and that vexes me.

". . . My mother-in-law writes us that the gentleman who caused such excitement at the Bourse was Achille Degas. I saw the report of the incident among the sensational news items. The newspapers here are full of the accident that took place in the Solent several hours after our departure from Cowes. You must have read about it in the Paris newspapers. The queen's yacht sank another yacht; there were dead and injured. I am surprised that such disasters do not occur more often, considering the number of boats in this country. But do not worry, we never do anything imprudent."

Madame Morisot, who was taking care of Berthe's relations with the art dealers, wrote to her daughter on August 3:
"Your dealer complains that you have not told him your prices. I reminded him that I had just told him that you relied on him, but this embarrasses

him, and it is an arrangement that he does not like. He is asking 600 francs for the Gennevilliers landscape. I said that was all right, but he smiled and said that one never gets what one asks; moreover, he has to take his profit, and finally, he says, paintings are not selling this season, and it is, indeed, a shame to expose good paintings to cheap witticisms. Some people, he says, have told him that the Gennevilliers canvas is abominable and that they would prefer it blank, while others find it beautiful. It is admired by the Vicomte and his son. There have been quite a number of inquiries about it, as well as about the water-colour, but so far all this has not seemed serious to him. He has no news for you and wants to know what you will take for the big landscape. This was an old man who was alone in the gallery. Do you know him? Is he the owner? I shall return there with your ultimatum. Three of your things have been in the window for the last two weeks. Blanchot on his donkey looks quite well, the water-colour is excellent, and the big landscape, placed at the back, seems to me very effective. This painting has your brother-in-law's wholehearted admiration."

87

On August 21 she wrote to Berthe:
"Well, I am not surprised, my dear *chou*, that you have lost a little of your enthusiasm. I think that the English clientèle would not suit you at all, and that one thrives only where one has become acclimatized. Perhaps with a lot of money, and cutting a figure of some importance in London, you would succeed in making yourself known and appreciated more readily than in France, on account of that special protection which the English spontaneously extend to originality. But if you continue to be what you are, you will require much time to attain the modest position you have already attained here. After seeing a great deal, and experiencing a great deal, I think that one finds one's own little corner is best. Where are you going to find yours? That is the main problem."

And in a last letter to Berthe in London, she wrote on August 28:
"I should come quickly to a decision about that position in the Orient, if only Eugène could find some employment here; it would be better to scrape along than to go far away and be forgotten, for the sole purpose of earning one's bread. I am not at all sure that Eugène would know how to make his fortune; I think he is too honest, for one thing – of that I am glad – and too carefree for another, and finally I do not know whether such a radical change would be good for the health of either of you."

Puvis de Chavannes had also written to Berthe on August 3:

"And so you are in an earthly paradise! Accept all my compliments there. But how much butter, how much tea, how much awful bread, how much of Great Britain! But a poor little French potato field with a brook trickling through it has a great deal of charm too – don't you ever think of Gennevilliers amidst all your splendour and your ladies? It is true that you have English blood in your veins – didn't you tell me so? At all events, there is a family likeness, you speak the language, and one might even say that you see with English eyes – in short, you really are half at home there.

"As for me, I have not yet got over an odious pleasure trip to England that I took a long, very long time ago. The recollection of it still sickens me, as it did from the very first day; it revives in me the most violent antipathy for the existence one had there, from every point of view. One more day, and I should have died of it (here you may keep any unkind thoughts to yourself).

"If I am not too undeserving, give me a detailed account. You must be literally swimming in water-colour. Do you see many people – are you well – will you stay a long time – will you return to your peninsula – are you satisfied with yourself – are there many mirrors there – are they kind?

"Now it is my turn. I am working a great deal, still in Neuilly – the street-cars have begun to run, and now one goes from Saint-Augustin to the Boulevard du Château like a shot. It is very convenient. In any case I don't use them very much – but this spares me the interminable directions that I formerly had to give people eager to visit me.

"I had again to be a godfather. It is an additional duty, and an additional jolt to my wallet. Is there any worse practice? Nothing is more false, more silly, and more stupid than this custom among respectable people of mulcting each other. Such false duties should be replaced by charitable acts, and the money spent so stupidly on stupid gifts to a rich child should go to a poor child. It is almost like a sin – but try to make vanity listen to reason. I literally see no one whom you know. I have not seen Stevens since the opening of the Salon – this Salon where I did not meet you even once . . . It is true that as an intransigent you had no reason to be strolling about in the camp of the Philistines.

"I am leaving you on this note of regret, and with regret, but everything has an end, even a sheet of paper; I shall not conclude, however, without telling you that if friendship has an end, mine for you will finish only with me. My cordial regards to Monsieur Manet."

On her return from England Berthe went back to Maurecourt to visit Edma, and then stayed for some time with Yves at Cambrai. Her husband, who remained in Paris, wrote to her:

"I feel very lonely without you; I miss your lovely chatter and your pretty plumage a great deal. May the inhabitants of Maurecourt, who look a little sad, benefit by it . . ."

In a later letter addressed to Berthe at Cambrai, Eugène wrote:

". . . There is going to be an exhibition at the Dudley Gallery. Work must be sent in before October 6. Do you want to send the pastels you did in London? You might add the one of Marguerite Carré. As for oils, the little steamboat you painted on the river would look well if framed, I think.

"If you want me to, I'll show it to Edouard. I am going to order the frames . . .

"Edouard gave me the circular letter of the Dudley Gallery. I see that only oils are to be sent. That is very vexing. Tell me what you want to do . . .

"Master Poussin yesterday showed me your pictures, your little Gennevilliers group, with great solemnity. He has not sold any, but he must have got many compliments, judging from the way he displayed them to me. I was greatly pleased to see them again; they are really charming, and they seemed to have improved. I told him about your pastels. He will be glad to have them; he seems to be entirely devoted to your painting.

"My letter has been interrupted by a visit from the two mothers-in-law. I brought out all your pictures in review before them. Great success. The *Ground de constructor*, with the children, May and the fat Poulot, aroused your mother's enthusiasm. My mother asks me to convey many compliments. I must bring Edouard to see them . . .

"Edouard is preparing to leave for England; he is more sure of himself than ever. He has borrowed ten thousand francs and is affluent for the moment . . . This morning I met your friend Claudine at Gennevilliers . . . You made a great impression in this little village, where everyone asks about you . . . There are good pens in Maurecourt. I don't think that either you or Edma spoil your mother very much.

"Tiburce, that good-for-nothing, has asked for his bonds, in order to squander them, just as he has done with everything else. You haven't made him a bit more sensible . . . It seems to me that you are taking a long vacation; my mother keeps asking me with a worried look where you are. As though you were on a spree . . ."

Another letter of Eugène at that time reads:

"*Ma chère amie,* your letter of Sunday was very nice. I hope you will follow it up with others written with the same ink, as our friends of Gennevilliers say . . .

"Yesterday I had dinner with all the cousins, who stared at each other like china dogs . . . Your friend Edouard is not well. He has begun a picture, he says, which will annoy all the painters anxious to work outdoors and paint in clear colours. Not a drop of black; Turner must have appeared to him in a dream . . .

"I dropped in yesterday at Achille Degas'; he is worried about the outcome of his case. He has been advised to have it tried in the court of assizes. The judges of the Correctionnelle court would find him guilty."

In his last letter to Berthe at Cambrai he said:

"*Ma chère amie,* you spoil me; your letters are very affectionate and very gracious. Do not measure my devotion to you by the length and frequency of mine. I am very busy, first, putting my affairs in order, then working, or at least trying to finish the work I began at Cowes . . ."

In the following winter Berthe and her husband lived in Mme Morisot's apartment at No. 7 Rue Guichard. In April, 1874, the second exhibition of the Impressionists took place, and Degas wrote to Berthe on this occasion:

"Dear Madam, I do not know whether you have been notified that this is the moment for sending your pictures. The opening will be Thursday morning, the 30th of this month. It is therefore necessary that you send in your work on Monday or Tuesday, and that you come if possible to take care of the placing. We are planning to hang the works of each painter in a group together, separating them from any others as much as possible.

"I beg of you, do come to direct this. And then I want to ask your permission about two things. I expect to show an old sketch of a portrait of your sister, Mme Gobillard, and a portrait of your husband sitting by the side of a road. Of course I shall not do this without your consent."

For this exhibition Berthe Morisot entered the following pictures: *Au Bal* (Donop de Monchy Collection), *Le Lever* (Choquet sale, De Ganay Collection), *La Toilette, Le Dejeuner sur l'herbe, Vue du Solent, Ile de Wight, West Cowes, Le Bateau à vapeur* (Monet Collection), *Plage de Fécamp, Chantier, Percher de blanchisseuse* (Donop de Monchy Collection), two English landscapes, a female figure, three English seascapes in water-colour, and three pastels.

In a letter to one of her aunts at that time, she wrote:

"If you read any Paris newspapers, among others the *Figaro*, which is so popular with the respectable public, you must know that I am one of a group of artists who are holding a show of their own, and you must also have seen how little favour this exhibition enjoys in the eyes of the gentlemen of this press. On the other hand, we have been praised in the radical papers, but these you do not read. Anyway, we are being discussed, and we are so proud of it that we are all very happy. My brother-in-law is not with us. Speaking of success, he has just been rejected by the Salon, he takes his defeat with as great good humour as possible."

It is well known that this exhibition provoked strong reactions among the public and in the press. Eugène Manet was on the verge of fighting a duel with Albert Wolf, whose article in the *Figaro* began thus: "Five or six lunatics, one of whom is a woman . . ." and ended as follows: "There is also a woman in the group, as is the case with all famous gangs. Her name is Berthe Morisot, and she is interesting to behold. In her, feminine grace is preserved amidst the frenzy of a mind in delirium." 90

In September, while on a vacation at her sister's, Berthe received from her husband a letter that ran as follows:

"The entire tribe of painters is in distress. The dealers are overstocked. Edouard talks of cutting down expenses and giving up his studio. Let us hope the buyers will return. The present moment, it is true, is unfavourable. Developments are taking place in Europe that would enable France to recover her rightful place, if it were not for the fact that we have been governed since 1870 by . . . (*script illegible*).

"Read the newspapers; they are interesting. Your grandfather spoke to me of speculation. He appeared to be a great expert on the subject.

"Braquemond, whom I met at Sèvres, asked about you. He inquired as to what impression his porcelains made on you. He has some of them at the exhibition of the industrial arts that is going on now. I shall wait for your answer before going to see them.

". . . Take advantage of this to paint some pictures, they . . . (*script illegible*) while waiting for them to be sold.

"You cannot imagine what a good husband my mother believes me to be. She thought I would go to fetch you. If the money situation did not counsel prudence, I should be quite capable of doing it."

DEATH OF MADAME MORISOT
IMPRESSIONIST EXHIBITIONS – BIRTH OF
JULIE MANET – BOUGIVAL – NICE

IN October 1876 Madame Morisot died after a long and painful illness. Berthe received the following letter of condolence from Puvis de Chavannes:

"Dear Madam, first of all I must tell you how much I share your grief. Not having had the honour of seeing you for many months, I did not know during that time how apprehensive you were about your mother. I was all the more shocked by your sad black-edged letter from which I learned everything at once.

"As for your question, I must unfortunately answer in the negative. My relations with the person to whom you refer, and whom incidentally I like very much, have never gone beyond a formal exchange of courtesies, without the least trace of intimacy. Today I regret this for I should have been very happy to be able to render you any service, however slight. Kindly receive, dear Madam, my expression of deep sympathy and of respectful devotion."

The Eugène Manets no longer having any reason to stay at Passy moved closer to the centre of Paris. They rented an apartment at No. 9, Avenue d'Eylau (the present Avenue Victor Hugo), a few steps from the Place de l'Etoile.

In the spring of 1877 Berthe took part in the third Impressionist exhibition. On this occasion she received the following letter signed by Renoir and Caillebotte:

"Madam, we wish to inform you that we have rented an apartment for our exhibition at No. 6, Rue Lepelletier. We are happy to think that you will participate as usual.

"We shall keep you informed about everything. At all events, we hope that you will be present at our meeting on Monday at five o'clock, at the home of Monsieur Legrand, 22-*bis* Rue Laffitte . . ."

Degas also wrote to her:

"Dear Madam, Caillebotte and Renoir must have already written to you that the premises are rented and that on Monday (tomorrow) there will be a general meeting at the home of M. Legrand, at No. 20 or 22 Rue Laffitte (next door to an optician). But I am writing this anyway, just for the pleasure of doing so and of sending you my best wishes. I do not know whether your husband remembers that last year he promised to exhibit with us. Your very devoted, E. Degas.

"The meeting is at five o'clock. A momentous question is to be discussed: is it permitted to exhibit at the Salon as well as with us? Very important!"

Berthe exhibited *Tête de jeune fille, La psyché, La terrasse, Jeune femme à sa toilette, L'Amazone,* ten pastels, three water-colours, and two drawings. It is with reference to this exhibition that Puvis de Chavannes wrote to her:

"I resent a little what you told me the other day about certain congratulations. You have forgotten those, although they were very sincere, which I gave you three years ago, I believe, during the very first hour of a certain exhibition on the Boulevard de la Madeleine, which was inaugurated under the auspices of a torrential rain."

In 1879 Berthe Morisot was unable to prepare for and participate in the fourth Impressionist exhibition because her health had been greatly under-' mined by the birth of her daughter. She wrote to Yves: *92*

"Well, I am just like everybody else! I regret that Bibi is not a boy. In the first place because she looks like a boy; then, she would perpetuate a famous name, and mostly for the simple reason that each and every one of us, men and women, are in love with the male sex . . . Your Bibi is a darling; you'll find mine ugly in comparison, with her head as flat as a paving stone. Edma's photograph has dispelled all my illusions about her . . . All poor Julie has to offer is her fat cheeks and her pretty complexion . . . Another piece of news, less distressing: Eva Gonzalès is married . . . Don't accuse me   *93* of being neglectful, my dear, I think of you and your children continually, but my life is becoming complicated, I have little time, and then I have my days of melancholy, my black days when I am afraid to take up a pen for fear of being dull. The death of the poor dear duchess made me pass through one of these bad phases. Mme Carré told me the other day, laughing at my looks: 'I think you have lived too long'. Well, this is true. Inasmuch as I see everything that I have known and loved disappear, I have lived too long. The loss of friends can no longer be replaced at my age, and the void is great."

She was referring to the death of the Duchess Colonna. And she added, regarding her doctor's recommendation that her daughter spend a season at the seashore: "I have no faith in his prognosis, and I am too poor to try the experiment. Life is largely a question of money, which is not at all to my taste . . ."

In another letter to Edma, Berthe wrote:
"Julie or Rose is like a big inflated balloon; she has been baptized (this came as a great shock to some people) and vaccinated. Two necessary chores are thus behind me . . . My daughter is a Manet to the tips of her fingers; even at this early date she is like her uncles, she has nothing of me."

To her niece she wrote:
"I should love to see you, my little niece, you whom I regard a little as my elder daughter. And then I should not mind showing you my little Bibi who

in reality is not as ugly as in her photograph, and is sweet as an angel, though horribly quick-tempered . . . I am sure that you will love your little cousin very much when you know her; she likes to laugh and play so much! She is like a kitten, always happy, she is round as a ball, she has little sparkling eyes, and a large grinning mouth."

In 1880 the fifth Impressionist exhibition was held at No. 10 Rue des Pyramides. Berthe showed fifteen of her works, among them *Eté* (Tate Gallery), *Hiver, Femme à sa toilette, Le lac du Bois de Boulogne, L'avenue du Bois sous la neige, Au jardin,* and *Un portrait.*

The Eugène Manets spent that summer, like the preceding one, at Beuzeval-Houlgate. In October Berthe lost her grandfather Thomas. He died at the age of ninety-two, of a congestion of the lungs contracted as a result of running after an omnibus. On this occasion she wrote a letter expressing the wish that her grandfather's house in the Rue Franklin should not be sold, but this wish was not realized.

On December 28 Berthe received an easel from her brother-in-law. An accompanying note said: "My dear Berthe, do not be surprised to receive this latest style easel, very handy for pastel; it is my modest New Year's gift."

In 1881, as in the preceding years, the Impressionists organized an exhibition of their works – the sixth; Berthe sent a *plein air* study of her daughter and nurse, a young woman in pink, a portrait now in the Santamarina Collection in Buenos Aires, a portrait of a child, a landscape, and several pastel sketches.

That same year the Eugène Manets rented a little house at Bougival that they were to keep for several years. Berthe painted a great deal in the garden, using her daughter as a model. In a letter to a friend she wrote about her daughter:

"How grateful I am to you for your fondness for my sweet Chichi. Since you ask about her habits and tastes, I shall tell you that she likes the street more than anything in the world, that she makes advances to all the children in Bougival, and is very popular there. From every door one hears, 'Good day, Mademoiselle Julie'. When she is asked her name she answers very politely, 'Bibi Manet'. This made two cocottes walking along the bank laugh till they cried. They no doubt thought that she was the daughter of the famous Manet put out to nurse in this village of boating girls.

96

"Mama is much less attractive than the daughter; she is ageing visibly and is still at work.

"Dear friend, you still have a lot to learn; the love of art, as you call it, or simply the love, the habit of any work, does not diminish with the years. It is this that reconciles us to our wrinkles and white hair.

"Chichi is charming but leaves much to be desired as an intellectual companion; and I live in such great solitude that I should be worthy of pity if I did not find something to keep me busy. You know that I have always had a need for activity, and now this need is gratified only by my work, Bibi, and reading. I have no friends left, of either sex; some have deserted me, and you, you are far away! And I have lost the dear duchess . . ."

Berthe became attached to this house at Bougival. She and her husband gave notice that they intended to vacate their apartment in Paris while awaiting the completion of the house for which they had acquired a lot in the Rue de Villejust, between the Bois and the Avenue d'Eylau. In order to build this house they took a loan. Although this project occupied much of their time, they spent a winter in Nice where Berthe painted a great deal, and from where she wrote to her brother Tiburce:

"I won forty francs at Monte Carlo – not enough to support me for very long . . . I have almost made up my mind not to continue this Nice experiment indefinitely, and to go to Italy. There is nothing to keep me here; the people are dreadful. At this season Monte Carlo is the only attraction, and I am determined not to succumb; it is an irritating temptation . . ."

Then she received the following letter from Edouard Manet, dated December 29, 1881:

"My dear Berthe, since I should rather send you nothing than a shabby present, I shall content myself for the time being with my best wishes. I am sure I'll find a way of making it up during the year . . . Will you take a little trip to Italy? I should like you to visit Venice and to bring back from there some paintings that would certainly be very personal.

"I went to see your house recently, but it is so covered with scaffolding that it is impossible to say how it looks; it is being worked on . . .

"This year is not ending very well for me as regards my health. However,

Potain seems to think that there is room for hope, and I conscientiously follow his prescription.

"Portier has not yet sent me his portrait, although I have written to him about it. Today I had a visit from the good Fantin who came to congratulate me, and then one from Faure, who was radiant because he is included in the New Year's promotion, and has even commissioned me to do his portrait."

It was only at the end of the winter that the Eugène Manets were able to carry out their project of a trip to Italy. But they did not succeed in reaching Venice. After stopping in Genoa and in Pisa, they went to Florence, where their daughter fell ill of a severe bronchitis. This prevented them from continuing their journey and compelled them to return to Nice, where Berthe received the following letter from Edouard Manet:

"I have just had a visit from that terrible Pissarro who told me about your coming exhibition. These gentlemen don't appear to get on together. . . . Gauguin acts the dictator. Sisley whom I also saw wants to know what Monet is going to do; as for Renoir, he has not yet returned to Paris.

"I am surprised that Eugène did not remember how cold it can be in Florence. We spent two very frigid months there once.

"It would be a good thing if, in the future, you did not frighten my mother too much about Bibi's health; it puts her in a fearful state. As for myself, I have been better these last two days. I have given up my cane, which is something.

"Business is bad. Everyone is penniless as a result of the recent financial events, and painting is feeling the effect. Susanne asks me to send you her love. Pertuiset is in Nice at the Grand Hotel."

The disagreements among the artists represented at the seventh Impressionist exhibition, to which Manet refers in his letter, were caused by the intransigent attitude of Degas, and they persisted despite the conciliatory efforts of his friend Henri Rouart. On returning to Paris Eugène Manet prepared Berthe's entries; she remained in Nice because she did not want to bring her daughter back to Paris before spring. During that period the following exchange of letters took place between them.

Eugène to Berthe, March 1, 1882:
"*Ma chère amie,* I am writing this to give you a brief account of what I

have done about your exhibition. When I arrived in Paris I went directly to the Salle des Panoramas. I found all of the brilliant group of the Impressionists busy hanging quantities of canvases in an enormous hall. Everyone was delighted to see me, especially because I have come for the purpose of exhibiting your works. Then I went at once to Bougival where I could find no one. The locksmith, with great difficulty, opened all the doors for me. I took the finished Nice canvases – Julie with Pasie in the Robin garden, Julie with her perambulator (a small canvas), I and Julie playing with her houses (unstretched canvas). I particularly liked Pasie sewing on a bench. Gustave agreed with me. Shall I enter it? I brought back the other canvases and deposited them last night Rue Saint-Honoré.

"I shall return this morning to Portier and the Rue Saint-Honoré to attend to the framing. Your paintings will probably be placed on easels, for there is no place left to hang them. I have forgotten to mention that I also brought back your pastels, all this in a driving rain.

"The temperature is very pleasant despite the rain. The changes are less sudden than in Nice. I am writing this at six in the morning in Gustave's study. I have no fire, yet it is not in the least cold. I am very comfortable here. Gustave lavishes me with attentions. I am waiting impatiently for a letter from you; write to me every day as you promised you would.

"The trip is very easy. I made it without fatigue. The worst part of the journey is between Nice and Marseille. There is a twenty-five minutes stop for dinner. The train was very crowded when we left, but emptied somewhat at Marseille. Only two passengers, I and a respectable grocer from Grenelle, remained in my compartment. I slept as if I were in my bed; the night was cold only for a moment after we passed Lyon. At eight o'clock I had an excellent cup of chocolate at Laroche (thirteen-minute stop), and I arrived in Paris at a quarter past eleven.

"All the rest of the day was devoted to your affairs. I did not see my mother until the evening. Edouard seems improved. He is delighted about his decoration; but financial success does not seem to come to the Rue Saint-Pétersbourg any more.

"The Impressionists have all asked many questions about you and wanted to know whether you would come to see the exhibition.

"The painting you began in your room is very good. Finish it and send it. Give me the size of the canvas and I will order a frame for it in advance. Your pictures at Portier's seemed very good to me.

"Much love to you and Bibi. I embrace you."

In a later letter Eugène wrote:

"Now, to come back to your exhibition. I returned there this morning at eight o'clock. It is sure to be a success. Sisley is most fully represented and has made great strides. He has a painting – a pond or a canal surrounded by trees – which is a real masterpiece. Pissarro is more uneven, but he has two or three figures of peasant women in landscapes that are far superior to those of Millet in drawing and colour. Monet has some weak things side by side with some excellent ones, particularly winter landscapes – ice drifting on a river – which are quite beautiful.

"Renoir's painting of boatmen looks very good. The views of Venice are detestable, real failures. A scene with palm trees, very good. Two very pretty figures of women. Gauguin and Vignon, very poor. Vignon has relapsed into his imitations of Corot, an unfortunate influence. The unhappy boy looks quite sad and is aware of his inferiority. Caillebotte has some very boring figures done in blue ink, and some excellent small landscapes in pastel.

"This morning only your portrait of Marie had been placed. It was not well lit nor was it at the right angle. Portier had to have it adjusted. Durand-Ruel is devoting himself entirely to the exhibition and must have stirred up the press. Wolf was showing the exhibition to his friends with praise. He asked to see your pictures. Nivard has promised your frames in two days. Vignon has lent me a white frame in which your Nice beach looks very well. I have ordered similar frames for the other pictures.

"Vignon told me that he does not know anything about how the exhibition is organized. Degas remains in the society, pays his dues, but does not exhibit. The society still uses the name of 'Independents' which he gave it.

"All the upper part of the walls is hung with Gobelin tapestries which are very beautiful. The pictures are hung in three rows.

"I hope that you will send something within a week; don't forget to tell me the size of your canvas. Your *Blanchisseuse* is very much improved, as well as all those of your Nice pictures that are framed. My portrait is very good, it is beautifully drawn, and the colour is excellent. I shall return this evening (the exhibition is open until eleven o'clock).

"If I see that your picture of Marie does not look better than it did this morning, I shall have it placed on an easel . . . I saw the picture of Pasie again when I returned to Bougival in the afternoon, it did not seem to me sufficiently finished. Gustave claims that it is your pictures that interest the public most. Do something for this poor public."

Berthe answered him:

". . . You went to Bougival, and I see that it is the big picture of Pasie sewing that you have been referring to. I thought that I had scraped out the head the last time I worked on it. Pissarro and Edouard saw it and neither of them seemed to be lost in admiration of it. However, if it looks less bad than the others, put it in. I don't want to have too many; five or six are enough.

"Is the *Marie* that Portier has bad? I thought of showing it, and then of the *Blanchisseuse*, and the small picture of Bibi and Pasie, the only one which Edouard likes; he wrote me that again yesterday. That makes three, plus a few small pictures, either of Nice or of Bougival. However, I leave it entirely up to you, and whatever you do, I won't complain, this is a solemn promise.

"Bibi eats the honey they make here and is thriving on it; the chocolate disappeared with papa who needed it for his journey; she has not asked for it once. Today I had my lunch with her, my digestion having suffered severely yesterday from a mixture of mayonnaise and sauerkraut. As a result I did not dine last night, and this morning I felt the need of eating something wholesome.

"I miss you very much, and yet I would feel much less badly if everyone here did not try to console me in my widowhood; people knock at my door (you know how much I like that when I am at work), and offer to take me out. Yesterday I had to listen to all of Mlle Fulmann's philosophy and agree with everybody about the beauty of the sea.

"Since the weather is so good, could we not go to Bougival right away? If you don't think so, take the cheapest thing you can find in Paris; I shall be satisfied with anything as long as it is clean and healthful for Bibi. The Champs Elysées quarter, near your ministry, seems the most advisable."

From Eugène:

"Have you read the *Figaro*? I am sending you the other newspapers that mention the exhibition. I was there last night, this morning, and twice during the day. At night it looks very pretty, the lighting is excellent.

"I have ordered a white frame for your picture of Marie on the porch. Nivard promised it for tomorrow. Don't be upset because the newspapers do not mention you. The fact is, you cannot be seen while all your colleagues have done their utmost to be seen. Make a special effort. You can do two canvases size twenty or thirty in a week. Your landscape of the Villa Arnulfi is charming, and you did it in no time.

"Get Esther to sit for you in her big hat, or one of the young American ladies. They will be very flattered.

"Pissarro asked Edouard to take part in the exhibition. I think he bitterly regrets his refusal. I have the impression that he hesitated a great deal.

"I have just been told at my bankers' that the creditors of the Banque de Lyon have been repaid in full.

"A great deal of work is being done on the house in the Rue de Villejust. The stucco is being put on and the flooring brought in. The house is shaping up well. After the Genoa palaces the rooms are nothing but little boxes. Still, the balconies are nice, and the roof terrace is very pleasant. The coat-of-arms above the studio window is a failure; there wasn't enough stone. The other sculptures are simple and fairly well executed. In short, it looks pretty well. They are putting on the banisters. It was impossible to walk on the stairway today, but it seemed spacious and well lighted."

From Berthe:

"Bibi is in Guigui's bed and is sleeping soundly. She has been as good as can be since your departure. She said this morning that she did not think often of Nounou but a lot about papa. We lunch together every day; this delights her, and as for myself I am glad to escape from the insipid chatter of my neighbours. I also think that my digestion will not be as bad as a result of this change of diet.

"I cannot get over everything you did for me in that first day; it seems to me that you are working yourself to death, and all on my account. This touches me deeply and vexes me at the same time. I am a little dumbfounded by your announcement that you have taken the picture of you and Bibi – this picture seems perfectly absurd to me. Please, look at it a second time. Besides, I am working on the picture begun in my room, I shall send it if I can, and that will make a good many Bibis, won't it? If my pictures are to be seen on easels, that is at very close quarters, one must not show things that might appear grotesque. However, you will see how they will impress the other exhibitors, and one can always make a change.

"Thank Gustave in my name for the hospitality he is so kindly showing you, and give him my greetings.

"We took a walk with Bibi in the country, in a very pretty place, in a direction we have never taken together. The ground was cut by little streams; we had to ask the washerwomen to help us step over one of these obstacles, and your daughter, who is not brave, has developed such a fear that she begs me not to go there again. Her happy little pink face is a pleasure to look at and consoles me for your absence."

From Eugène:
"You will have twelve canvases including my portrait. Only nine are listed in the catalogue that I am sending you ... I am also sending you a review by that philistine Claretie, who is bitter-sweet about the Impressionists.

103

"The hall was rented by Rouart for 6,000 francs a year and a share in the receipts. Rouart and Degas have since withdrawn. The first day the admissions yielded 950 francs.

104

"Keep visitors out, see people only at night, and lock your door when you are working.

"I have a good mind to ask Durand-Ruel to show your Marie with the lavender parasol, done last year, in his gallery Rue de la Paix. Give me your opinion on this. I took its frame for my portrait. I came back in the nick of time, my chief had written to Florence insisting that I return.

"I went back to the house today. Morize had already ordered the studio baseboard to be curved; he has a mania for curves."

In a subsequent letter he wrote:
"I hope that your paintings will be hung tomorrow. Nivard was to bring your frames and the glass today. Edouard is to come there tomorrow morning and give his opinion. He agrees with you concerning my portrait. We shall look at it when it is in place and then decide.

"It was a good thing I came back. Morize was about to run wild and curve everything that could be curved. I have asked him to send me a sketch of the foyer to enable you to judge for yourself what he has done. We shall have it changed or corrected if you don't like it. He is going to make little plans of the studios and the adjoining apartments, to put in the shops selling artists' materials where people often make inquiries about studios to let. The workmen are now putting on the stucco in the entrance and the staircase. The courtyard seems enormous ...

"The Impressionists, especially Renoir and Sisley, are doing well. Durand-Ruel gets 2,000 francs for a Sisley. Give me your prices. Edouard says one must ask high prices. However, he has just sold two pictures to Faure at low prices, Faure has cheated him. He is preparing a painful fiasco for himself at the exhibition. He keeps doing the same picture – a woman in a café – over and over again."

Still later he wrote:

"Your pictures were put up this morning; all are in gray frames with gold ornaments. *Marie* has been reframed, taken from the place where it did not look well and placed on an easel in the main room. It is now in the best possible light. Bibi with Pasie (Robin garden) is placed below Marie; its white and gold frame improves it enormously. Facing it on an easel are: on top the *Villa Arnulfi*, in the middle *La Blanchisseuse*, and below *Bibi et son tonneau*. My portrait is in the entrance hall in the somewhat unfavourable place the *Marie* had occupied before.

"Edouard who came to the exhibition this morning says that your pictures are among the best, and he has changed his opinion about the effect of my portrait. Duret who has returned from London congratulated me on your paintings. I have no doubt about your future success. I have asked 500 francs for each of your small pictures, 1,000 for *La blanchisseuse* and for *Pasie et Bibi*, and 1,200 francs for *Marie*."

Berthe wrote:

"It is impossible to set up one's easel because of the wind. I have worked in my room too much; with a model like Bibi one can advance only very slowly, unless one wants to risk ruining everything. It was going well, but it is not going well any more; I am not despairing of getting it into shape again, although it will take longer than you think.

"Am I not a failure at the exhibition? I have a feeling that I am, but I have become very philosophical. That sort of thing no longer depresses me as it had formerly.

"Bibi has found a little friend; it is the tiny Russian girl. They don't understand each other at all but they adore each other; they never stop hugging. They are playing around me as I am writing this. They are very sweet to watch. I notice that when Bibi plays with other children she is very overbearing – the other child, though she loves her very much, is terrified by her."

In another letter she wrote:

"I received the newspapers last night and read them with great interest. Sisley and Pissarro seem to get all the glory. Why not Monet? This surprises me. I can see from here that my poor big *Marie* is a caricature. I don't think she has been badly reviewed at all. What does Edouard say of the exhibition as a whole? Has he been there? It seems to me that there are some good things despite Wolf's stupid article.

"I usually pass on the *Figaro* to Mlle Fulmann and to Mme Labarre; I was going to give them this issue as I had given them the others, and I was amused in advance by imagining the questions they would ask me about the Independents, but Pasie spilled a whole inkpot over it and I had to throw it into the fire. Wolf's prose thus got only what it deserved. Is it possible to have less artistic sense than this creature, and to be more unbearably arrogant?

"Have you met Miss Cassatt? Why did she back out? Our friend Vignon seems to have a nice little success; not much mention is made of Guillaume though he has talent, and particularly a more clear-cut personality. Gauguin and I seem to play the part of the comic characters. Or am I mistaken? Do not be afraid to tell me, since being far away I am very philosophical." *105* *106*

From Eugène:
"I am looking for a furnished apartment in the neighbourhood of the Gare Saint-Lazare and the Parc Monceau. I think I can find something for 200 or 250 francs.

"Do not work yourself to exhaustion; what you have is sufficient. There are not many visitors – 340, 350.

"I am sending you the plan drawn for the foyer by Morize. He could not resist his passion for curves. The window above the staircase facing the opening is of the same shape and dimensions as the one over the foyer of your entresol. It is to be filled with either opaque glass or stained glass. On the third wall of the foyer, which faces the stairway, at the same height, there is a similar opening above the passage between the foyer of the entresol and the stairway of the studio. The three openings will serve to light the foyer at the foot of the principal staircase. The foyer will have a coat of white stucco trimmed with green. The walls of the staircase will be covered with white stucco bordered with stucco looking like large-veined red marble. I should have preferred square openings. Could we not cover these windows and openings with a green trellis?

"Follow freely your architectural taste and come to the rescue of your architect. The walls of the *porte cochère* are in white stucco and in stucco imitating stone."

In another letter he wrote:
"I feel that as an artist you have benefited from me considerably. One of the reasons I came back was to exhibit your works; now I see that I have succeeded in organizing an exhibition that will in no way detract from your

reputation. Portier who reflects the general opinion seems to have made a complete aboutface. He says he will sell more of your pictures. Your pastels are not yet in the exhibition; they will be tomorrow.

107 "I am sending you an article by Burty who has not seen all of your exhibits . . .

"I have not yet been able to discover the reason for Degas' and Miss Cassatt's withdrawal. A stupid Gambettist newspaper (*Paris*) says tonight that as a result of this withdrawal the Impressionist exhibition was 'decapitated'.

"Marie no longer has a frame; I used it for my portrait. I am going to order another inexpensive frame, and give her back her own.

108 "Duret who knows what he is talking about thinks that this year's exhibition is the best your group has ever had. This is also my opinion . . .

"Plasterers, carpenters, masons are busily working on the house. I gave Morize 3,600 francs; this filled him with zeal. The staircase will look very well."

From Berthe:

"I read your letter of last night with much pleasure; everything you tell me is pleasant to hear and reassures me about my exhibition which I thought must be ludicrous. You do not tell me what Edouard thinks of the exhibition as a whole; I think I can read between the lines that he was only moderately satisfied with it. Am I mistaken?

"The prospect of leaving discourages me a little from beginning anything here; however, in a little while I am to decide how to pose the lady with the parrots. If I am satisfied, I'll try to paint it very quickly; if not, I shall not do anything at all under the pretext that I must leave in a hurry . . .

"I have just had lunch and now continue this letter. I have begun my lady with the parrots; I was surrounded by all the boarders while working. I don't think I have posed her very well; however, one could do something very pretty with her. I thought all the time what Edouard would do of her, and as a result I naturally found my own attempt all the less attractive. I have begun it in the garden with a very pretty, quite exotic background – palm trees, aloes, lawn."

From Eugène:

"I forgot to tell you this morning that the architect wants a detailed drawing of the 'Jesus' window of which you made a sketch. Please send it to me as soon as possible.

"I have just returned from Epinay and Gennevilliers. Everything is in bud and there is a smell of spring in the air. This flat country is lovely everywhere . . .

"Has your success encouraged you, and are you busy at *La dame aux perroquets?*

"Nature in our part of the country is even prettier than in the south. It is softer and hazier.

"Renoir is ill with pneumonia in Marseille. I think he has made great strides . . . Your pastels must have been brought to the exhibition today. Work on the house is progressing rapidly. Send your ideas and suggestions. What is to be done in the courtyard? Where shall the fountain be placed? It would be a good thing to give the house a pleasant appearance as soon as possible and to plant early.

"I have just received a letter from Tiburce informing me that he has been appointed secretary to the Minister of the Sudan Provinces and that he is leaving for the Sudan in a fortnight. He asks me to send him an ice-making machine, vegetable seeds, and an *appareil Dussonide* . . ."

From Berthe:
"Last night I went to see Sardou's *Odette* with Mme Conneau; the performance is much better than I expected. All the references to Nice are received with laughter and applause; the theatre was pretty well filled; yesterday's performance was the third. But how false all the modern theatre is, eternally revolving around the same themes! You see that I lose no time in your absence, but I decidedly prefer outdoor pleasures. My walk the other day at Monaco was infinitely more pleasant to me than that stuffy evening."

From Eugène:
"Yesterday I met Miss Cassatt at the exhibition. She seems to wish to be more intimate with us. She asks to do portraits of Bibi and of you. I said, yes, gladly, on condition of reciprocity.

"The reason for Degas's abstention is Gauguin's hostility toward him. Degas has a seat at the Opera, gets high prices, and does not think of settling his debts to Faure and Ephrussi. Faure is a great success at Nice; have you seen him there? The Nittis are joining the household of Princess Mathilde. They held a great reception attended by Mme Adam, where Raffaelli performed a Napolitan dance. This calligrapher has an astounding success."

In a later letter he wrote:

"I have rented a spacious apartment, fairly well furnished, with every thing you need, at No. 3, Rue du Mont-Thabor, near the Tuileries.

"I am convinced that a month in Paris will not seem longer to you than a week in Nice. You will be near your exhibition. It is really very interesting. I spent an hour there this morning waiting for Portier. He sold your Maurecourt pastel to Brandon for 300 francs.

"I have just read a dispatch from Egypt, according to which the Egyptian government will be interpellated in the Egyptian parliament (Egypt now has a parliament) on the appointment of M. Morisot, a European, as secretary of the Sudan government. I hope he will think of sending some samples of gold dust to Edma. Poor Adolphe has been worried about his investment of 2,000 francs, which was the source of Tiburce's fortune."

DEATH OF EDOUARD MANET – DEATH OF EVA GONZALES – IMPRESSIONIST EXHIBITION IN LONDON – THE HOUSE IN THE RUE DE VILLEJUST – THE MANET SALE

TOWARD the middle of March Berthe returned from Nice with her daughter. The house in the Rue de Villejust was not yet completed, and the Eugène Manets, after staying several weeks in a small furnished apartment in the Rue du Mont-Thabor, went to their house in Bougival where they spent the summer and the winter of 1882-83.

Edouard Manet, who was very ill at that time, had rented a house at Rueil in which he spent the summer with his mother and his wife. The Eugène Manets who were his close neighbours visited him a great deal. It was in the garden at Rueil that Manet painted his last landscapes and made a sketch of his niece seated on a watering can. The following winter he painted scarcely anything except flowers; his last work is a bouquet of lilacs and roses in a Japanese vase.

On March 9, 1883, Berthe wrote to Tiburce:

"I am sorry to have missed you yesterday; I was at the Rue Saint-Péters-bourg. Poor Edouard is very ill; his famous vegetarian has very nearly dis-patched him into the next world."

Manet died on April 30. In May Berthe wrote to Edma in answer to her letter of sympathy:

"My dear Edma, thank you for your affectionate letter, and thanks also to Adolphe, who wrote Eugène a note that touched him very much. These last days were very painful; poor Edouard suffered atrociously. His agony was horrible. In a word, it was death in one of its most appalling forms that I once again witnessed at very close range.

"If you add to these almost physical emotions my old bonds of friendship with Edouard, an entire past of youth and work suddenly ending, you will understand that I am crushed. The expressions of sympathy have been intense and universal; his richly endowed nature compelled everyone's friendship; he also had an intellectual charm, a warmth, something indefin-able, so that, on the day of his funeral, all the people who came to attend – and who usually are so indifferent on such occasions – seemed to me like one big family mourning one of their own.

"I shall never forget the days of my friendship and intimacy with him, when I sat for him and when the charm of his mind kept me alert during those long hours."

After the death of Edouard, his wife Susanne went for some time to her native Holland, and her mother-in-law wrote to her informing her of the death of Eva Gonzalès, which had occurred following her confinement, while she was making a funeral wreath for Edouard Manet:

"I am very comfortable with Eugène and Berthe who both take good care of me with great thoughtfulness and affection. I am trying to fight against the despondency and the chaos that I feel in my mind following such great grief.

"You have received a letter which gives you good financial news. Answer at once, or have Léon who has become a consummate business man answer it for you. This piece of good news has given me an idea: I should be very

111

happy if you consent to join me in renting an apartment in Eugène's house. Berthe says to tell you how very pleased she would be to have you. . .

"Berthe says to tell you that she has attended to Edouard's grave. They – she and Eugène – went to Passy where they bought a plot in the cemetery. Eugène is going to buy one for himself next to his brother's. The poor boy is greatly mourned. I receive letters of condolence and sympathy from all quarters.

"Eugène and Berthe have brought me very sad news. Poor Eva died this morning, or yesterday, from a blood clot."

In her following letter Mme Auguste Manet wrote:
"Berthe and Eugène went to see Eva's poor father, who is completely prostrated. Poor Eva was covered with flowers. She had them in her hair, in her hands, and on her poor face which had become the colour of wax, and was still beautiful despite this change. Jeanne was busy looking after the infant who is very much alive, and quieting the nurse who was completely upset, saying that such a death would bring bad luck to her. I am still very much pampered and looked after by Eugène and Berthe. There is not much room except in her studio. This troubles me greatly."

Berthe Morisot wrote to her friend Sophie answering her letters of condolence:
"I know, my dear friend, that you have understood how painful the spectacle of that terrible agony was for me. Edouard and I were friends for many, many years, and he is associated with all the memories of my youth; moreover, he was such an attractive personality, his mind was so young and alert, that it seemed that more than others he was beyond the power of death."

A little later she wrote again to Sophie from the Rue de Villejust:
". . . Amidst all my occupations and the labours of moving, time has passed leaving a surface of indifference and forgetfulness in its wake . . . I have no furniture yet to seat visitors, but my doors and windows can close, and workmen no longer clutter up my house. Won't you come to see me?"

Berthe now worked in her new garden which her husband had planted for her, then she returned to Bougival from where she wrote to her brother on July 10:
"My dear Tiburce, a letter from Edma informs me that the exhibition

you have undertaken in America is not going as well as you had hoped. Write me exactly where you stand, who are your exhibitors, etc. . . . You could have come to see me in the Rue de Villejust; I wasn't miles away, a quarter of an hour's walk and the mere wish to see me would have sufficed, and I might have been of greater use to you than our friend Chavannes who is as difficult as a plough to set in motion. It occurred to me this morning that Antonin Proust might be helpful to you in finding a position of some sort . . . *113* I can easily introduce you to him. Answer me . . ."

On August 20 she wrote:
"My dear Tiburce, I hope that you have been satisfied with your conversation with Proust's secretary, although it would have been preferable to see Proust himself. I had taken it into my head that you two would surely like each other and that this interview might result in some good opportunity for you.

"I stayed only a little while in Paris, Bibi's whooping-cough was becoming wicked there; here she is visibly improving, and I hope that she will be soon rid of it. Yves did not want to come fearing that Paule would catch it. She is at Limoges, with her friend Louise Haviland, and she likes being there. *114*

"As for me, I am more or less alone; Eugène sleeps in Paris and spends part of the day there. Mme Manet is extremely ill, she had a stroke of paralysis and can no longer speak. She stays in bed, her face is frightening; her sons maintain that she is quite rational, but she does not seem so to me. Gustave was called back from his tour. The sight of this poor woman able to utter only little plaintive ah-ah's! is terribly distressing. The doctors cannot make head or tail of it, and do not know whether she will live or die. It would be horrible if she were to remain in this condition for years.

"As for your undertaking, I always meant to tell you that you should pay a visit to Fantin-Latour, Rue des Beaux-Arts; he had great success abroad; he is a very delightful man – if he wants to be. There is also Cazin, and Lerolle whom I have mentioned to you, and who has been successful. And *115* then I should like you to send letters to Monet and to Renoir. Monet is at Poissy, Villa Saint-Louis. Both sent paintings to the last exhibition, and your exclusion of them seems to me rather ungracious; they are men of immense talent. There are Sisley and Degas who are fully recognized but who will refuse to send anything; it would therefore be only a polite gesture on your part. If you talk with Mlle Cassatt, she might be helpful to you; her address is 13 Avenue Trudaine; she is intelligent. Yours, Berthe M.

116   "Have you sent anything to Sargent, the American? We were at Nice together; he left suddenly for Paris when we were about to be introduced to each other. He is supposed to have spoken of me in the most flattering way. He is very successful and a pupil of Carolus Duran."

As Tiburce was leaving for another distant journey, she wrote to him again:
"My dear Tiburce, I don't know why everyone, and you above all, thinks he has the right to doubt my feelings. Yesterday I went from Paris to Bougival, sadly pondering the past and the future, wondering whether we were fated ever to see each other again, and saying to myself how ridiculous our nonchalant farewell had been. Then your last words came back to me; why do you say that I never write, while actually it is you who never write? If I use the telegraphic style, it is only to humour you, and, in all sincerity, I have never thought that a letter from me could give you any pleasure.

"And so, send me one of your latest photographs, not the one where you are so tall, tall, but the other. . . I am sending you Bibi; she is all I love, all I have left of youth and beauty, and I do not want you to forget that you have a niece, a niece who will some day grow to be a superior woman. . ."

117   In the fall of 1883 Berthe Morisot participated in an exhibition of the Impressionists in London where she showed *Femme dans un jardin, Femme étendant du linge,* and *Sur la plage.* During the winter the Eugène Manets moved definitively to the ground floor of their house in the Rue de Ville-
118   just. Berthe Morisot used the high-ceilinged drawing room as her studio. High up in one wall was a window, opening from a bedroom, whose design was patterned after a window in the Eglise du Jésus in old Nice.

Only one of her works was displayed on the wall – a copy of a fragment of a Boucher in the Louvre, *Vénus demandant des armes à Vulcain.* She hung it above the mirror, while waiting for the painting that Claude Monet had promised her for this place.

119   The winter of 1883-84 was devoted to organizing the exhibition, and later to the sale of the works of Edouard Manet, about which Berthe wrote to Edma on December 31, 1883:

"My dear Edma, I received your letter this morning and I hasten to return your New Year's greetings. Although you seem to be the happiest woman in the world, and although I do not know of anything that you may lack for your happiness, I am sure that you are a little too reserved to give happiness to others, that you do not desire sufficiently to share your life with theirs. Is it your fault? Is it mine? I no longer know. . . And so let us both say *mea culpa*, and let us begin the year of 1884 under new auspices.

"I know of nothing more destructive of a correspondence than to have one's letter answered a month after it has been written, when one no longer remembers a word of what it contained. But you tell me that I am witty, and I, who no longer receive compliments from anyone, am enchanted, and aided by my poor memory I let myself believe that I write you nice letters . . .

"No, I don't believe it . . . I am not so foolishly conceited. I acquire only one quality as I grow older – that of becoming simplicity personified.

"Do you know that the exhibition of the works of Edouard Manet opens at the Beaux-Arts on January 5? Mme Riesener asked me very seriously whether you would not come to Paris to see it. I think that it will be a great success, that all this painting so fresh, so vital, will electrify the Palais des Beaux-Arts, which is accustomed to dead art. It will be the revenge for so many rebuffs, but a revenge that the poor boy obtains only in his grave."

In another letter to Edma, dated early in 1884, she wrote:

"My life is not as amusing as you think. I do go to the Beaux-Arts, but the days of trysts are over. I have not collected the newspaper articles; in my opinion they are all rather poor whether they praise or condemn. I completely agree with Degas who says that he does not attach the slightest importance to them. However, if I can find any, I shall send them to you.

"On the whole, the exhibition is a great success. The informed public is surprised by the vigour of his work when it is thus shown in its entirety. There is a sureness of execution, a technical mastery that overwhelms us all.

"I regret that you cannot see all this. On the morning of the opening, Stevens, Chavannes, and Duez were saying: 'Since *Père* Ingres we have not seen anything as great', but we, the truly faithful, we say, 'It is far greater'. *120*

"The auction of the paintings in his studio will take place early in February, and there is every indication that it will be a success. I often meet your friend Fantin. His bad disposition becomes more pronounced as he grows older; but he always asks about you. Degas is always the same, witty and paradoxical. I am beginning to develop close friendships with my colleagues, the Impressionists. Monet insists on offering me a panel for my drawing room. You can imagine whether or not I will accept it with pleasure."

Several days later she wrote:

"Here I am again. I am sending you the catalogue, not of the exhibition at the Beaux-Arts but of the auction at the Hotel Drouot. Do you want to buy any pictures? I am sure that at this question your husband will jump out of his chair and you will think me a little crazy; but it is certain that it is with such ideas of wisdom and extreme caution that one misses all good opportunities. In the old days, it would never have occurred to father or mother to use a thousand-franc or even a five-hundred franc note for a purchase of this kind, but today Faure is offered twenty thousand francs, which he refuses, for *L'homme mort*, which he bought for one thousand, and [*illegible*] for the *Bal de l'Opéra*; as a good speculator he is waiting till their value increases further.

"I want to buy some if I can; I have even the ambition to own a large one, counting on the inheritance from Maman Manet.

"I have marked with a cross those of the smaller ones which I like best. All the heads in pastel are pretty but I think they will be sold relatively high. If you answer me on this matter be sure to indicate the catalogue numbers. I think you must leave a margin of 500 to 1,500. If you do not think this idea is absurd, answer me.

"I am negotiating to sell my *Enfant aux cerises* by Edouard; it is a relatively average piece but it had an enormous success at the exhibition. I am asking 5,000 francs for it and I will get it. I have bought for 1,700 francs a little corner of the garden which is a jewel, one of the prettiest things he ever did. I also have a magnificent sketch of Mme Manet in the garden.

"I have nothing in which to wrap the catalogue today; you won't receive it till tomorrow. I think that everything would sell at extremely high prices if we were not in the midst of a depression. Don't mention my buying projects to anyone for if they were known they could be harmful to the auction."

Immediately after the auction she wrote:

"It's all over, and it was a fiasco. Following the victory at the Beaux-Arts the auction was a complete failure. I got for you, for 620 francs, the picture of the departure of the steamboat. It is not a nocturne; it is a daytime scene, with a crowd swarming on the dock. It is a very pretty piece. If you want it tell me right away; I shall have it packed for you; if not, I shall keep it to resell at a profit, not that I do not like it enormously, but in this rout the brothers thought they had better step in, and we spent twenty thousand francs. It is true that I have three big pieces, *Le linge*, *Madame de Callias*, and *La jeune fille dans le jardin*, and some small ones – a singer at a café concert, two pastels, a torso of a woman, and some oysters. It was certainly more advantageous to buy the smaller canvases rather than the big ones, but the former were bringing relatively high prices whereas the large ones would have gone for nothing if we had not intervened. Anyway I am brokenhearted. The only consolation is that everything has fallen into the hands of connoisseurs, of artists.

"In all, the auction brought 110,000 francs, whereas we were counting on 200,000 at the least. Times are bad, that is certain, but no matter, it is a severe blow. Did you see, in the studio, *Madame de Callias*, a woman in black reclining on a sofa with Japanese fans hung in the background? It is a marvel that will go to the Louvre.

"As for *Le linge*, you know it. *La jeune fille*, a girl sitting under rose bushes, is just as large, but much less finished.

"Anyway, here I am with a whole gallery, our future inheritance from Madame Manet has been eaten into, but no matter, one can only laugh.

"Answer me about the picture of the boat; do exactly as you please."

She wrote to her sister again on the subject of that picture:
"I shall show the picture to Adolphe; he will take it if he likes it and leave it if he does not, but I cannot exchange any with him for I have given all the small ones to Gustave; moreover, only the still life was not high-priced, and you had written me that 600 francs was your maximum. As the days go by we are resigning ourselves to the result of the auction. We take into consideration the fact that times are bad, that people are reluctant to spend money, that those who bought the pictures represented an elite – not because of their well-lined pockets but at least because of their good taste – and that they all now value their pictures almost as they value their own lives and will never part from them except for their weight in gold; and all this gives us hope for a more complete vindication in the future. I am sure that you will be enthusiastic about *Madame de Callias*; I am in love with it, I think that I prefer it to *Le linge*. At all events I shall not let it go except to the Louvre, and if this does not come to pass in my lifetime, it will in Bibi's."

Berthe thought that her choice of a picture representing the departure of a steamboat was an appropriate one for her sister, since Edma's husband was a naval officer. But when Commander Pontillon saw that the captain was on the bridge, such a violation of the rules was more than he could endure, and he refused the painting. The Eugène Manets then presented it to Degas, who thanked them in these words:

"You wanted to give me a great pleasure and you have succeeded in doing so. May I also tell you that I deeply feel the many delicate meanings conveyed in your gift . . . I shall soon come to see you and thank you."

Le linge and *La jeune fille assise dans l'herbe* decorated the two principal panels of Berthe Morisot's studio. Claude Monet had promised her a large canvas for the panel above the mirror, and he wrote to her about this from Bordighera on March 30, 1884:

"Dear Madam, for quite a long time I have wanted to write to you because you must think that I have completely forgotten your panel; but no, I have not forgotten my promise. But I came here with the idea of staying a month, and it will now soon be three; I have been seduced by this delightful place; I have started many things; naturally I had many failures and have had to paint out a good deal. All in all I have had a lot of trouble, and by now I no longer know whether the paintings I am going to bring back are even passable.

"I intended to stop near Marseille in a place where I had seen something I wanted to do precisely for your panel. But having extended my stay here, I must return directly home. If you are not too afraid to come all the way to Giverny, we might look over together the paintings I am going to bring, and see whether there is anything suitable for a decoration. I shall be home in about twelve days; you will have only to notify me of your visit by a line the day before."

On August 5 he wrote to her from Giverny:
"I came to Paris yesterday hoping to be able to pay you a visit, but unexpected errands deprived me of that pleasure. When I come again (very soon, I think) my first visit will be to you. I have, however, hoped that you would remember your promise and come to spend a day at Giverny, with M. Manet and your lovely little girl.

"Your panel is almost finished, and would be finished in three or four days if I were not obliged to go on a trip with my children; but on my return it will be done quickly; then I shall go to see you and we'll arrange for your visit to me."

The summer of 1884 was the last that the Eugène Manets spent in

Bougival, and during it Berthe worked even more than in the preceding years. The following letter she wrote in answer to Edma who had sent her the diary of her eldest daughter:

"It is very sweet of you to have sent me Jeannot's diary, which I find very nice and which touches me deeply. However, I know how much the admirations of our youth are dispelled with the years; after she has acquired all the lucidity of mature age, she will judge her aunt quite differently, that is to say, as she deserves. She is sweet, this little darling, and to record her thoughts every day is an excellent idea; nothing forms one's style more effectively. And by this I mean not the habit of turning out fine phrases but of putting one's thoughts into words. It even seems to me that we ought to be very lenient, to condone lack of correctness, provided that the feeling is real, and that the ideas are personal.

"Correctness will be the natural result of practice and constant effort, especially when one devotes oneself to this study from early youth. I could never write four consecutive lines that made sense, owing to my laziness as a young girl, to the great difficulties I experienced – if I had made an effort it might have degenerated into originality. All this perturbs me because I have just been glancing through the diary of Marie Pau. Do you know it? I read the most laudatory articles about it, and I am deeply disappointed. What shocks me is to see this girl of fourteen write as grammatically as if she were twenty-five; all this in a monotonous correct prose which savours neither of life nor of youth, and which drags on listlessly from the beginning to the end of the volume. In truth, I think that the 'not bad' is further removed from the good than is the bad. Don't you think so?

"In short, let Jeannot develop freely; if I were you I would be particular in the choice of reading – no drivel, nothing sentimental, nothing affected, as many good old French authors as possible. We are all born monkeys before we are ourselves; therein lies the danger of bad examples.

"Paule too seems to have a certain fluency of style which I am urging her mother to cultivate. Why should there not be as much chance of success in a literary future as in an artistic one? In England all the women are going in for novel writing; I think there is a great future for the new generation in that; all these husbandless *bachelières* will want to take up their pens.

"I don't know what makes me write all this, and in addition so illegibly that you won't be able to read it. Don't go blind on account of this, it is not worth the trouble.

"Tell me what your husband thinks of the situation in China; it seems to me that Jules Ferry who has so far been merely ridiculous is becoming insufferable."

Called back to Paris because of her mother-in-law's failing health, Berthe Morisot took advantage of the beautiful autumn of 1884 to work in the Bois de Boulogne; her husband went to the south of France to accompany his brother Gustave, the municipal councillor, who was very ill. She wrote to Eugène:

"It delights me to know that you are there and to follow you in my thoughts in that pretty countryside that I love so much; my poor Bois seems ugly in comparison. If you discover a bankrupt proprietor, a villa for a mere song, think of me, and above all, enjoy all these splendours while you are there. I embrace you, my dear friend, and I envy you the scent of the mimosas. Do you at least recall some tender memories?"

Eugène answered her:
"I went to make some drawings at our favourite spots, but everything is changed, ruined . . . It is even hotter than the year when we were here, one can work outdoors from eight in the morning on. Then I went to look for the villa of our dreams. I have been offered an old one of rather large size, well situated, all the way up on the crest of Cimiez, with a view of the whole valley of Nice, at the fork of two roads, for next to nothing, on condition that we buy the surrounding land at 30 francs the meter – it is a large amount of land, no less than 1,000 meters. This land is planted with big olive trees and a few orange trees. The house would cost 30,000 francs with the land. One would have to spend at least 10,000 francs to restore it and make it look attractive. Do you know anyone who would go halves with you in this speculation? Ask your aunt Chevalier or make the money with your paintings. Try to rouse Durand-Ruel."

Gustave Manet died before the end of 1884; Madame Auguste Manet died early in January 1885 without having learned of the death of her youngest son. At that time Claude Monet wrote to Eugène:

"It is by chance, reading the newspaper, that I learned of the death of your brother Gustave. I am very shocked, and greatly aggrieved, for we were old acquaintances, old friends . . ."

Claude Monet and Gustave Manet had actually met long before there had been any relation between Edouard Manet and Claude Monet, who were somewhat irritated by the fact that their signatures were almost identical. One day Monet said to Gustave Manet: 'This Manet, the painter, is he any relation of yours?'

"He is my brother", Gustave answered.

In the course of the same year Monet once more wrote to Berthe Morisot on the subject of the promised painting:

"I have not been in Paris for three or four months, otherwise you would certainly have had a visit from me, for you must have been thinking strange things about me since I promised you this famous picture that has never come. I must confess the truth: on my return from the seashore I realized that what I had begun was so bad that I no longer had the courage to finish it. Now I have resumed work on it and I expect to bring it to you in about a week, probably, but I must ask you to be indulgent – I am very much afraid you won't like it. It is not a picture but a very crude decoration – or perhaps not crude enough; however, it must be seen hung; then, if you don't like it you must tell me so frankly."

At that time Puvis de Chavannes had not met Monet, as is shown by the following letter he wrote to Berthe Morisot on June 5, 1885:

"I was indeed planning to come to see you on Thursday, to be forgiven as well as to meet Monet, that inspired painter of water, but I realize that this is impossible. I am very regretful, please believe me, and tell your visitor as much; I should have been very flattered to know that he is one of my friends. My best regards to M. Manet, and to you, dear Madam and friend, my respectful devotion . . . The *bonhomme* wishes to be remembered to Mlle. Manet."

The last sentence of the foregoing letter refers to a call Puvis de Chavannes had once paid to the Eugène Manets when they were not at home. On their return their little daughter had told them: "The *bonhomme* was here".

TRIP TO HOLLAND – THE CIRCLE OF FRIENDS OF THE RUE DE VILLEJUST – JERSEY – VALVINS

I N 1885, after a dreary winter, wishing to divert her daughter who was recovering from scarlet fever, Berthe organized a *mi-carême* costume ball for children. Julie was dressed as a Greek girl, just as her mother had been at a similar party given many years before at Passy, when she and her sisters were a sensation, with Yves wearing a Directoire costume and Edma dressed as a bacchante. On reading an account of the costume ball by Léon Leenhoff (Mme Edouard Manet's son) in *L'Impartial*, a newspaper he published at Gennevilliers, Edma wrote to Berthe:

"We were thrilled by the newspaper article, my dear Berthe, and we have been waiting for you to give us your own version. My son is utterly dejected at the thought that he could have seen this performance and enjoyed all these delightful things as a member of the family. How did you manage to gather together so many parents and children, you who maintain that you no longer know anyone? I see that a very successful children's party took place in your elegant home, and I congratulate you on your success, for when one goes to the trouble of organizing such affairs, one should at least be satisfied with the result. I am sure you knew beforehand that Bibi would be a success, you must have been proud of your daughter. Was she not the loveliest of all? You don't say a word about painting, no doubt you think I do not deserve to be kept informed."

Berthe Morisot's existence was now divided between her studio, her little garden, and the Bois de Boulogne – these were the places where she worked. Referring to the dissensions among the Impressionists, which were at that time hindering the organization of an exhibition, Berthe wrote to Edma:

"I am working with some prospect of having an exhibition this year: everything I have done for a long time seems to me so horribly bad that I should like to have new, and above all better, things to show to the public. This project is very much up in the air, Degas' perversity makes it almost impossible of realization; there are clashes of vanity in this little group that make any understanding difficult. It seems to me that I am about the only one without any pettiness of character; this makes up for my inferiority as a painter."

Although she proved unable to get her fellow artists to agree on an exhibition, she continued to paint with unabated ardour. Engrossed in her work, it was only at the end of the summer that she thought of leaving Paris. She and her husband planned to go to Italy, but an epidemic of cholera forced them to change their minds. Expressing her disappointment that her project of working in Venice was once again frustrated she wrote to Edma:

"I am not myself these days; perhaps this is only because of the change of season, but the burden of life seems hard to bear. I had made up my mind and I had persuaded Eugène to spend a month in Venice, and these accursed quarantines make it impossible for me to carry out my plans. I know from the Italians themselves that they take advantage of this opportunity to show their dislike for everything French, and they create countless vexations for us ... Yet I had a strong wish to go abroad and to find sun and warmth, to walk in the galleries and the palaces, and to see an art that is different. In this respect northern Italy is incredibly rich. Paris certainly has a thousand things to offer, and there is undeniably always something new to be seen; and yet, if you continually live here you reach the point of saturation."

After paying a visit to Yves Gobillard at Vieux Moulin, in the forest of Compiègnes, the Eugène Manets went to Belgium and Holland instead of to Italy. Berthe made only a few sketches at Amsterdam, and painted but little at Rotterdam, from where she wrote to Edma:

"*Ma chère amie,* I received your letter just as I was leaving, having suddenly resolved to go to Holland instead of to Italy. I think you would like this country very much, particularly Amsterdam. I am enchanted with it, but the season is already too far along, and it is almost impossible for us to work outdoors. At the same time everything that passes before your eyes here makes you yearn to paint. The temperature is still very pleasant for walking, and the light and the sky have infinite charm.

"Eugène was bored in Amsterdam, and we were spending a mad amount of money in a hotel too grand for us, so that we have fallen back on Rotterdam, and this I regret, for although the city is very beautiful, it is less characteristic, less Dutch. I have not yet seen The Hague; it is within walking distance; I do not know whether I shall like the museum, but that of Amsterdam was a disappointment. Rembrandt's famous 'Night Watch' seemed to me of the most disagreeable blackish brown, and, except for a charming portrait by Rubens, the other paintings are quite insignificant ...

"At Harlem I became acquainted with the work of Franz Hals, and there again I was disappointed. I had expected it to be better, judging from the figure in the La Caze gallery. His paintings show extreme skill, but they are commonplace. At least such was my first impression, and Bibi did not give me time to have a second one. Although she likes painting, museums bore her; she keeps tugging at me all the time to get it over with as soon as possible, and to be taken for a walk in the country."

After they returned to Paris, the Eugène Manets often invited their friends Degas, Monet, Renoir, and Mallarmé to their home. They did not lead a social life, and went out only to dine in the homes of these friends, or with Miss Cassatt and the Emile Olliviers. They preferred this restricted but choice circle to more mixed company, and made no attempt to go beyond it.

On January 11, 1886, Berthe Morisot made the following entry in her notebook:

"Visit to Renoir. On a stand, a red pencil and chalk drawing of a young mother nursing her child, charming in subtlety and gracefulness. As I admired it, he showed me a whole series done from the same model and with about the same movement. He is a draftsman of the first order; it would be interesting to show all these preparatory studies for a painting, to the public, which generally imagines that the Impressionists work in a very casual way. I do not think it possible to go further in the rendering of form; two drawings of women going into the water I find as charming as the drawings of Ingres. He said that nudes seemed to him to be one of the essential forms of art."

Just as she had done the year before, she organized a children's theatrical performance, this time of Molière's *Médecin malgré lui*. "The ingenuousness of our actors is one of our attractions; they are aged between five and thirteen", she wrote in her invitation to Geneviève Mallarmé. At that time Eugène wanted Mallarmé to write a "lampshade ballet" to be performed by the same children. But Mallarmé never wrote the ballet.

This spring Berthe again tried to get her colleagues to agree to an exhibition; she was successful, but not entirely, since Monet, Renoir and Sisley abstained. On the other hand, Odilon Redon, Seurat, and Signac took part in it. The exhibition was held in a hall situated above the restaurant "La Maison Dorée", at No. 1, Rue Laffitte, from May 15 to June 15.

Among other paintings Bertha exhibited several canvases done from a little seventeen-year-old model, Isabelle Lambert, of whom she was very fond, and whose premature death was greatly to affect her. Puvis de Chavannes referred to Isabelle in a letter about this exhibition, addressed to Berthe, and dated May 14, 1886:

"Dear Madam and friend, I count on your kindness and indulgence to excuse my delay in answering you, which was quite involuntary. I can blame many things for this, but not myself, for as soon as your exhibition opened I visited it to restore my serenity and to purify my vision by contemplating your charming works. Among others, there is a standing figure of a pretty girl whom I recognized, having seen her several times at your studio, and which is a marvel of tones – her pose is very provocative . . . Subtle, very subtle, and inimitable too – which is the main thing.

"Aside from you, here and there, very interesting things, among them F –'s *Gommeux Noctambule*, quite remarkable. Degas seemed to be full of vigour. As for the gentleman you do not like, and whose name I could not decipher in your letter, I no longer like him, since you dislike him."

In June the Eugène Manets went to Jersey. From there Berthe wrote to Claude Monet:

"I am far from Paris. I cannot go to admire your work at Petit's, but almost every day I receive letters filled with accounts of your successes, and I wish to compliment you on them. I hear that Renoir too has very fine things.

"I regret being unable to see all that and to measure for myself the degree of the public's intelligence. This time, will you conquer the public once and for all? I have been here for three or four weeks, I no longer know, it seems like an eternity.

"I have a bay window overlooking the sea, and a garden which is a mass of flowers. You could do marvellous things with it. As for myself, I do not even try, being here on a weekly basis, and holding myself ready to leave at any moment. Although one lives here comfortably and inexpensively, I do not understand why people are so enthusiastic about this island, which does not compare with our own coast, and involves being seasick both coming and going."

The climate of Jersey did not prove beneficial to Eugène Manet, who fell ill on returning to Paris. To divert him during his convalescence, Berthe gave regular Thursday dinners, which were attended by Mallarmé and the painters, and Jules Devoy, a lawyer, cousin of the Manets. Since Claude Monet did not live in Paris, he was not one of the habitués. On November 1, 1886, he wrote to Berthe from Belle-Isle:

"I have only now received your kind letter that you addressed to me at Giverny, and I hasten to answer it, for I am living in a place where the mail service is rather slow because the mail boats operate most irregularly at this time of year; therefore do not hold it against me if my letter is delayed.

"A thousand thanks for your kind invitation; I regret that I am unable to take advantage of it, for the time being at least, but rest assured that immediately after my return, in about a month, I shall come to see you.

"I have been here for almost two months. It is a terrible, sinister place, but very beautiful; it has seduced me from the very first moment, and the ocean is so beautiful that I have embarked on a number of studies, and the more I work the more I am enchanted; but what terrible weather. I work in rain, in wind. In other words, I am quite carried away; perhaps I am on the wrong track, but I keep on."

As he had promised, he wrote to Berthe from Giverny, on December 5:
"I have just arrived, and expect to go to Paris next week, probably Wednesday; and so, if convenient to you, I shall come to dinner at your home on Thursday, that is, a week from tomorrow. You see, I have not forgotten."

On December 10, Berthe wrote to Mallarmé:
"Would you do us the favour – you and Mlle Geneviève – of coming to dine with us next Thursday. Monet will be with us, Renoir also, and my husband and I will be delighted to spend a little time with you. I should also like to tell you how much pleasure I had reading your charming article in the *Presse indépendante*. My best regards."

Mallarmé wrote her in reply:
"I am put in a quandary by your graciousness. I am invited for Thursday by someone who is to introduce me to the old and admirable Barbey d'Aurévilly; if it were anything less important than that, I should break the engagement and take refuge in your home which is so pleasant. It is a piece of bad luck for me; I never visit anyone, and I should have so liked to see Monet and Renoir also." *132*

In May 1887, Berthe Morisot was represented in the exhibition that Durand-Ruel organized in New York, and later in the international exhibition at Georges Petit's, where, in addition to her paintings, she exhibited a bust of her daughter. Wishing to have Rodin's opinion, she asked Monet to serve as intermediary. Monet wrote to her from Giverny: *133* *134*

"Forgive me for not having kept my word, but it is not my fault: I was unable to see Rodin as he did not appear at the dinner. But I have just written to him, and I am sure that he will be glad to visit you and be of service to you. As you will be able to judge for yourself, he is the best of men, with an exquisite taste, which is rare in sculptors.

135   "I have just learned that Pissarro has answered Petit that he accepts; thus he no longer fears to find himself in bad company, and his convictions are shortlived. Unfortunately, I dare not hope the same from Degas. Do work hard so that this time success may be decisive for all of us."

The Eugène Manets asked Renoir to do a portrait of their daughter, who posed in an embroidered English dress, holding a cat. By coming to lunch Renoir was able to divide Julie's sittings into two parts – he was accustomed to ask his sitters to pose for longer periods than was Berthe Morisot. Renoir

136   was then in his Ingres period and painted section by section. He often talked about Mme de Bonnières, whose portrait he was also painting, and who had to have a juicy chop brought to her to give her strength to pose; on the other hand, he said, she always stood upright in the cab taking her to a ball, in order not to wrinkle her gown.

During the summer of 1887, the Eugène Manets went for a few days to stay with Mallarmé at Les Platreries, between Valvins and Samois, where he occupied a farm house, and where he had only a tiny study, hung with old cretonne decorated with large roses. When Eugène asked him whether he was not writing anything on his sailing boat, Mallarmé answered: "No, I am leaving that great sheet white."

A little later the Eugène Manets took a short trip into Touraine, and they visited the chateaux of the Loire. Then they went to the chateau of Vassé in the Sarthe to visit the Vaissières, Manet's cousins. There Eugène received the following letter from Mallarmé, dated August 21:

"I have thought of you during this great heat; tell Mlle Julie that the brook has been 'mowed,' and that a gangplank was thrown across it for her. The water has cooled off after the storms, but we often bathe throughout September; the sun will warm the fine days soon, and nothing is lost.

"Your letter fills me with envy; I too have skies of distant green, but I lack flowers, and I fancy that your eyes are spared this suffering, the worst of all privations. At times I would give the centuries of a tree for a few pinks. A Lenôtre garden! It haunts me with its yews; as I see it, it has not many flowers, but it is like a decorative home, an old intimacy recalled while travelling; all this was waiting for Mme Manet's exquisite perception.

"I have worked over a good many poems that are being published, and now, before undertaking anything, it is myself that I am going to rework a little and restore my strength that Paris strips me of each year.

"Come and interrupt me. Your visit will be a little fête for all of us; the brook and the woods are preparing themselves for it.

"The ladies join me in waiting for you."

On her return to Paris, Berthe received from Mallarmé an issue of the *Revue indépendante*, addressed as follows:

> *Apporte ce livre quand naît*
> *Sur le bois l'aube amaranthe,*
> *Chez Madame Eugène Manet,*
> *Rue au loin, Villejust, quarante.*

> [When the amaranth dawn emerges
> Above the woods, take this book
> To Madame Eugène Manet,
> Far off, Rue de Villejust, number forty.]

The hospitality that the Eugène Manets received from the Vaissières brought them closer together with their hosts, and Berthe Morisot did a pastel portrait of their eldest daughter. Then the Thursday dinners were resumed. The Emile Olliviers joined the older habitués. Eugène Manet had been a great friend of Emile Ollivier's in his youth, and had gone with him to Italy on a journey which had included Edouard Manet.

Degas, who liked Mme Ollivier, wrote:

". . . of course, with the greatest pleasure. But if you see me falling asleep at Mme Ollivier's feet, be so kind as to tell her that it is because I am tired from moving . . .

"It was indeed he, Eugène, your husband, dear Madam, who wrote me asking me not to answer if I could dine with you on Thursday. I did as I was ordered. I must also do as you wish, and assure you that I shall be very glad to see M. and Mme Ollivier again. And so, it is agreed, till Thursday, and many thanks. Regards."

Another occasional guest at Berthe's dinners was Astruc; he came with his wife and his daughter Isabelle, whom he called *la biche au bois*. Fantin-Latour and Puvis de Chavannes came but rarely. As for cousin Dejouy,

though an assiduous guest, he found this milieu and Berthe as strange as the dinner menus, which also were unusual, with dishes such as rice Mexican style, or chicken with dates.

At that time Mallarmé planned an edition of his prose poems illustrated by his painter friends. The cover bearing the title *Le Coffret de laque* was entrusted to Lewis-Brown, Renoir was to illustrate *Le Phénomène futur*, and Berthe Morisot *Le Nénuphar blanc*. Degas and Monet were also to illustrate one poem each. In December Berthe mentioned this matter in a letter to Mallarmé:

"It would be kind of you to come to dinner Thursday. Renoir and I are quite bewildered; we need explanations for the illustrations. Do not consider yourself obliged to write to me; no answer will mean that you accept, and I shall absolutely expect you."

Mallarmé wrote in reply:

"I am answering nevertheless because I am disturbed by your bewilderment: fortunately, your smile appears in the background. . . All this time I have had to wait – and I am still waiting – for the size of my volume to be decided; in the meantime I am sending you, as an instrument of torture, the page to be illustrated which is the last piece of the enclosed publication. Until Thursday, then. My wife is ill, and she asks you regretfully to accept her apologies for the long delay, and I am instructed to send you her regards."

The project was not carried out; only Renoir made his illustration which was included in the volume published under the title *Pages*.

Toward the end of that winter Berthe Morisot suffered a severe illness. Claude Monet wrote to her from the chateau of La Pinède, near Antibes:

"Dear Madam, I have learned that you are ill and that I might have been the cause of this. I should be very happy to hear that everybody is well now, but I do believe that the terrible winter you have had was the real cause of this nasty grippe. Here we had the backlash of the cold spell, and during two weeks the weather was frightful, quite unbearable. Fortunately the sun quickly gets the upper hand here.

"I am working a great deal; I am having great difficulties, but I dare not yet say that I am satisfied, for another period of bad days might spoil everything I have undertaken. Moreover it is so difficult, so tender, and so delicate – particularly for me who am inclined to go about things violently; the truth is that I am making a great effort.

"I do not expect to return before April – just in time for our exhibition. I hope that you have been able to work, and I urge you to prepare as many entries as possible. There will doubtless be fewer of us than last year, and for that very reason it is imperative that the exhibition be all the better.

"Renoir is near Marseille, at Martigues; I have not heard from him for a long time, but he seemed satisfied with the place. Unfortunately I fear for him that he has had worse weather than we had here.

"Excuse this interminable scrawl."

On March 14 Berthe wrote him in reply:

"I think that you are very kind to reproach yourself on my account; the real truth is that the bad weather and my age are the only causes of my illnesses; I am becoming a bronchial old lady. At last I am on my feet again, and engaged in a pitched battle with my canvases. Do not depend on me to cover much wall space, I am not doing anything worth while despite my desire to do it, and the endless series of dark days we are having this year is an added obstacle. Your sun makes me envious as do other things too . . . even your 'violence'. You are being coy, but I well know that you are in good form, that you are doing delightful things, and I hope as much from Renoir, for it is you two who will make the exhibition.

138
139

"The other day, at the older Goupil's, I saw pictures by Pissarro that are much less *pointillé*, and very beautiful; it seems to me that they might be liked. I went there to see the nudes of that fierce Degas, which are becoming more and more extraordinary.

140

"We often talk about you with Mallarmé, who is very devoted and full of friendly feelings for you. He has lent me *Ten o'clock* by M. Whistler. I went to great pains to read his very literary English, without much profit."

On his return to Giverny, Monet wrote to Berthe:

"Dear Madam, I have not yet been able to come to see you since my return, having gone to Paris only yesterday, and for only a few hours, during which I was busy with previous engagements.

"You have heard about all the trouble we had with Petit. After working so hard it is not pleasant to be treated in this way. There was talk about an exhibition at Durand's; this project was not at all to my liking, and on reaching Paris I gave it up at once for many reasons that it would be too long to go into.

"But this morning Renoir tells me that this exhibition is taking place, indeed that it opens on Saturday, and that the young Durand, without even having consulted me, proposes to put in pictures of mine owned by him and by various collectors. Considering that I am going to oppose this by every means at my disposal, since this is my right if it is a paying exhibition, I think it is my duty to let you know this in advance, not in order to influence you in any way, but because I don't want you to be surprised and to believe that I am a quitter, as they will certainly say. I have given evidence of my good intentions, and I have proved to you that my greatest wish was to exhibit with you.

"I expect to visit you as soon as I come to Paris for a day or two, and I hope that you will be kind enough to come to Giverny one day.

"Be assured, you and M. Manet, of my friendship."

Renoir wrote to her:
"Dear Madam, since I shall not have the pleasure of seeing you tomorrow – I am in the country trying to paint a landscape or two – I must inform you that Durand-Ruel is preparing an exhibition for May 18; the only expense will be that of sending one's pictures.

"I think the exhibitors will be the same as those at Petit's, except for Monet who will not participate.

"All my regards to you and to the lovely little future competitor, Julie Manet.

"A handshake to your husband."

The exhibition was held at Durand-Ruel's, from May 25 to June 25; it was smaller than originally planned. Berthe sent three paintings, one pastel, and one water-colour. Monet wrote to her later:
". . . You must think that I am quite forgetful, don't you? I wanted to come to see you and to tell you how good I thought your pictures at Durand's were. I have been very busy here, going to Paris only occasionally for a few hours; and then I hoped that you would arrange with Mallarmé to come to Giverny.

"Have the Goupils at least notified you that they were giving an exhibition of about ten paintings that I sold them? I should be very pleased to have your opinion."

She wrote in answer:
"Thank you very much for kindly remembering me and for your kind words about my wretched pictures at Durand's. I am all the more touched

because, as you know, the show is a complete fiasco, and it seemed to me that each of us had his share of responsibility in this disaster, of course Renoir and Whistler less than the others; but all this the public cannot understand.

"As for you, you have conquered this recalcitrant public. At Goupil's one meets only people who have the highest admiration for you, and I find that there is much coquetry in your request to me to give you my opinion – I am simply dazzled! and you know it quite well. If you insist I shall tell you that the picture I like best is the one with the little red-brown tree in the foreground; my husband and I stood in ecstasy before it for an hour.

"I saw Mallarmé on Thursday. I should be quite surprised if this charming man did not express all his admiration for you in a delightful letter. Both of us are still very eager to see you at Giverny, and I hope that next month the weather will be less unpleasant than this month.

"Please, give my best regards to Mme Hoschedé."

Enjoying their apartment and garden in the Rue de Villejust, and being close to the Bois de Boulogne, the Eugène Manets did not feel the need to leave Paris that summer. At the request of Edma who was planning a trip to England Berthe sent her information about London.

"I am enclosing a little note made by Eugène who remembers our peregrinations in London more accurately than I do. . . Eugène mentions the Marquess of Westminster and Lord Sutherland. I think I visited others, but I don't recall the names. You will find there extremely beautiful Gainsboroughs and Reynolds'. Also, spend a long time at Kensington. From the picturesque point of view, I most enjoyed the boat trips on the Thames, and excursions to Greenwich and to Kew. I did not go to Windsor, which Eugène recommends, and we regretted this.

"I suppose you will return via Dover. If so, do as I did: take the boat from London to Ramsgate and Margate; the crossing is really very beautiful and not to be feared at all from the point of view of seasickness. If you go to Southampton, you should make an excursion to the Isle of Wight. It is worth the trouble; I am giving you my own itinerary. We were very satisfied with it, and when I was in London, Tissot told me that it was the prettiest that one could follow.

"Eugène thinks that it is very daring on the part of three women – a feeble mother and two inexperienced daughters – to face the difficulties and the great traffic of London."

Cher Madame.

Non seulement montmartré
ressemble à Chamonix. mais
j'ai de plus très mal aux reins
est-ce mon grand age. ou
un rhume. je vous dirai ça
quand je pourrai aller vous
voir. veuillez mon Bordives
prié de ne pas avoir le
courage de franchir le lac
de boue qui nous sépare.
j'irai vous dire bonjour dès
que je pourrai bouger.
j'espère que malgré ce
vilain temps ça ne va pas
trop mal chez vous.
mille amitiés a tous
Renoir

Jeudi

On Sunday, July 22, she wrote to Mallarmé:

"Next Thursday, I think, will be your last Thursday in Paris; you would give us great pleasure by coming to spend it with us.

"Bibi's godfather [Dejouy] has just been appointed member of the council of the bar association; we shall put flowers at his place. I shall expect you unless you advise me to the contrary; if you do come I shall invite Lewis-Brown also. Yours."

During that summer there was constant talk of a visit to Valvins. On September 2 Mallarmé wrote to Berthe Morisot:

"Here we are in September, dear lady, and there is not much sun. How are you all, and do you still feel like spending a week in the country? Will you go so far as to set a date?

"As for your inquiries, before I look more extensively, I can tell you this: that Mme Biard would put at your disposal half of her house (two bedrooms, a maid's room, and a living room) at the price of sixty francs.

"With the lovely garden along the water, and the trees overarching, I doubt that there is anything better. . .

"Miss Cassatt seems to count on you a great deal, and I encourage her. Degas has written to me from Cauterets promising his drawing for the twentieth of the next month; as for you, I know your punctuality, and nice Lewis-Brown has shown me something charming; do not deny it.

"I have not written to you because I was travelling. I let myself be enticed to Royat for half of August; here, back home again, I remember how charming your visit was last year.

"The water is cold, Mademoiselle Bibi. Geneviève and her horse, a real one this time, dip in it every day.

"Good-bye to the three of you from the three of us; I hope to see you soon."

But Berthe Morisot wrote him in reply:

"The answer is no, unfortunately, *cher ami* (I shall call you *cher maître*, if you prefer). We make this decision after much thought, having many reasons that are as sensible as they are dreary for remaining in Paris.

"Mme Biard's proposal was very tempting, at least it seemed so despite my husband's prejudices against this poor woman. He had an unpleasant memory of quilts on beds (he could easily have taken them off).

"In a word, we are leaving you entirely to your work and to your solitude, and you are less to be pitied than we who are living on our lovely recollections of last year.

"I have still been planning to send you my masterpiece – not charming at all, though full of good intentions, but Lewis-Brown instead of meeting me at the printer's shop, as he promised, is being horribly lazy about it.

"I am working fairly well, trying to take advantage of these beautiful days so rare this year; this is one of my sensible reasons for remaining in Paris.

"Many regards from me to Miss Cassatt when you see her, and very affectionate regards from all of us to Mme Mallarmé and to Mlle Geneviève."

Bibi i Nassi

THE VILLA RATTI AT CIMIEZ

IN the fall the Eugène Manets left for the south of France. They rented the Villa Ratti at Cimiez, a green and white country house in the Italian style, surrounded by a large garden full of olive, orange, fig, and pepper trees, bamboos, and aloes woods. Berthe reported to Edma:

"I have been settled here about a week. I am delightfully comfortable, and the temperature is such that I miss my light dresses which I left in Paris. We have plenty of room; poor Nice has suffered a great deal as a result of the disasters of these last years, and everybody goes to Cannes or other fashionable places, so that here at Nice spacious villas with large gardens planted with orange trees are available at very reasonable prices; formerly these were prohibitive.

"We are on a hill, with Nice at our feet and the sea beyond. Right beside us, near the Roman ruins, there is a very picturesque monastery, more Italian than Italy itself, and we are in the midst of real country. We are outdoors from morning till night. We lunch in the garden. I think that all this will be beneficial to everyone's health. Julie is like a rose in bloom. This morning we went down together to buy *bella sardina*; we were a little short of provisions, and her cheerful little face, as she trotted in the narrow streets of the old town, was a pleasure to see. I am very happy to see this setting again, since I am not interested in new places."

On November 1, Mallarmé wrote to her:

"Dear lady, here is a note from Valvins where your roses have followed us; they are on the mantlepiece, making up for the poor autumn outdoors. Instead of leaves, drops of rain are falling on the windows, which I would otherwise keep open; for despite the winter landscape we have late summer temperatures. And thanks to your flowers it is a little like Nice.

"But since the newspapers mention a new mode of locomotion that will take one to Marseille in two hours, I think that I shall not content myself with the prolonged hothouse weather here, and that I shall visit you this winter, even if I must take the ordinary railway, yes! If I can manage it, that is, my dear friends.

"Did you have a pleasant trip? I thought of you all a great deal the night of your departure; my pupil's indisposition did not persist; and now, this Thursday, eve of All Saints, all I know, through Mme Suzanne, is that you are 'out of town', and my letter will be forwarded to you from the Rue Villejust.

"I am still working a great deal on my lectures, four of these to be given next year. Do not emigrate each winter, unless of course you bring back many marvels. Do you still use the little album?

"I saw Blanche (Jacques, without his nurse) on Sunday. He told that according to a letter he received Renoir is depressed and discouraged, and that Whistler, who is away from London, may one day settle in Paris.

"This is all that I remember here, in this woodland silence, before the bells start ringing for All Saints.

"Regards to Manet, who I see is settled and in good spirits. Kisses for Mlle Bibi, and Geneviève joins her mother in giving thanks for the roses. Thank you."

Mallarmé's mention of Blanche recalls the visits Jacques used to pay, as a child, to Berthe Morisot, accompanied by his nurse who waited for him in the hallway while he watched Berthe paint, standing behind her like a well-behaved boy.

Berthe wrote in reply:
"Here is our address, my dear friend: Villa Ratti, montée de Cimiez. We are a little in the mountains, on the site of the old Roman city, near a monastery; it is very Italian, very rural, and in my opinion delightful.

"We have a large garden, more precisely an orchard, with many orange trees; their fruit will be yellow next month; this would be a good time to come. As you almost promised me this, I am positively counting on your visit.

"The house is very spacious; there is a room for you, with a glimpse of the sea beyond the tree tops. Julie finds it very poetic, this room of Monsieur Mallarmé. Unfortunately the trip is very long, even in a sleeping car with a corridor which is a great help. There was a magnificent moon which afforded me a glimpse of a very beautiful part of France that I had never visited.

"I saw Renoir on the eve of my departure, not in the least sad, very chatty, and fairly satisfied with his work; he says he will come to see us on his tricycle! I also received a note from Mme Hoschedé in which she says that Monet expected us all summer and had prepared beautiful surprises for us – figures in a landscape. This is one of the things on my conscience, and it is partly your fault.

"For my faded flowers you have rewarded me by a very kind and charming letter. I shall send you more, this time from my garden; this is a method of correspondence customary in this region, and quite within my means. In return you will send me your charming prose. . . I don't want to bore you, but please think occasionally that we have no one to talk with in our villa, which once belonged to the Chevalier Ratti.

"Julie is writing her memoirs and learning to play the mandolin; this will supply a lovely motif for the album; but don't imagine that I am working on it!"

There was plenty of space in the villa Ratti: in addition to Mallarmé, Berthe hoped in vain to receive Yves Gobillard and Puvis de Chavannes. The latter wrote to her:
"Dear Madam and friend, you have written me a most amiable and charming letter which I would have answered without delay if I had not wanted first to know where I stood regarding my trip to Italy and the possibility of

dropping in, en route, at your villa on the Riviera. Alas, my lovely trip is out for this year. The Sorbonne would grumble; Baudoin, my companion and pupil, is recovering slowly; the end of the autumn is mild; in short, I am staying – and then, indeed, of all the countries that have become impossible for us, Frenchmen, Italy is perhaps the one to be most avoided. I have heart-rending details about this from an artist who has recently returned from there, very much chagrined.

"And so, it is in Paris that I shall see you again; in Paris, which is restless and tosses about like a sick man – how cheerless all this is!

"Adieu, dear Madam and friend; remember me to your husband."

Renoir, for whom a room was also reserved, was unable to come because of illness. He wrote:

"My dear friends – I am of course using the plural – my answer will be a little late because I am painting peasant women in Champagne so as to escape the expense of Paris models. I am doing laundresses, or rather washerwomen, on the banks of the river; moreover I am taking advantage of the springlike weather that I hope will continue for some time, since I promised to bring back something. All this will explain my delay, now I have only to answer your letter. The white house and the orange blossoms both tempt me, and above all the sun, yet despite that I cannot answer, yes. It is not that I should not like to come, but I have to paint my washerwomen, and then to move. If all these complicated matters go as well as I wish, I shall try by the beginning of January to visit the white house and my friends who live in it.

"Ah, if I only could get on well with my washerwomen, how glad I should be to paint a few people sitting under the orange trees! I shall write to you and if it is not too late I hope to visit you in January. I hope that the beautiful sun agrees with all of you, and that I shall find you glowing like gold (horrible idea!)

"It is very sweet of you to have thought of your friend who thanks you and wishes you continued good weather and good health. Many, many regards."

On December 29 he wrote again, this time to Eugène Manet:

"My dear Manet, I am still hoping that my displacements can be carried out without difficulty: this will enable me to visit you and to see whether the climate of orange trees agrees with you. We have had here a fairly sunny winter for the north; it is true that I am in a country where one takes advantage of the slightest ray of the sun that passes unnoticed in Paris because there one is too busy, and the houses are too high.

"I am becoming more and more rustic, and I realize a little late that winter is the really good time: the fire in the large fireplaces never gives you a headache, the blaze is cheerful, and the wooden sabots keep you from being afraid of cold feet, not to mention the chestnuts and the potatoes cooked under the ashes, and the light wine of the Côte d'Or. It is with regret that I return to Paris where the starched collars forgotten for months will again get on my nerves, but I hope not to stay there long enough to have to endure these tortures. The blue sea and the mountains constantly lure me; only if I cannot afford to go shall I linger beside the studio stove, unless I get many orders for portraits, which would surprise me a great deal."

In a subsequent letter he wrote:
"My dear Manet, I must say farewell to the oranges and to the pleasure of seeing my friends. I am held captive: I have caught cold in the country, and I have a facial, local, rheumatic etc. paralysis. . . . In short, I can no longer move a whole side of my face, and for diversion I have two months of electrical treatments. I am forbidden to go out for fear of catching another cold. It is not serious, I think, but up until now nothing has improved. I need not tell you that I am bored with being kept here in this dark and foggy weather; I shall let you know when I am better, this will be my solace. Otherwise I am all right; I have no pain. I have waited a little to tell you this news, as I hoped to find a medical man who would cure me. My hopes were frustrated, and so I am forced to tell you about my illness; this is the least I can do.

"I hope that unlike me all of you are well and that I shall find you glowing with magnificent health. My regards."

He thanked the Manets for a package in these words:
"Wonderful. These lemons are ridiculously fresh, to quote Courbet ('so beautiful that it is ridiculous'). I was touched to discover the humble violet. I am writing this only to acknowledge the safe and sound arrival.

"I am having trouble with my eyes, just to imitate Degas. And we shall talk about General Boulanger when I can write without tears falling on my paper." *146*

Throughout their stay at Cimiez the Eugène Manets attended only one social function – a reception aboard the Lancaster, an American warship anchored at Villefranche, whose captain was the father of a friend of Julie Manet. Berthe wrote to her friend Sophie Canat:

"Your picture of our life here is all wrong. We are never on the Promenade des Anglais; our villa with its beautiful shade trees is all that we need. I am busy with Julie's lessons and also with my painting; we often walk in the mountains following the goat paths, though they are a little beyond my strength – my hair is as white as snow, and my legs are a little stiff.

"As for society and parties, none at all, or at least as little as possible. I am enjoying my freedom thinking with some terror of the day when I shall have to take my daughter to dances."

A little later she wrote to Edma:

"This place is delightful; I am working, I am doing aloes, orange trees, olive trees – in short, a whole exotic vegetation that it is quite difficult to draw . . .

"I have worked as much as I could; the result may seem meagre. . . . I should like to capture some of the charming effect of the surrounding vegetation. I am working myself to death trying to give the effect of the orange trees. I want it to be as delicate as it is in the Botticelli I saw in Florence, and this is a dream that I shall not realize. . . . I do not understand why this country here does not serve as a studio for all young landscapists: aside from its beauty one enjoys here an unchanging weather that makes possible the most careful studies. I won't say that work is easier here, for the landscape is fiendish, of an outline that does not permit of approximations and of colours that one never finds. It is extraordinary how much of Corot there is in the olive trees and the backgrounds. Now I can understand the title he loves – *Souvenir d'Italie*".

On one occasion Mallarmé acknowledged a gift of flowers from Berthe by the following quatrain:

> *O fin de siècle, hiver! qui truques*
> *Tout, excepté le sentiment,*
> *J'aime quand tu mets gentiment*
> *Aux camélias des perruques.*

> [O end of century, winter! It disguises
> Everything except emotions.
> I love the pretty wigs
> It puts on the camelias.]

In a subsequent letter, dated January 15, 1889, he wrote:

"My dear friends, the new year has brought me an unexpected deluge of work, and illness to one of my dear friends, Villiers. But I have delayed up *147* until now answering a pile of letters, among which one has been weighing heavily on my conscience – your letter, as you may guess.

"And I regret that I cannot come in person instead of sending it. Even aside from friendship, and the pleasure of pressing the hands of both of you, it would be nice to spend some time among your flowers rather than to stay in this opaque and frigid fog, which this afternoon prevents me from seeing anything on my sheet of paper, despite the fire and the lamp. More than ever our feet are caught in the sticky existence which is the lot of those Parisians who refuse to be engaged in business, public or private, but instead dream. But just to dream of the Villa Ratti, something I often do, is not enough for me! I wish I could appear there, were it only for one day . . ."

On February 17 he wrote to Berthe:

"Dear lady, here I am to press your hand and to give you a handful of news, so that you may be present here in a way, not merely constantly remembered by your friends. Who can tell?

"Renoir is better, I am told; will you see him? And his painful condition that was feared to be definitive has turned out to be only a bad cold, without after-effects.

"The exhibition of painters–engravers at Durand-Ruel's offers exquisite *148* trifles; I know of two drypoints that should be there.

"The good Lewis-Brown, very much distressed by the loss of his wife's little granddaughter, now and then attends to the printing of your (and my) picture; but thanks to Degas, to whom I am going to send a quatrain on legal paper, the publisher can take his time. His own poetry is taking up his attention, for – and this will be the notable event of this winter – he is on his fourth sonnet. In reality, he is no longer of this world; one is perturbed before his obsession with a new art in which he is really quite proficient.

"This does not prevent him from exhibiting, on the Boulevard Montmartre, next to the incomparable landscapes of Monet, marvellous works – dancing girls, bathing women, and jockeys. Monet who has been charmed by the white waterlily done with the famous three crayons, is following your example and doing an illustration for my book. Leaving the concert we saw the Cassatt ladies, whom you have bedecked with your flowers, and Saturday *149* we, or perhaps only I, will dine with them.

"I am working in the dark. Here is an additional bit of diary, specially for you. I want to know what all of you are doing under your blue skies, and whether water-colours are being prepared for the poems, and what you are painting. What is Mlle Bibi reading? Well, Manet, I voted for the general, in obedience to my daughter; she and her mother who is weary of the winter send you kisses, my ladies, and would like to follow them. I greatly wish to find Nice in the garden of the Rue Villejust this spring, and I shall say frankly that I can hardly wait."

Berthe answered:
"My dear friend, it is kind of you to send me such a charming new entry, and I feel very guilty to have delayed all this time telling you how delighted I was. Fundamentally I am like Julie; you disturb me a great deal, and this, as well as the fact that I am working badly serves me as an excuse. This country is too beautiful for me.

"Now I want to think only of the water-colours, and to try to be worthy of you will be an added difficulty for me. The carnival is on. We have been terribly cold these last days, and we have had rain which distressed Bibi; she has a mauve domino – this colour is fashionable in Nice – and she intends to take part in all the festivities. These celebrations would be pretty if only the organizers had a little taste and imagination; the people co-operate with a goodwill that is charming, but there is nothing French about the pranks. This is incidentally the feeling one has all the time – that one is not at home; you can imagine whether I shall be delighted to see Paris again, and particularly our Thursday faithful.

"I am lost in conjectures about Degas's four sonnets: are they poetic, or only variations on the tub? Give him my regards, and also tell him that Mme Emile Ollivier continues to be his fervent admirer."

On February 15, Monet wrote her from Giverny:
"I thought that the winter here would be beautiful, and I anticipated the pleasure of doing effects of snow or frost, but the weather has been uninterruptedly atrocious, and what is worse, changing, so that I have done nothing good, and now it is too late for me to go away. I am counting on the first beautiful spring days to catch up, but while waiting I do nothing but fret. . . I have nothing of great interest to tell you. I go to Paris less and less frequently, and anyhow people there are only engrossed in politics. There are always the same exhibitions; your humble servant has also his own, quite

unpretentious, at Van Gogh's, but the public pays it no marked attention."

On March 7, Berthe Morisot answered him from Nice:

"My dear Monet, may I drop the 'dear Sir,' and treat you as a friend? Your letter has given me all the more pleasure because I was beginning to think that you had completely forgotten me. I have hoped throughout the winter that you would come somewhere in this region, or even, despite your prejudices against Nice, to the villa Ratti. I am in a delightful place which you could have put to good use; I do not. I am working a great deal, but nothing comes of it. It is horribly difficult.

"I know through Malarmé that you have marvels at Van Gogh's, and indeed I regret that I am not there to see them. I shall make up for this by going to see you on my return. This will not be before the beginning of May. I am so comfortable here, and the country is so delightful, that the only thing I miss about Paris is my friends. My husband is very much better, my daughter looks like a peasant girl, and since we shall certainly not budge throughout the summer, I feel that it is better to take as' much advantage as possible of the beautiful spring days."

Monet answered her from the Creuse:

"As you can see I am once more a little out of the way and at grips with the difficulties inherent in a change of surroundings. The place here is terribly wild; it reminds me of Belle-Isle. I came on an excursion with friends, and I was so charmed that I have been here for a month; I thought I was going to do amazing things, but alas, the more I try the more difficult I find it to paint what I should like to. With all that the weather is frightful, rain every day, and terribly cold. Therefore I need quite a bit of courage to persist, but since I am here I must go on to the bitter end. I hope that you have less inclement and more favourable weather; I also hope that you will bring back many good paintings."

In a letter dated Palm Sunday, Mallarmé wrote to Berthe:

"Dear Madam and friend, when will you be back? Winter is dragging on here; we need a paint brush with any kind of colour to change this; you alone can do it. I have a vague intention of making some sun for my ladies at Valvins, from the day after-tomorrow to the last Tuesday of this month, but I shall not succeed. We shall watch for your train going by quick as lightning (but this will perhaps be at night). Ah, it would be a good thing if you could get off for a few hours, long enough for all three of you to shake the south out of your clothes!

Berthe replied:

"We shall indeed pass close to you on Friday the 26th, but without stopping. We shall think of you, and you for your part, pity us for we shall be encrusted with black soot for twenty-four hours."

A few days after arriving in Paris Berthe received Mallarmé's answer to her invitation to dinner. He wrote:

"We have just arrived from Valvins, where I would have written a note in answer to your kind invitation had we not been engrossed in strange occupations. What double pleasure it is for me not to be at the Salon at this moment, and to think of the travel sketches you will show me Thursday evening! Yes, with all my heart I accept your invitation to dine *en famille*, and I should be happy to see you all even before that, if tonight and tomorrow, at the college, I did not have to get rid of a pile of papers accumulated on my desk during my fortnight of fresh air."

THE SUBSCRIPTION FOR THE OLYMPIA
MALLARMÉ'S LECTURE ON VILLIERS
DE L'ISLE ADAM – MÉZY

IN the spring and the summer of 1889 the Eugène Manets often visited the Exposition Universelle, which was held at that time. They were particularly attracted by the Javanese dancers and the retrospective exhibition, which included a room devoted to Edouard Manet.

At that time Claude Monet conceived the plan of opening a subscription for buying the "Olympia" from Mme Edouard Manet in order to present it to the Louvre. He encountered many difficulties, and only by dint of great perseverance and devotion did he succeed in getting the painting accepted by the Luxembourg museum. The Louvre refused it on the ground that not enough time had elapsed since Manet's death. On November 10, 1889, Berthe Morisot wrote to Monet:

"My dear Monet, I saw Chavannes a week ago, and I promised to write to him on the subject of the 'Olympia' subscription. You have no idea how formal and complicated he is (this between ourselves, please). All the same he is a charming man; but the idea that he might appear to be in disagreement with the administration upsets him. He would like you first of all to ascertain the administration's goodwill. I told him that neither you nor I thought this necessary; to this he replied that someone should at least talk about it to Proust."

On November 13, Monet wrote to Berthe:
"The subscription is successful beyond my hopes; it has reached 18,000 francs; thus the amount required will be easily covered. All the important painters have contributed; this is a very good thing, although I have learned that in various quarters a great effort is being made to spoil our plan. Proust seems to be backing out."

Berthe wrote him in reply:
"Everything I have heard confirms the administration's hostility which you have mentioned before. I have no way of influencing the authorities, and even if I had, I should think that an intervention by the family would change the character of the subscription. You alone, with your name and your authority, can open doors if they can be opened at all. I was told that someone (whose name I do not know) had gone to see Kaempfen to sound him out, that Kaempfen had angrily assured him that so long as he was there no Manet would be admitted to the Louvre, and that thereupon his visitor rose saying: 'Very well then, we shall try to get rid of you, and then we shall bring in Manet'."

On January 22, 1890, following the publication of an article in the *Figaro*, Monet wrote to Berthe:
"You have probably read Calmette's article on the subject of the 'Olympia' in yesterday's *Figaro*. This Proust is a contemptible fellow and he has a peculiar way of understanding friendship. What a cad he is to set himself up as arbiter, to pass judgment on the 'Olympia,' and to maintain that in organizing this subscription we are not interested in what will happen to the

painting, as if we were asking for charity. I am indignant because I see clearly that the purpose of all this disgusting campaign is only to thwart our undertaking, but since I have no need of M. Proust, I am writing him to give him a piece of my mind, and now that war is declared we shall fight on to the end . . ."

Eugène Manet, for his part, wrote to the *Figaro* to protest against the article which suggested that the subscription was a piece of charity in behalf of Manet's widow.

After this summer which was interrupted only by another visit to Vassé in the Sarthe, the Eugène Manets resumed their Thursday dinners. On one occasion Renoir, unable to come because of a grippe, sent the following letter of excuse:

"I regret this indisposition all the more because it deprives me of your pleasant company and of an opportunity of using my poor though sincere talents to comfort this great and sweet poet whose words are a music greatly to my taste. Try to do it for me and better than I could."

On another occasion he accepted Berthe's invitation in the following words:

"I think that you are cruel toward yourself and 'uncle godfather', and since you refuse to believe that people are coming for your sake, I shall tell you that I shall come in the hope that the girl with the beautiful hair is still with you. So there you are . . . A thousand regards."

On February 12, 1890, Mallarmé, upon returning from Belgium where he had given a lecture on Villiers de l'Isle Adam, wrote to Eugène: "Dear friend. Till Thursday, then. I'll come with Geneviève and with the lecture."

Eugène Manet was enthusiastic about the lecture and immediately asked Mallarmé to give another reading of it in his home. He arranged a soirée for February 27 to which were invited friends of Mallarmé and of the Manets.

Monet wrote from Giverny: "Of course I'll make the trip, and I'll be delighted to do so. But I'll have to appear in full dress."

It was before a small but select public that Mallarmé, short and erect, began with these words into which he put all his personal charm: "One dreamer has come to speak to you of another . . ."

This soirée is referred to in the dedication that he wrote on the reprint
of the lecture which he gave to the Eugène Manets:

Vous me prêtâtes une ouïe
Fameuse et le temple; si du
Soir la pompe s'est évanouie
En voici l'humble résidu.

[You lent me famous ears and
the temple; while the splendour
of that evening has evaporated
here is its humble residue.]

Eugène Manet was not only a devoted friend of Mallarmé's, he also had
boundless admiration, almost veneration for him. One morning he was
surprised to find Mallarmé carrying wine from his cellar, and he was greatly
upset at the thought that a man of such intellect should be compelled to
perform such chores.

Because of his bad health Eugène had to spend part of the year outside
Paris. In the spring of 1890 the Manets began to look for a country house.
One day, after many a fruitless search they stopped, without great expecta-
tions, at Mézy. But they were thrilled by a walk to the promontory of Gibet
which dominates the Seine, and they rented a house there. On April 14
Berthe wrote to Mallarmé: "Dear friend, come to dine with us on Thursday;
you cannot refuse, this is a farewell dinner."

On April 28 Mallarmé wrote to Mézy:
"Dear friends, so you have gone taking with you those Thursdays which
I shall miss. Last Thursday, when I received your letter, I was preparing to
go to see you to say good-bye, and not alone, but in company with my friend
Marras, your guest of a famous evening, who wanted, having left Versailles
for Paris, to pay you a visit as soon as he became settled . . . And now the
rain which is blotting out the very memory of the countryside from one's
eyes does not frighten you at all; in reality you are right: the leaves reappear
as soon as the rain stops, greener and bigger.

"As for the address for the material, we have received it, thanks. My only
way of living through the spring is to drape myself in its colours, with a
dash of gray and ennui in my heart."

As soon as she was settled Berthe wrote to Mallarmé:

". . . I have worked a great deal to prepare a room for you; nonetheless, my dear friend, you are forewarned. Wednesday I shall go to Miss Cassatt to see with her those marvellous Japanese prints at the Beaux-Arts. At five o'clock I shall be at the Gare Saint-Lazare, in the waiting room of the Mantes line. If you wish to join me there we shall travel together; you would spend Thursday with us and Friday morning you would take another express that will bring you to Paris at nine o'clock, that is to say, in time for the college, if you have classes. All this, of course, if the fresh air of the country tempts you, if the weather is good; but you would give us great pleasure. The landscape will be less pretty later on . . . No need to answer me if you come."

Mallarmé answered, nevertheless:

"Dear friend, yes; and although silence, according to your kind letter, is an affirmative answer, I feel I should write the monosyllable. And so, a little after five o'clock, Gare d'Amsterdam, near your ticket window; but – this is my only but – I must return Thursday night for I have classes Friday at dawn."

At Mézy Berthe painted a great deal. She set up a studio in the barn, in which she posed a boy from the village as St. John, naked except for a sheepskin, to whom Mallarmé later alluded in a letter. She also used as a model a girl of a rather uncouth aspect, whom she had met in the village carrying a basin of milk. Berthe's first painting of her was the canvas that Claude Monet bought in 1892 at an exhibition of her works at Joyant's. Berthe planned to visit Monet with Mallarmé, whose letter referring to this project was addressed as follows:

Sans t'endormir dans l'herbe verte
Naïf distributeur, mets-y
Du tien: cours chez Mme Berthe
Manet, par Meulan, à Mézy.

[Take no nap in the fields
  Naïve postman. On your toes!
Run to Madame Berthe Manet
  At Mézy, near Meulan.]

"My dear friends, here it comes, this Fourteenth of July, a bit clouded over, and I keep looking in your direction and thinking of you. As for those gentlemen, your neighbours, there was an intrigue against them at Versailles. If everything goes well I shall arrive tomorrow evening, travelling alone, alas, by the same train as last time. Are we still planning to go to see Monet on Monday? Should I write to him?"

Those "gentlemen of the neighbourhood" were pigs in a pig farm belonging to the mayor of Mézy. The Manets had applied to the authorities in an effort to get rid of them, and Mallarmé served as their intermediary.

Berthe replied:
"Thank you, dear friend, for being faithful despite the rain. . . We have not seen Monet again, nor received a letter from him; this may mean that he is expecting us without fail or that he is engrossed in work; you shall decide which it is, and do whatever you think is right; we shall follow your example . . . The naïve postman was quite dumbfounded and I quite enchanted."

Finally Monet's answer came, dated July 11. He wrote:
"We are very much at fault, but I hope this will not prevent you from carrying out your promise on July 14; or better on July 13 if it is convenient to you. We shall be very happy to see you with your husband and your friend Mallarmé, and I hope you will raise my spirits a little, for I am in a state of complete discouragement. This fiendish painting has me on the rack, and I cannot do a thing. All I accomplish is to scrape out and ruin my canvases. I realize that having gone a long time without doing anything I should have expected this, but what I am doing is beneath anything.

"You must be cursing the weather, just as we are. What a summer! Here we are in a state of distress; my pretty models have been sick. In short, we had trouble upon trouble, which has prevented us from paying you a visit."

On Sunday, July 13 the little party left Mézy for Mantes in a carriole, and took the train to Vernon. They spent the day and dined at Giverny. Monet, to compensate Mallarmé for not having made an illustration for him, offered him a canvas. Mallarmé did not dare choose the painting he preferred, but finally took it, urged by Berthe Morisot – it was a landscape of Giverny showing the smoke of a train. Mallarmé returned radiant, his painting on his knees. "One thing that makes me happy," he said in the carriole, "is to be living in the same age as Monet."

The following night Mallarmé returned to Paris with his precious burden. Renoir came several times to stay at Mézy, sharing Berthe Morisot's models or setting out early in the morning to make little sketches of the surrounding countryside. Knowing that he was always expected he would come with his suitcase, unannounced.

Mallarmé, on his vacation at Valvins, wrote to the Eugène Manets:

"My dear friends, even though I do not want to know the exact date and even though I believe that this return of the summer begins my vacation anew, the idea that the first communion will take place in September haunts me, and I wish to remind you that in my thoughts I am not far from you.

"I think of the little lady in white each time I see gossamer threads floating by on the river. How are you at Mézy? And those celebrated gentlemen of the neighbourhood? Do they now make their presence felt only by their laments?

"I am thinking of St. John and I regret that I am no longer young enough to clothe myself thus, so as to have a pretext for never again becoming a city dweller.

"We have a piebald horse, and we speak of you each time we drive along the road where you had your misadventure, already of too distant memory. Ah, would you were here! The boat plies back and forth across the river. For a month I was not well, overworked, good for nothing but fishing. Now that I am at work again I bend over my little desk; I regret that this should not take place among certain Persian tapestries I know.

"*Au revoir*; I press the hands of all of you, and the ladies send a kiss – there is also a kiss from the old tutor to his pupil soon to be wearing a veil of tulle."

Mallarmé refers in this letter to Julie Manet's first communion that her parents, although not practising Catholics, caused her to make together with the other children of the village. He also mentions an accident that had taken place at Valvins several years previously, involving his daughter's English dog-cart and a rented pony. In the following letter, after referring to the fact that the sick curate of Mézy had been replaced by three priests, he reports a more recent and more serious accident:

"And so the black nightmare became triple, and you had to know enough to satisfy three abbés. Julie came through it all unscathed, candle in hand, like a flower; it's all for the best. I somehow think that it is you who will preserve the lasting impression. Ah, but she had previously hurt her hand, Manet writes me. What a piece of bad luck! I hope that it is all over now. We too had a terrifying accident: the horse bolted into the river with the carriage and was drowned. Some day I shall tell you about it.

"After our many troubles we are going to Paris, to come back on All Saints, for three days, for a brief dazzlement by the golden woods. That is why I am answering by a letter and not by a personal appearance."

On returning to Paris Mallarmé received the following letter from Berthe:
"My dear friend, October is with us, the end of vacation, and magnificent weather. If you still have any longing for the countryside, think of us; we shall remain here until the end of the month unless something unexpected happens.

"I received your letter a few days before the first communion; I owe you my apologies for not having thanked you for your kind remembrance, but I was quite nervous, in complete rout, with the sick curate being replaced by fellow priests who terrified me.

"Our friend Renoir spent several weeks with us. I have not yet seen Monet again: I have given him permission not to visit me because I feel that he is immersed in his work. But if you come I shall write to him."

At Mézy the Eugène Manets spent the autumn evenings reading. Berthe was at that time engrossed in Marie Bashkirtseff's diary, to which she refers as follows: "My admiration is dampened because of her mediocre painting; the 'meeting' and the rest are awkward, commonplace, almost stupid, and very difficult to reconcile with her alert style, with so much intellectual boldness and grace. I associate in my mind two books by women: *Récits d'une sœur* and hers. The truth is that our value lies in feeling, in intention, in our vision that is subtler than that of men, and we can accomplish a great deal provided that affectation, pedantry, and sentimentalism do not come to spoil everything."

On returning to Paris Berthe wrote to Monet:
"It is true, my dear Monet, that I appear to have forgotten you, but this is only an appearance for I have thought of you a great deal throughout the week of the re-opening of the Luxembourg, and every morning I hoped that you would come to dinner. It is this hope that stopped me from giving you

154

my impressions as soon as possible; and I owed them to you. Incidentally, they are absolutely identical with yours, as regards both the 'Olympia' and that strange museum devoted to French art. It seems to me impossible that the 'Olympia' should not be transferred to the Louvre, for this painting is simply admirable, and the public seems to be beginning to realize this. At all events we have come a long way from the kind of stupid jokes that used to be made about the picture.''

At the end of 1890 Berthe was very ill. After recovering she wrote to her sister Edma:

"I am well now but I have not yet got over the moral shock; I felt the embrace of death, and I am still terrified at the idea of all that might happen after I go, particularly to Julie. Have I ever told you that according to my will Mallarmé would be her guardian? But, how many buts . . . If Eugène too went, or if he fell seriously ill, would you undertake to care for the child?

"You ask me what I am doing. My attempts at colour prints are disappointing, and that was all that interested me. I worked all summer with a view to publishing a series of drawings of Julie. Worst of all, I am approaching the end of my life, and yet I am still a mere beginner. I feel myself to be of little account, and this is not an encouraging thought.''

A little later she wrote:

"Thank you for your affectionate letter; in a word, this is what I had – a rheumatic heart. Perhaps it is not as dangerous as it may seem to the patient, but the sensation is absolutely that your life is ebbing away, and since this will eventually happen one day or another, it is better to make arrangements concerning your loved ones.

"I have always thought life to be a very precious thing, and I shall do everything in my power to live as long as possible . . . Thank you for answering 'Yes' so sweetly and for assuring me of your affection for Julie.''

During the winter of 1890–1891 the Thursday dinners continued. In addition to the former habitués there were now Régnier and Wyzewa; the occasion for meeting the latter was his article on Berthe Morisot published in *L'Art dans les deux mondes*. At that time Durand-Ruel continually exhibited impressionist works, and Berthe refers to a visit she made to this gallery in the following entry in her notebook:

"Met Pissarro in the Rue Laffitte; he complimented me on my pictures at Durand's, I was overjoyed. But then I was cruelly disappointed – I found

155

156

my painting hung in the corridor and it is horrible. Julie looked frightful: one can see only the harshness and the effort that went into it. I was so unpleasantly surprised that I complained to young D. about the place that was given me; he answered that my paintings looked even worse in the rooms (*sic*). 'If so, remove them!' Then Chavannes arrived, the whole house escorted him. P. and I standing aside made philosophical remarks on the subject of success. At least Chavannes is a gentleman, he complimented me on my dress, my hat, and my paintings; he asked my permission to accompany me for a few moments. On the sidewalk I thought suddenly that I had probably left without saying good-bye to young D. and I told Chavannes of my doubts. 'You didn't say good-bye to him but he didn't notice.' – 'That is true, there is no use being polite when you are there, everyone is interested only in you.' – 'You are very irritable today.'

"Then, changing his tone, he said to me: 'It is strange that I should meet you today; for several days I have been thinking of you with great intensity, and not only of you but also of your mother.'

"The mention of my mother of whom no one ever speaks touched me deeply. I said to him: 'Really, I would never have thought you capable of this.' – 'Well, this happens to me, I have a great power of evocation and I often live in the past; I was seeing Passy again.' "

On April 6, 1891, Puvis de Chavannes wrote to her on the subject of her pictures exhibited at Durand-Ruel's, reproaching her for snubbing the Salon:

"Sunday morning I went to D-R's, and what I saw does not change my opinion in the least: you are very much at home there, with all your qualities. Nevertheless I regret that you are not regularly exhibiting at the Salon . . . But I am convinced that you will end up by returning there."

Early in the spring of 1891 the Eugène Manets returned to Mézy where it rained a great deal. Berthe wrote to Mallarmé:

"My dear friend, I am writing to you from Mézy; I have a fire in my room; you must have one at Valvins, I imagine. I have great sympathy for the ladies, tell them this; but I am not sorry for you because you were terribly dictatorial about this departure. Eugène refuses to admit that he was wrong; he is not aware of the deluge and does not even allow me to say that the menus are monotonous and insufficient.

"I have brought along your book, which I am reading with the greatest delight; so far this has been my only pleasure at Mézy, and I am reading it very slowly so as to make it last through the season. I also heard from my sister that your *Corbeau* was a great success at the Vaudeville. Let me add *158* my applause to that of the public although you hold women in such contempt.

"Do you know what Degas said about you and me? I shall tell you on the Fourteenth of July. In the meantime, my best regards. At the opening I met young Desboutins who is anxiously waiting for his quatrain." *159*

Although Berthe was living at Mézy at the time, she attended the opening of the Salon where she met her artist friends. Degas stayed in the Salon from morning till night, lunching there and thoroughly scrutinizing every picture.

Mallarmé wrote to Berthe from Valvins:
"My dear friend, I am taking advantage of a beautiful sunny day, because I do not like to answer my friends in rainy weather: when one is in the country rain might appear to be the motive for one's writing. Moreover the sight of a letter to be answered preserves something of the presence of the person who wrote it; and it seems that less is preserved after the letter has been answered . . . Furthermore I am either lazy or hard at work. As for you, are the apple trees sitting for you? And the little girls with flutes under them? . . . Thank you for glancing through *Pages*. As for *Le Corbeau*, I was at the Vaudeville, and I am still angry about it, even after going to the country, because of an impression of trashy work which is left with me and of which I cannot rid myself.

"What could Degas have said? This intrigues me to the utmost, but perhaps it is not too slanderous since I am in your company; hence I am somewhat reassured . . .

"The ladies ask me to send you a thousand regards. No, Eugène is not dictatorial, nor am I. I spend my life giving in, except perhaps in literature, but this is the least of it.

"If any of you suffer from hay fever, I urge you to ask M. Dejouy to get for you Mlle Cassatt's Corbelic Smoke Ball (what is that? I hear you say). It is doing wonders for Geneviève.

Later, on July 9, he wrote:
"My dear friends, what an absurd summer – not only because of the storm, but because I won't see you, and because I'll never know what Degas

said. I expected to spend July in Paris, whence I might have fled to Mézy; but my daughter is away at the seashore with her friends, and I am immobilized at Valvins with my wife whose health is not too good. Ah, what bad luck that we should be so far apart, though both on the Seine. You above all are among the few I should be so happy to have as neighbours. Otherwise I am working, and in my leisure time, trying to grow older.

"I am very unsociable. I had a visit from Whistler, that is all; I discreetly spared him a walk in the woods, but he was jubilant at the Palace [Fontainebleau] where your name, Madam, was frequently mentioned in connexion with the Empire furniture that you liked. As for painting – the orchard, the studio – how many things I should like to know of which you will perhaps judge that I am unworthy; but I want you all to know that I think longingly of last year. Our regards."

On July 14, Berthe wrote him in reply:

"How sorry I am, my dear friend, to write 'July 14' at the head of this letter. Do you really want to know Degas's secret? Well, what he said is rather unfair to me, and flattering to you. Are you satisfied? As for me, I do not feel humiliated a bit since it is only a question of your superiority. Moreover, it is an old story, it is not the most recent remark he has made, but such as it is, you will hear it only at Mézy.

"Eugène told you, did he not, that we were negotiating to buy a château; we are carried away by the desire to be in a beautiful setting before we die, and this is both tempting and unreasonable, so that I dread all possible outcomes. But how annoying not to be able to guide you through my palace while I still feel I have rights there.

"Your sentence, 'I am working and trying to grow older' describes me perfectly. If only you could always speak for me! I am not dissatisfied with myself, and it is wrong of me to say this because it will bring me bad luck.

"I have not seen Monet, I have seen Renoir for a moment with his family. I shall tell you about this later . . . In short, I am writing to you like a sentimental young girl, to make you realize that I miss you today, and without mentioning it to Eugène who always accuses me of boring my friends. Yours."

Renoir had brought to Mézy his wife and his son Pierre. He had not previously introduced them to the Manets – a remarkable circumstance in view of their close relationship. As usual he had arrived unexpectedly; he had dispensed with any formal introduction, and as a result the first moments of the visit were marked by some awkwardness. Then the Manets took him to see the château referred to in the foregoing letter to Mallarmé. The Renoirs stayed for dinner, and by evening Mme Renoir no longer seemed a new acquaintance.

Shortly after this visit Renoir wrote to Berthe:
"I have just written to a model. I am resuming work in the studio while waiting for better things. A month has gone by during which I have done nothing but look at the sky . . . It would have been delightful to work a little with you, but, but . . . I am postponing this pleasure until better days. Forgive me if I do not take advantage of your kind hospitality. I am going to paint outdoor pictures in the studio. Your devoted friend."

Nevertheless he came for a short visit to Mézy, after which he wrote, on August 17:
"I have been this morning to see M. Apprin who tonight will send you the *porte-toile* complete with two canvases. I forgot my pointed stick. I shall come for it one of these days, don't bother about it. Moreover I am not sure that I did not leave it somewhere in the fields.

"I would have returned last night to take advantage of the good weather and your kindness, but I found my boy quite ill with some sort of dysentery. I had the doctor who told me it was not dangerous but that he required a lot of nursing. In short, I shall not leave him before he is entirely recovered. He is much better even this morning, though his digestion is still quite upset. This good weather breaks my heart, but I shall go tomorrow to Argenteuil if everything goes well. I can leave in the morning and be back in the evening; I shall not be far away should he have a relapse.

"I am busy looking over my sketches. I think it isn't going too badly. My model has just arrived. I will buy some dresses. And so I shall let you work. Be sure to finish your painting with the cherry trees. I shall send something to the Champ de Mars, so try to do the same. We must put ourselves in evidence. I send you all my wishes for success. Give my regards to the young ladies and to Manet. A thousand regards. I have another stick, don't bother about it."

The paintings referred to in this letter are those of the *Cerisier* – two large canvases on which Berthe was working in her studio from a sketch and numerous studies made outdoors. At that time she was also working on her paintings of a nude shepherdess reclining and of another shepherdess dressed.

Towards the end of the summer Berthe wrote to Edma:

"I was almost surprised to see your handwriting, my dear Edma, but as you say it would ill become us to indulge in mutual recriminations since both of us behave in the same way. However, I am constantly aware of the fact that life is moving on and that it is high time to reveal what is in one's heart. I very often think about our life of old, about all of us.

"I am at Mézy; it is raining almost incessantly; the place is too pretty to be spoiled, but it is becoming sad. I have decided to give up the house at the end of the season, and this makes me doubly regret the fact that you did not come to Maurecourt; that was our last opportunity of meeting this summer.

"I am working less than I should like to because of the weather. I have pretty models – local children; but all this cannot be described. I have projects, many projects, but little work done. As I grow older, painting seems to me more difficult and more useless.

"We have not bought a château; there is one for sale near the village, so extraordinarily cheap that for a moment we had the idea of committing this folly. It is extremely pretty. Eugène was crazy about it, and Julie too. But we will be reasonable; the house in Paris is quite enough . . ."

The Manets had decided against buying the château of Mesnil, which was then put up for auction without finding a purchaser. Thereupon new negotiations took place, as can be seen from the following letter which Mallarmé wrote to Berthe on September 29:

"My dear friend, you see that I have waited till the eve of your return to think of you – no, you won't believe this; I have not written before simply because I have been watching the brook flowing by and being rippled by occasional gusts of wind – there is no other reason. Perhaps also because my mind usually wanders far off each time I put some sentences together, and it seems to me that I create distance between myself and those to whom I am near in my thoughts when I make sentences for them. This is a cause of defeat which would never have occurred to you!

"But please believe me that I am haunted by the château, and that I often make bets with myself as to whether you own it or not. It would be so becoming to you; there is a certain dark brown cloak that I see hanging on the panelled walls of an old drawing room or rustling past the rows of dahlias in the park . . . you shall have to answer me by a note from Paris.

"This mild autumn, which will continue, should bring you back only at the end of the month; as for ourselves, we shall leave tomorrow regretting that we do not leave desolation behind. There are, however, your Thursdays in store for me, and some Sunday evenings. Otherwise, Paris evades me. "You have been working, I should like to have a look. My hand to Manet. Good-bye, my pupil. Until soon."

Berthe wrote him her news:
"My dear friend, we shall stay another week for the weather is marvellous. If you want to see the château, this is the time to come for we seem to be becoming seriously interested in buying it. I do not even know any longer whether I really want it, but the present owner is very anxious for us to take it. The deal was off, but now it is on again. If you should be tempted to spend a last day in the sun, and Mlle Geneviève as well, we would be delighted, and in the event you wished to spend the night, I have two beds to offer. I am writing all this in the conditional mood because I should not wish to bore you for anything in the world.

"Renoir has spent a few days with us, without his wife this time. I shall never succeed in describing to you my astonishment at the sight of this ungainly woman whom, I don't know why, I had imagined to be like her husband's paintings. I shall introduce her to you this winter.

"I am in a hurry to return to Paris; I think that women never like the country wholeheartedly. At all events, I shall see you soon, and thanks for your letter; it is delightfully pretty, and almost touching."

Mallarmé wrote to her from Paris:
"My dear friends, until soon, but, alas, not under your trees, and this year I shall know the château only in my dreams and from your descriptions.

"This is a stormy end of vacation, the college has already half devoured me trying to finish off its prey, I am struggling and cannot let go before giving it a few blows. The ladies join me – Geneviève with regrets – in sending you their last regards from this distance. Soon, soon."

Before leaving Mézy Berthe received the following letter from Renoir:
"I must if possible apologize to you. I could not go to see you. I wanted to come to tell you not to bother with that canvas of last year. I left it deliberately. If I took it, it would be to cut it up and paint over. I thought that you could do the same. I wanted to go to get my stick and my umbrella, but as

soon as I am in Paris I cannot budge. Sometimes it is because of the models; this week it is Durand who tells me every day that he will come to see me, and who does not come; I do not care but I am always being kept in. In short, at this moment I am in process of giving a patina to a genre painting (the kind that sells).

"I do not know whether my letter will still find you at Mézy, but I hope it will. I received your letter concerning my umbrella, this makes one that has been retrieved. I and my family have lost five umbrellas since this spring, all new. I have just bought one for two francs, and this one I am sure not to lose.

"Regards to Manet and to my little friend. I hope to see you soon in Paris."

mercredi matin

Mes chers amis

Sauf un mot de vous me
décommandant, demain j'irai
vous demander une chaise au
dîner de famille ; parce qu'il
me paraît qu'il y a un peu
longtemps qu'on ne s'est vu.

votre, à tous
Stéphane Mallarmé

DEATH OF EUGÈNE MANET
EXHIBITION AT JOYANTS – THE RUE WEBER

BACK in Paris, the Eugène Manets resumed their Thursday dinners. Berthe recorded some of the table talk:

"Degas advised Charpentier to publish an edition of [Zola's] *Bonheur des dames* for New Year's Day, with samples of materials and lace trimmings as illustrations on facing pages. But Charpentier did not understand the joke.

"Yesterday Astruc said that Carolus [Duran] was nothing but a sedulous ape, and that left to himself he would always prefer the glitter of paste to a precious stone . . . One day Degas said referring to Caillebotte: 'He has the stubbornness of a hunchback, and therein lies his talent.'

"Mallarmé admires Richepin's *Mer* only with reservations: 'It is a song sung by a beautiful voice, but a little coarse.'

160

161

"Last night Renoir said that in literature as well as in painting talent is shown only by the treatment of feminine figures. He said this, I think, a propos of the pretty Natasha in *War and Peace*.

"Mallarmé finds more beauty in men than in women. He uses countless circumlocutions to say this to me; my answer is that all this is quite indifferent to me . . ."

Eugène Manet's health, which had been quite precarious, became worse in January 1892, when Berthe wrote to Mallarmé:

"The weather is hideous; Eugène is on his feet again but he is so terribly thin that he barely fills his place at the table. Therefore I shall take pity on you and let you have your freedom on Thursday the 14th. Would you postpone your visit till Thursday the 21st? No answer will mean, 'yes'. How considerate I am of you, dear master!"

In the course of the months that followed Berthe expressed to Mallarmé her growing anxiety concerning her husband's health in a number of notes. This anxiety was justified: Eugène Manet died on April 13, 1892. Among Berthe's notes written in that period there are the following lines:

"I have descended to the depths of suffering, and it seems to me that after that one cannot help being raised up. But I have spent the last three nights weeping. Pity! Pity!

"Remembrance is the true imperishable life; what has sunk into oblivion, what has been blotted out was not worth the trouble of being lived, hence was not. The hours of happiness and of grief remain immutable, and have we need of material objects to be contemplated as relics? All this is so crude. It is better to burn the love letters . . .

"I should like to live my life over again, to record it, to admit my weaknesses; no, this is useless; I have sinned, I have suffered, I have atoned for it. I could write only a bad novel by relating what has been related a thousand times."

But Berthe, displaying great strength of character, concealed her grief in order not to cast a cloud over her young daughter's life. She found escape in work which she interrupted reluctantly to keep business appointments. She had now to attend to her affairs, on the subject of which she wrote to Mallarmé, whom she had appointed guardian of her daughter:

"I am distressed, my dear friend, that you did not wait yesterday; I returned a few moments after you had left, and I had news for you. Shortly

Dimanche soir

Le temps est atroce et Eugène
est si terriblement maigre
qu'il ne tient pas sa place à
table. Donc, j'ai pitié de vous et
vous rends votre liberté pour
Jeudi 14. Voulez vous remettre
à Jeudi 21 ?

Pas de réponse voudra dire
oui. Comme je vous ménage,
cher Maître !

Berthe Manet

you will receive a note from Gustave-Adolphe Hubbard, deputy of the Seine-et-Oise, attorney, my counsel in this complicated liquidation. You, in your capacity as guardian, are to take charge of everything. He will give you explanations, and will ask you for an appointment for this purpose. This solution calms me a little. I was in the clutches of that wretched notary, and I had the feeling that being at the helm I was causing the bark to founder, thus failing in my duty toward my daughter as well as toward the memory of Eugène.

"This handsome boy whom you will meet – he looks like an Indian god – seemed to me a saviour. He is confident, he has the élan of youth . . . In short I entrust myself to him! I have dragged my widow's weeds, my papers, my grief to all those horrible businessmen; this could not go on."

Joyant, who had proposed to Berthe Morisot to have an exhibition of her works in his gallery, wrote to her:

"Forgive me for insisting, but have you considered the possibility of having an exhibition, around May 15, of your paintings, pastels, and drawings (about forty of them) at my gallery (Boussod and Valadon, Boulevard Montmartre)?"

This exhibition was held from May 25 to June 18. Gustave Geoffroy 162 wrote the preface to the catalogue. The works shown were from different periods, including a number lent by collectors, and were particularly appreciated by Degas, Monet, and Renoir. This success encouraged Berthe to work assiduously.

On the occasion of her husband's death Théodore de Wyzewa wrote to her:

"Madam, I was absent from Paris when I heard of your loss; that is why I did not tell you sooner the great grief it caused me. I vividly remember M. Manet's extreme kindness to me. He seemed unwell when I met him, and I was deeply touched by his nobility and courage.

"If only, Madam, you could now rest after your hardships of so many years! and if only painting could take your mind off your sorrow, if only you could devote yourself to it entirely! I have always sensed, Madam, that your feelings were so exalted and your disinterestedness so unalloyed that I have always feared to offend you by telling you how much I admire your talent. But I believe more and more firmly that after the death of Manet only Renoir and you have preserved the qualities of the painters of past times; that you alone, with Renoir, are an artist among pupils or teachers; and each time I see your works I am so deeply enchanted that I do not know of any that I cherish more.

"And now please forgive me for having confessed this to you. I still dream of an article or book in which I should at last be able to put down my ideas about your art and that of Renoir in a form that might please you. But I am doomed to write only things that I dislike on subjects that I dislike.

"And yet I should like to convey to the ten souls kindred to mine which must exist in this world, the admiration and the joy that everything you do gives me."

He wrote to her again on the occasion of her exhibition:

"Madam, thank you with all my heart for your cordial invitation that I so little deserve and that touches me deeply. But until the end of the month I too shall be immersed in moving and settling.

"I rented a little house at Sèvres where I expected to spend the summer, but I have just learned that it is haunted, so that I must live elsewhere because I am superstitious and perhaps over-nervous.

"But are you leaving that château of which Renoir gave me such an interesting description? Are you leaving it to return to Paris, or are you going to spend the summer at some other place where I could, in July or in August, pay you my respects, and present all my thanks and apologies?

"At all events I must thank you also for the joyous occasion which your exhibition is. You know what deep and personal affection I have for your paintings; I find them all the more delightful when I see them brought together."

On the day of the opening of the exhibition Renoir wrote to her:

"Your colleague is happy to tell you that your dread of a fiasco is itself a fiasco. It has gone very well; they have already sold the ducks, the large painting which I think is entitled *La Véranda* and some water-colours. In short, everybody is satisfied, and I compliment you. Regards."

Puvis de Chavannes did not congratulate her until July 22:

"Madam and friend, I saw you yesterday without being able to speak to you, since I was on a roof and you were in the street. At that moment I was stricken with regret and remorse, the regret of not being able to press your hand, the remorse for not having yet told you what I have indeed often thought, namely, how charmed I was by your exhibition. Never before have

the rare and the distinguished found an equal interpreter with such variety. I left these modest rooms absolutely enraptured."

As for Degas, he gave her the greatest pleasure he could give her by telling her that her somewhat vaporous painting concealed the surest draftsmanship.

Instead of fitting out the château of Mesnil as she would have liked when her husband was alive and both of them wished to "see themselves in a beautiful setting before dying", Berthe was compelled to let it after making only the most necessary repairs. It was from the château that she wrote to the young and pretty Louise Riesener:

"Thank you, my dear Louise, for all the nice things you say to me about the exhibition, and also for your interest in my château. I have just let it for three years at a modest price – 2,500 francs, but at any rate it is let, and I am freed from the expenses it involved.

"I have been here for three weeks supervising the workers, having hangings installed, painting – in short, attending to all these ruinously expensive things, and I find this house prettier and prettier.

"It was certainly a find, and I have a great satisfaction thinking that some day Julie will enjoy it and fill it with her children. But as for myself, I feel mortally sad in it, and am in a hurry to leave. During my husband's last days, his mind was haunted by this château, so that his memory is present here evoking all the sadness of his illness.

"To return to the beginning of my letter: I was very gratified to learn about what took place at Joyant's. I left Paris the day after the opening, which, needless to say, I did not attend. Renoir is in Spain, Mallarmé is busy, and, as you can imagine, Miss Cassatt is not one to write me about an exhibition of mine.

"I came back one morning when I had business with my notary, and your charming cousin assured me that there were many visitors – but not at the time I was there. I was quite aware of that myself.

"All in all, I shall tell you very frankly that the whole seemed to me less bad than I had expected, and that I did not dislike even the very old pieces. Let us hope that in twenty years from now the new ones will have the same effect upon me."

Berthe Morisot also decided to leave the ground floor apartment of the Rue de Villejust for a smaller flat. For this reason she spent the summer in

Paris, trying to take advantage, while she still could, of these surroundings
that she loved, that were partly her own creation, and that suited her so
perfectly. At that time she worked a great deal from a very young model
sent to her by Zandomeneghi, a blonde girl whom she painted with a cat, *163*
then with a fan, and asleep. She also painted her in the garden, and later
beside a pond.

Her friends were out of Paris. Renoir wrote to her from Pornic:
"Every day I want to write to you and I do not because I am in a very
bad humour. I have ended up by being stranded at Pornic where I am
teaching my son to swim; so far so good, but I should be painting landscapes. The country here is quite pretty, and that is why I am so cross. To
paint landscapes is becoming for me an ever greater torture, all the more so
because it is a duty: obviously this is the only way to learn one's craft a
little, but to station oneself out of doors like a mountebank, this is something
I can no longer do.

"In my moments of enthusiasm I wanted to tell you, 'Do come', but then
I am seized by the boredom of the seashore, and I do not want to play on
you a bad trick by telling you to come to a place where I am so bored, a
place I should quickly leave were I alone. Nevertheless I went to Noirmoutiers; it is superb and quite like the south, far superior to Jersey and
Guernsey, but too far away, much too far. If I were bolder, there would be
lovely things to do there, as everywhere else for that matter.

"I have gone so long without writing to you that I no longer dare to ask
you how you are, whether you have stayed in Paris, or whether you have gone
to Touraine, as you intended. Are you still worried about where to live?
This is something I want to put out of my mind, I find it so troublesome. To
relieve myself of the studio problem I toyed for a while with the idea of
going to Algeria with some friends, but I think it is bad to be always travelling. I shall write to you when I have painted an interesting landscape.

"Now I can only wish you a better humour than mine, and above all good
health; the same to my excellent friend Julie. Your friend."

On September 23 Mallarmé wrote her from Valvins:
"My dear friend, can one see Mesnil from the train a little beyond Gargenville? On two occasions, on my way to Honfleur and on returning from there,
I jostled everyone in the compartment in my rush to the window, and I saw
something that looks indeed like the façade of a château.

"We are finishing our vacations at Valvins, as usual. We had a great deal of trouble, at Honfleur and here, because of the state of my wife's health; she now seems a little better. Aside from that, our double fugue would have been nice. I have written so much for myself that my correspondence has suffered, as it did because of the good weather; and to celebrate the holiday I shall grant myself a day of wandering into friendly homes, yours to begin with. Have you found one? But first of all, have you not left Paris? Have you not been tempted by Renoir and the Loire? You see that I know nothing about you; and of course it's my fault. But we often talk about you . . .

"How is the work going? This luminous season is favourable, and I am looking forward to adorable things when I see you early in October. Unless – and I don't want to think of it – you have been beset by worries. How is Mme Gobillard? And M. Dejouy, does he keep well?"

Yves Gobillard was seriously ill at that time; Jules Dejouy was paralysed after a stroke he had had the previous winter. In her answer to Mallarmé's letter Berthe wrote:

"I do not write, my dear friend, because my sadness increases with the passing of time.

"Thank you for having at last thought of me and for having written first; I knew that you had left in poor health and I wanted very much to hear about all of you.

"It may well have been Mesnil that you saw – something long, sad, a high Mansard roof, a cluster of big pinetrees cutting across the front. The railroad passes near-by, a little before Gargenville when coming from Paris. I returned there last week with Julie and young Rossignol, my only faithful companion of this summer's solitude; the park and the château were spoiled by the presence of my tenants. No, I no longer miss it.

"I have asked the count to let me stay until January; this way I have a great deal of time to think about this boring problem, whereas actually I should have hastened the solution.

"This is what you have to do: write to Maître Massé that you are giving him full powers and return the document to him directly from your Paris apartment. This is the advice of Maître Dejouy, still paralysed. I saw Renoir at the funeral of poor little Durand. He had come from Noirmoutiers and was to return there the following day. His wife and his son greatly enjoy the bathing, but he is bored to death.

"You can see that I am incapable of writing. Come to see me when you are back in Paris; I shall be very much pleased. My regards to all. Julie is returning the greetings of her guardian."

On October 7, she wrote to Sophie Canat:
"You have understood perfectly, my dear friend: I do not write because my heart is filled with sorrow. But your letter was among those which I have put aside intending to answer. The affectionate memory that you have kept of Eugène touches me deeply: not everyone realized how kind and intelligent he was.

"In brief, my dear friend, I am ending my life in the widowhood that you experienced as a young woman; I do not say in loneliness, since I have Julie, but it is a kind of solitude none the less, for instead of opening my heart I must control myself and spare her tender years the sight of my grief.

"The situation of Yves is also heart-rending. Am I callous? For the past few days I have begun to be hopeful; the reports are somewhat better; the other day I showed a letter to Doctor Martin, and he thought on the basis of it that the progress of the disease was temporarily arrested.

"I hope that your health is good, and I also hope that we shall meet again here. We now constitute a circle of old ladies of bygone days. Is not life strange? To think that we have already reached this point."

In the fall Berthe and her daughter took a short trip to Touraine. She made a few copies at the Tours museum and painted some landscapes. She wound up her trip with a brief stay with her husband's cousins at Vassé. Back in Paris she rented an apartment in the Rue Weber, where she had a studio built of two or three maids' rooms on the top floor. She spent most of the time in that studio; her daughter and occasionally other young girls served her as models. In good weather she worked in the Bois de Boulogne to which she was even closer now than when she had been in the Rue de Villejust.

Renoir wrote to her:
"I have waited for this note of yours to come to see your new establishment. You must feel strange there. I shall find you still unsettled. This will take some time.

"I shall come tomorrow around five o'clock just for a minute, as I shall come to dinner another time. I have begun a torso that prevents me from going with you to Mesnil. I regret this, but Thursday I must go to Argenteuil, and then to Louveciennes. That makes a great deal of country for this harsh season.

Mardi

Voilà Zoé au lit.
Ne venez pas ce soir.
A bientôt, j'espère.
amitiés
Degas

"I am dreaming of the south – if only it were not so far. And so I shall come to see what you are like when you are no longer in your own home. But one gets used to such things, you will see . . . I hope that you and Julie are well."

Later he wrote:

"You must have been very much annoyed about that business, but I hope that this note is not too late; it will be a matter of luck for my wife is in Burgundy and I am in the Midi.

"I have often thought of you but I have completely forgotten my role of family adviser. I have thought of you all the more because if you want to see the most beautiful country in the world, it is here; one has Italy, Greece, and the Batignolles all in one, plus the sea, and if you want to make a beautiful and inexpensive tour, here is the way to do it.

"Take the train as far as Pas de Lanciers, thence the little line of Martigues, stop at the Hotel Rouget, see Martigues – the town, the very pretty and easily accessible mountain, the ponds, and the fishermen's houses; hire a carriage which for the sum of eight francs will take you to Istres by way of Saint Mitre, and will make the tour of the Etang de Berre, fifteen kilometres, one hour and a half. At Istres, a man named Marie, livery man, will take you, for five or six francs, to Saint-Chamas, which is the most beautiful of marvels; and I am not telling you to stop there although one eats pretty well; the sleeping accommodations are somewhat rustic; aside from that the people are very nice.

"From Saint-Chamas take the train to Pas de Lanciers which will bring you back to Martigues.

"I think this excursion is the most beautiful one can make in France. I have been here only since the day before yesterday. I have had a toothache all the time; if this terrible pain subsides a little, I think I shall work here for three or four days.

"A thousand regards. I hope that the letter from the Suresnes notary will reach you in time.

"Your friend Renoir. – Hôtel de la Croix-Blanche, Saint-Chamas, Bouches-du-Rhône."

After the death of her sister Yves Gobillard, which occurred in June 1893, Berthe Morisot was planning to go to the Havilands in the Limousin to paint the portrait of their daughter Eva. Renoir, a native of the Limousin, encouraged her in this project in the following letters, the first of which was written at the Gallimards' in the Calvados: *165*

"I have just arrived in Normandy; it seems to me very beautiful, but cold. I am going to take a walk which will make me decide whether the place is any good for painting. I hope it is perfect for I shall have to stay here longer than I wish.

"I should like to see you go to the Limousin; I found that region very beautiful, and I think this is the right time. I recall the wonderful chestnut groves on the hillsides.

"Take canvases with you; there must be spots where one can paint without going to the châteaux, and you will tell me what you think of it. Do not be concerned with me; I should reproach myself for having made you miss a pleasant place in order to revisit a place that you have already seen; despite all the beauty here it is cold, cold . . .

"Many regards to my little friend Julie and to you."

"I have just received your letter; I have stayed only a very short time at the Manoir. Decidedly, this part of Normandy does not appeal to me very much, though it is fairly beautiful, Therefore I have left the splendours to visit a part of Normandy that we do not know.

"I passed through superb places, Falaise, Domfront. I came back by way of Nogent-le-Rotrou and Chartres, which is a little marvel, both the cathedral and the city. I am now in Burgundy and shall return to Paris Thursday night. I shall see whether you are there.

"I wish very much that you would go to Limoges. I thought the region so beautiful the last time I passed through it in a train that I should be very happy to have your opinion; I was sure that there were pretty things there for you to paint, and if there is nothing to prevent me, I do not say that I shall not go to see this too; but I have been travelling a long time and I confess that I felt the need of staying quiet for a little while.

"And so I shall come to see you, and if you are not in I shall leave a little note.

"I am addressing this to Paris, hoping that you have not left since the weather is fine again, and that you will be able to give my best regards to the poet. I should have visited you and him too, but I always do the opposite of what one should.

"My regards to Mlle Julie and to you."

VALVINS – THE DURET AUCTION
SUMMER AT PORTRIEUX
DEATH OF BERTHE MORISOT

THE project of painting the portrait of Eva Haviland was dropped, and instead of going to the Limousin Berthe divided her summer between the Bois de Boulogne and Valvins. On August 10 Mallarmé wrote to her concerning an inn situated on the opposite bank of the Seine:

"I am frightened by the lateness of this date which I learned from the newspapers as I was taking my first stroll; for, except for my awareness that I have not seen you for a long time, I feel as though we have just arrived and as though I have been asleep a bit. However, I notice patches of green that will remind you of the Bois, though they are a little too abundant and too bright.

"Inquiries have been made at the inns; the one next door will be quite suitable . . . because one of the two ladies, Julie, is a hearty eater; but I have not said a word about that. It offers a room with two beds, overlooking the river, and meals for fourteen francs a day instead of sixteen. One is not wrong to entrust oneself to dreamers who are the only practical people; and now I have made a charming dream for myself, with details.

166
"All of us are well and say au revoir to you, including Laertes."

A little later he wrote:

"What is the matter? I hope, and the ladies as well, that it is nothing serious; nevertheless we are worried.

"The little inn is filled, and if Julie's health no longer causes you any anxiety, write to us one or two days in advance so that we may find for you the desired and perfect little shelter, at that inn or elsewhere."

On August 21 Berthe wrote in reply:

"No, nothing serious, my dear friend, simply a painfully infected finger. With the hot weather doing its share, she had several days of fever and sleeplessness. On Monday the doctor will tell me whether we may leave, and then I shall let you know.

"I think that the inn will be empty; the 'viper hunters' who stayed there have returned to Paris. You see that I am well informed.

"Best regards."

A little later she wrote him:

"Thank you for the trouble you took on our behalf; we shall arrive on Thursday by a morning train."

They stayed at Valvins from August 24 to September 4. Mallarmé, who did not like walking, occasionally let himself be persuaded to take walks in the woods, during which he spoke to Berthe Morisot about his work, and about his project for a book that was to be "The Book", and that one could open at any page and from any side. This project was never carried out. Berthe made water-colours in the woods or from the window of the inn, from which she also painted a little study in oil of Mallarmé's boat.

Back in Paris she wrote to Mallarmé:

"1.04 is the correct time; at least I was told so at the station, and I was triumphant; but we did not leave at that time, nor even at 1.15, and the express trains passed by without stopping. After all, I think you were right, or rather that I don't understand a thing.

"It was a great disappointment to be back in Paris to which one becomes attached in the long run, by force of habit, whereas even the shortest stay in Valvins makes you hate to leave it.

"Laertes was so tired last night that he crept into my suitcase and made himself a nest among the frills of your neighbour whom I admired so much. And this morning we feel so exiled not to be there with all of you that it is impossible to resist sending you a greeting and a little gossip, intended more for the ladies than for the poet."

Mallarmé wrote in reply:

"Everything has changed, even the wind, since your departure; the boat lies sleeping under the threat of rain. I am working without knowing too well on what, and am writing this on the side. Your stay here brought us a great pleasure – the feeling that I was taking walks with a dear friend in our neighbourhood; and only now do I realize how charming they were; while you were here everything seemed so natural.

"I know that you are dealing courageously with your troubles; how is Julie's finger (I am being asked about it), and when will you leave for the Limousin with your timetable? My wife has a little cough, Geneviève remembers a chatty and very special Julie in the woods; as for myself, I thought that she had a round and rosy face when she left.

"To look at the painting of the little sailboat is very satisfying.

"Thank you for your note. My best to both of you. Also to good Laertes, as Hamlet called him."

On September 18 Berthe and her daughter returned to Valvins. A few days later they went with Mallarmé to Moret where Sisley was painting a series of churches, which Mallarmé thought had been inspired by Monet's series of cathedrals. Berthe worked in the forest of Fontainebleau, and they took walks under the big beech trees that Mallarmé likened to a dance hall, which, he said, would be the scene of his daughter's wedding. After Berthe left, he wrote to her:

"The Manet ladies have proved perspicacious thanks to Laertes' keen nose. What weather! We stay indoors, with a fire going, meditating on the irony of the last fine days. I have been at Valvins less since you left it.

"In the evening I was taken aback at the sight of the closed inn, and I returned there the following day, finding it hard to believe that you had such a great talent for disappearing.

"Your departure was not confirmed to me until Sunday, at the Signorets' where the talk was only about the Manet ladies who created a sensation there. Madame Point met them on the avenue leading to the railroad station in the act of departure, Julie carrying a violin case. Early next week we shall escape from these dark days in our turn. *Au revoir*. I suspect that you will not go to the Limousin, nor even to Tours."

In October Edma Pointillon, whose husband had retired, returned to
167   Paris. This was the period of the Franco-Russian alliance; despite the general enthusiasm Berthe did not expect anything good to come of it.

On October 30 she spent the day at Giverny with Monet who showed her the changes he had made in his house, and his series of twenty-six cathedrals.

She often paid visits to Mme Edouard Manet, her sister-in-law; she liked on those occasions to enter the coach-house in which the sketches left by her brother-in-law were stacked.

The former habitués of the Rue de Villejust now came to see her in the Rue Weber; occasionally she went to dinner at Degas' where she usually
168   met Forain and Bartholomé. On Sundays she often took her daughter to the Lamoureux concerts, where she saw Mallarmé. "At the Concert Lamoureux", she wrote in her notebook, "Mallarmé said to me that music is to him like a lady manifesting her joy by her hair – an enormous head of wavy hair."

During that winter of 1893-1894 Mallarmé invited Berthe and her daughter to one of his Tuesday evenings, to attend a reading of a lecture he was to give at Oxford. But although she had often said to him facetiously: "Julie and I will dress as men and attend one of your Tuesdays", Berthe declined the invitation. She wrote:

"No, decidedly, the schoolbench would intimidate us too much. We shall see you on your return, rejuvenated by your triumphs; only let us know in advance so that we may be the first to celebrate them."

On January 12 Renoir wrote her the following note:
"Having received your letter this morning only, although it came last night, I could not avail myself of your kind invitation. I had and still have the grippe; last night everyone was asleep by nine o'clock.

"The weather is improving, spring is coming with great strides. Oh poetry! I shall therefore see this enchanting poet another time.

"Since rose-fingered dawn now rises a little earlier, it will perhaps be possible to paint."

Early in March Berthe suffered the loss of her friend Mme Hubbard as well as that of her cousin Dejouy. On March 13 she left for Brussels, accompanied by her daughter, to visit the museum and the Free Aesthetics exhibition where she showed several paintings. There she was introduced to the violinist Ysaïe. On the night of October 16 she boarded the train for Paris so as not to miss the exhibition preceding the Duret auction. The auction was held on October 19. She wanted to buy Manet's *Repos*, but through the fault of the person whom she had commissioned to acquire it for her it went to someone else. She did, however, buy a small portrait of herself by Manet. One of her paintings, *Jeune femme en toilette de bal*, was purchased by the Luxembourg museum.

169
170
171

On March 31 she received the following note from Renoir:
"Next Wednesday Mallarmé will give me the pleasure of coming to dinner at Montmartre, If the climb in the evening is not too arduous for you, I thought that he would like to meet you there. Durand-Ruel will come, and I am going to write to the above-mentioned poet to invite Régnier for me.
"P.S. I am not mentioning sweet and lovable Julie: that is of course taken for granted, and I think that Mallarmé will bring his daughter. I wanted to invite Degas; I confess that I don't dare."

A little later he wrote to her again concerning a portrait that he had begun in the Rue Weber apartment:
"Ten more days until the Manet exhibition.
"If you do not mind I should like, instead of painting Julie alone, to paint her with you. But this is what bothers me: if I were to plan to work at your house, something will always turn up to keep me from coming. On the other hand, if you are willing to give me two hours, that is, two mornings or afternoons a week, I think I can do the portrait in six sessions at the most. Tell me, is it yes or no?"

172

The sittings in the studio of the Rue Tourlaque took place in the morning, and sometimes Berthe and her daughter went to lunch at the Renoirs where Mme Renoir prepared an excellent meal for them.

Wishing to revisit Brittany which she had seen as a child, Berthe let herself be tempted by a poster in the Gare Saint-Lazare, and on August 8 she left for Portrieux on the bay of Saint-Brieuc, where she rented an old granite house called *Roche plate*. Mallarmé sent her the following letter addressed in verse:

Ce mot, qui sur elle planait
A Portrieux, la Roche plate,
Retraite des Dames Manet,
Dans les Côtes-du-Nord éclate.

[This note now flying to Portrieux
in the Côtes-du-Nord
is to burst open at Roche plate
The retreat of the Ladies Manet.]

"So you have gone, on your own initiative, to Portrieux; I refuse to believe a word of it; what made you go there rather than to Bagatelle, for instance?

"However it is true that we receive very charming cakes from there, reminiscent of sea biscuits and spice cake. As for the roses, Julie, they are of a kind that young ladies in comedies do not usually offer to their guardians; so I am more than flattered. As I look at Geneviève I imagine both of you under the muslin of your coifs, and I am delighted at the idea of the trio that before the end of September will be floating about thus clad among the poplars of Valvins. Are you painting a great deal? As for myself, I am letting myself live, for the first time in years, and I am idling my time away, influenced by the radiant beginning of autumn.

"One had lost all notion of the sun here. Once again the brook is with us, clear and broad; and now, I'll say good-bye to you, and go to my sailboat, where I shall continue to dream about all the things I have not included in this brief note.

"And Laertes, I suddenly wonder, how does he like the sea? The ladies put their hands in mine which affectionately press yours."

Berthe had invited Renoir to come to Brittany, but he wrote:
"It is my fate that each time you have everything to make me welcome and delight me, circumstances prevent me from taking advantage of it. This year I cannot go too far away, and I am going to Trouville for a little while only because it is no more than four hours from Paris; nevertheless it is possible that toward the end of September, if you have not left Portrieux, I may be able to come to greet you before surrendering definitively to my furnace. Since I saw you I have had several shocks. Pierre was again pretty sick, and I was obliged to leave suddenly for Burgundy where he was with

173

his mother. Fortunately everything turned out to be all right, and I escaped with a good scare.

"I am truly distressed at not being able to accept your invitation. I might have worked, but I have wasted my summer; let's say no more about it. I imagine that all of you are well since you have not mentioned anyone's health. Moreover Brittany is quite pleasant, not as rainy as Normandy. Unfortunately it is rather far away – fortunately so, because otherwise it would be crowded with dreadful people.

"And so, enjoy yourself; bring back some of those lovely sea views, which are so beautiful in Brittany, with the water clear all the way to the edge, and white-clad Julies against a background of golden isles. What a sentence! I have written it just to tease Mallarmé. Regards to sweet Julie, and the best of health to all of you."

On September 1 Berthe answered Mallarmé's question. She wrote:
"We made up our minds to go to Brittany just by looking at the little posters in the waiting room of Gare Saint-Lazare. You are inquisitive, dear friend, and so I begin by answering your question; now I want to thank you for the pretty quatrain that has arrived in magnificent sunny weather. Now *Roche plate* is immortalized; the quatrain will be a lovely souvenir of our stay here. If you had as much initiative as I have you would come here to become acquainted with it. I have enough room to put up all of you. But I realize that it is useless to insist, knowing how faithful you are to the charms of Valvins and to your brook, which I hope indeed to see again on my return if you are still there. I fear that you have already gone back to the Rue de Rome. My nieces are with me; we walk on the shore, in the open country, and everything would be charming if the place were not pretty, inviting me to paint it. Then despair sets in.

"Renoir could not join me, to my great regret, and his too, I think, at least so he says. He is consoling himself at Deauville with Gallimard. I have used up all my writing paper at Fermé, so that I am reduced to these little cards which induce me to write in a telegraphic style – Mauclair would certainly not like it.

"A thousand affectionate regards to the three of you. You won't see me with a coif, I do not wear one. Can you really picture me walking draped in white muslin between Geneviève and Julie? Yours."

Mallarmé's answer was again addressed in verse:

174

Leur lévrier industrieux
Aux dames Manet va remettre
(Côtes-du-Nord) à Portrieux
La Roche plate, cette lettre.

[Their diligent greyhound
Will deliver this letter
To the Ladies Manet at Roche plate
Portrieux, Côtes-du-Nord.]

"My dear friend, your explanation charmed me, as well as the fact that a poster made to ensnare simpletons should thus have determined the summer of one of the subtlest persons who have ever passed through the Gare Saint-Lazare. I shall follow your example. Hitherto I have been afraid that I would not find at the end of my travels the gorgeous gladiolus or the wrecked ship which usually adorns those misleading chromo-lithographs.

"We should be very tempted to visit you to verify their accuracy – yes, we could have done it from Honfleur – but, as you say, the woods and the waters here hold us under their spell, and the weather is really too gloomy to inspire any wishes.

"One of these days I am going to see your notary Pinguet to get a life certificate; I need it for my retirement, and I will be the first to be surprised if, having examined me, he gives it to me, so little do I feel myself to be living. And that is why I am waiting for you to come with Julie to bring everything here to life. Our best wishes to all of the lovely gynaeceum, of which Laertes is the sole defender."

On September 15 Berthe left Le Portrieux to take a little trip by mail coach. After visiting Ile Bréhat and spending the night at Paimpol she continued her journey by way of Tréguier, Lannion, Perros-Guirec, La Clarté, Trégastel and Ploumanach. Morlaix enchanted her, but after Saint-Pol de Léon and Kreis-Ker, Roscoff was a disappointment. She visited Brest where she enjoyed sailing in the harbour, and then went to Auray where she found the following letter from Renoir:

"I have a perfectly ridiculous piece of news for you, but completely contradicting the letter that you sent me and that I received today: namely, the arrival of a second son, who is called Jean. Mother and baby are in excellent health.

"Regards to sweet and charming Julie, and to the no less charming mother."

175

Berthe wrote in answer to Renoir that he would think for another ten years and then have a girl.

After stopping at Vannes, Berthe went to Nantes where she visited the cathedral and the museum and was pleased to find her portrait of Mme de Senonnes, and then took the train for Paris. She immediately resumed work, taking advantage of a mild October to paint in the Bois de Boulogne. She saw her friends and even let herself be taken by Renoir to attend performances of *Rose et Colas* and *Tante Aurore*. Degas had a passion for the former of these operettas. On November 14, Julie's birthday, she took her to the *176* Théâtre Français to see *Le Mariage forcé*, *La Joie fait peur*, and *Il ne faut jurer de rien*.

On November 21 Renoir answered her invitation to dinner as follows:

"I made an attempt to go out hoping that if I could not come to dinner I could at least see you for ten minutes, but my legs gave out and I was obliged to return home; therefore I shall be grateful to you if you present my apologies to the pleasant company, to our gentle poet, and to M. and Mme Lerolle who did me the honour of wishing to meet me; tell them that they do not miss much, that I alone am the loser because, decidedly, I am no longer good for anything. You have often praised Mme Lerolle to me, you said she was very charming; old young man that I am, I feel regretful. Regards to you and Julie."

She addressed the following *pneumatique* to Mallarmé:

"My dear friend, I do not know any more what I said to you at the head of that staircase; but I absolutely count on you tomorrow. Degas is not free! and the Lerolle ladies have not answered; hence, less and less formality."

Early in January 1895 Berthe received this charming invitation to the theatre from Mallarmé:

> "I wish to have at these oral games
> Julie, in a Gainsborough hat,

to hide me from view, because you will be in our loge, if it is agreeable to you, my ladies."

It was followed by this card:

"Box C instead of E; it is vast, although we will be numerous, and its proportions are favourable to the hat."

But Berthe wrote him in reply:

"Julie is sick in bed with the grippe; however the doctor assures me that I can leave her, so that I shall attend your apotheosis, but without that pretty hat in front of me. I beg to be forgiven for this."

177

Renoir went to Carry-Lerouet near Martigues with his young pupil Jeanne Baudot and her parents, and he urged Berthe Morisot to join him:

"My dear friend, the weather is fine, cool in the morning and in the evening. There is a comfortable room in this hotel. I don't know about the food; last year they told me that it was 6.50 a day; this year it is 7 francs, but I think that I shall obtain a small reduction for two ... Stay at the hotel Terminus in Marseille; reserve a room on the third floor from Paris – 8 francs for one with two beds, very clean, lunch 3 francs. To get to Carry take a boat near Marseille at 9 in the morning, arriving at Carry at 10-30; there is also an old coach leaving Marseille at 3 and arriving at Carry at 6-30. The carriage is at Number 5, Rue de l'Arbre. Regards.

"P.S. – Room at the Terminus: third floor at 4 and 5 francs; with two beds, 6 and 8 francs."

On February 10 he wrote:

"My dear friend, it is understood that if you come I shall leave the château for the simple inn with you. I have made sure that there is a fireplace in that inn, and if necessary there will be a fire. The weather has turned bad since yesterday.

"I found my view of the sea as beautiful as ever, but one misses the sun. We had snow all the way from Paris to Tarascon, and the cold was terrible; the frost on the window panes did not thaw, and so our joy was great when we arrived at Marseille in delightfully warm weather. In bad weather like today's it is very ugly. Provence needs the sun. Regards."

And the next day he sent another pencilled card with these simple words: "Warm and fine today."

But Berthe could not join Renoir in the south that she loved. She was unduly alarmed about her daughter's grippe. She feared that it was the beginning of typhoid fever, and then she caught it herself. Her condition became complicated with pneumonia which carried her off in a few days. On February 27 she sent this pencilled note to Mallarmé:

"I am ill, my dear friend, I do not ask you to come because it is impossible for me to speak."

On March 1, on the eve of her death, she wrote a letter to her daughter, which included at the end a line addressed to her niece:

"My little Julie, I love you as I die; I shall still love you even when I am dead; I beg you not to cry, this parting was inevitable. I hoped to live until you were married . . . Work and be good as you have always been; you have not caused me one sorrow in your little life. You have beauty, money; make good use of them. I think it would be best for you to live with your cousins, Rue de Villejust, but I do not wish to force you to do anything. Please give a remembrance from me to your aunt Edma and to your cousins; and to your cousin Gabriel give Monet's *Bateaux en réparation*. Tell M. Degas that if he founds a museum he should select a Manet. A souvenir to Monet, to Renoir, and one of my drawings to Bartholomé. Give something to the two concierges. Do not cry; I love you more than I can tell you. Jeannie, take care of Julie."

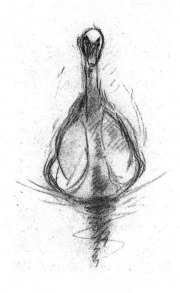

NOTES

1. Yves Morisot married a tax collector, Paul Gobillard. Her children were Jeannie, who married Paul Valéry, the poet, and Paule, who was a painter.

   Edma Morisot exhibited at the Salons of 1864, 1865, 1867, and 1868. She and Berthe were favourably mentioned by Emile Zola in his Salon review *Les Paysagistes* of 1868. After marrying Adolphe Pontillon, a naval officer, in 1869, she gave up painting. Edma had two daughters, Jeanne and Blanche.

   Tiburce Morisot was born in 1848 in Bourges when Berthe was seven years old. He became a civil servant.

2. Madame Morisot decided to send her three daughters to have drawing lessons so that each of them could give their father a drawing. Such skills were thought appropriate for the daughters of the *haute bourgeoisie*. Young women were not admitted to State fine art institutions in France until the end of the nineteenth century: the Ecole des Beaux-Arts in Paris first accepted women students in 1897 after a campaign led by Madame Léon Bertaux, but only permitted women to study from the nude model three years later, in 1900. Tuition for women generally took place in the studios of artists prepared to accept female students. The Académie Julian had a separate women's studio, and several women artists ran drawing schools for girls. Private academies were usually expensive, and a fine art education for women often depended on family wealth. Design tuition for women, especially working class women, on the other hand, was encouraged, and by 1869 there were twenty design academies for women in Paris.

   Geoffrey-Alphonse Chocarne, born in Boulogne in 1797, had first exhibited at the Salon in 1838. A pupil of Regnault, he advocated adherence to the classical tradition, and despised Delacroix and the Romantics.

3. Joseph-Benoît Guichard (1806–80) was Professor at the Ecole des Beaux-Arts in Lyons from 1862, and Director from 1871. In 1879 he became Conservator of the Lyons Museum. He exhibited at the Salon from 1831 to 1853, and was awarded a second-class medal in 1833. He taught Félix Bracquemond, who dedicated his book, *Le Dessin et la Couleur* to him. From 1868 until his death he directed a municipal course in drawing and painting for girls.

4. Morisot was registered as a copyist on 19 March 1858 as a pupil of Guichard, and again on 16 February 1865. In 1858 she copied Veronese's *Feast in the House of Simon* and *Calvary*. Other copies by her of Venetian paintings appear not to have survived. The later registration probably relates to her copy of Rubens's *Debarkation of Marie de' Medici at Versailles*.

Notes

5. Félix Bracquemond (1833–1914) trained with Joseph Guichard. He obtained a medal for painting at the 1866 Salon but after 1869 concentrated on printmaking. He exhibited at the Impressionist exhibitions of 1874, 1879 and 1880. He was the husband of the painter Marie Bracquemond.

   Henri-Jean-Théodore Fantin-Latour (1836–1904) studied under Horace Lecoq de Boisbaudran, and began copying in the Louvre in 1852. In 1858 he met the Morisot sisters, and he introduced Morisot to Edouard Manet in 1867. He was married to the painter Victoria Dubourg.

6. Jean-Baptiste-Camille Corot (1796–1875) studied with the landscapists Michallon and Bertin. Like them, he valued the oil sketch and the spontaneity of work done outdoors, preparatory to paintings executed in the studio. He travelled and painted outdoors in the spring and summer, before returning to Paris in the winter. He advised many young painters who came to his studio, among them Pissarro. His work was in great demand from the late 1840s, to the extent that by the 1860s he employed assistants.

7. Achille François Oudinot (1820–91) was a pupil of Corot and a friend of Daubigny. He exhibited at the Salon between 1845 and 1876.

8. It was here that Morisot painted her Salon submission of 1864, *Vieux chemin à Auvers*.

9. Charles François Daubigny (1817–78) was a landscape painter and a member of the Barbizon school. He played a central role in the development of mid-nineteenth-century naturalism.

10. Honoré Daumier (1805–79) was renowned for his political and social satire. He worked as a cartoonist on *La Caricature*, founded in 1830, and later for *Charivari*. He did oil paintings, sculpture, watercolours, and wash drawings and is associated with realism because of his unromanticized representations of the poor and the harsh characterization of his subjects.

    Jean Baptiste Antoine Guillemet (1841–1918) was a painter. Through the Morisot sisters, he met Corot in 1861–2, and became a pupil of Oudinot. He also attended the Atelier Suisse, where he met Pissarro, Monet, Courbet and Cézanne. He posed with Morisot for Manet's *Le Balcon* in 1868. Like Manet, he did not exhibit with the Impressionists, preferring to submit to the Salons.

11. Léon Riesener (1808–78) was a painter. In addition to being part of Morisot's circle, he was a friend of Renoir, whose *Hommage à Léon Riesener* appeared in the magazine *La Vie moderne* on 17 April 1879.

12. Duchess Castiglione Colonna was a sculptor and painter who worked under the name Marcello. She painted a portrait of Morisot in 1875.

13. Aimé Millet (1819–19) was a sculptor and painter. A pupil of David d'Angers and of Viollet-le-Duc, he exhibited at the Salon from 1840 and won a first class medal in 1857.

14. Charles Busson (1822–1928) was a landscape painter.
    The ages mentioned here are incorrect: Morisot was twenty-two.

15. Jules Ferry (1832–93) became a Republican deputy for Paris in 1869, and served as Prime Minister in 1880–1 and 1883–5. He was responsible for the law of 1882 making primary education in France free, non-clerical and compulsory; and for the completion of the conquest of Indo-China. His preoccupation with imperialism led to his fall from power in 1885. He was also responsible in 1879 for the establishment of the Museum of French Monuments, which aimed to portray the history of sculpture.

16. Charles-Emile-Auguste Durand (Carolus-Duran) (1837–1917) was a prolific and fashionable portrait painter. He attracted many students and had a lasting influence on the development of Salon portraiture. His portrait of his wife, the artist Pauline-Marie-Charlotte Croizette, was his first major Salon success in 1869.

17. Alfred-Emile-Léopold Stevens (1823–1906) was born in Brussels. He enjoyed early success at the Paris Salon, winning a third-class medal in 1853. He was acclaimed at the 1867 and 1878 Expositions Universelles. In the 1860s he was close to Manet and his circle, including Morisot. Sarah Bernhardt became his pupil in 1874, and in the 1880s many women painters studied at his atelier in the Avenue Frochot in Paris.

18. Camille Pissarro (1830–1903) was born at St. Thomas in the West Indies. He settled permanently in France in 1855, and was guided by Corot. He first exhibited at the Salon in 1859. He was the only member of the Impressionist group to exhibit at all eight shows, and he was instrumental in their organization and perpetuation.

19. The Salon was the official institution for the exhibition of contemporary paintings in Paris. It was established by the Académie in the mid-eighteenth century, and from 1831 was generally, though not consistently, an annual event.
    A description by the English critic P.G. Hamerton of the Salon of 1863 gives some idea of its magnitude and impact:

    > Entering . . . the visitors find themselves at the foot of a magnificent staircase of white stone, on ascending which they arrive at the exhibition of pictures, which is on the upper floor, and extends the whole length of the building in an uninterrupted line of rooms with tent-like ceilings of white

canvas to subdue the glare from the glass roof. There are three large halls, one in the middle and one at each end of the building, with a double line of lower rooms in between. The halls at the two ends open upon two other magnificent stone staircases . . . You . . . descend at the eastern end of the building, into the garden which occupies the whole of the immense nave, and there, under the broad glass roof, you see a great number of statues, each sufficiently isolated from the rest to admit of perfect examination . . .

(Quoted from Gerald M. Ackerman, 'The Glory and Decline of a Great Institution', *French Salon Paintings from Southern Collections*, Atlanta 1982, p. 8.)

There were thirty rooms of paintings, which were hung one above the other from floor to ceiling. To be 'on the line' meant that a painting was most favourably hung, at eye level.

The following is a list of Berthe's and Edma's Salon submissions during the 1860s: (BM=Berthe Morisot; EM=Edma Morisot)

1864   BM:*Souvenir des bords de l'Oise*
          Vieux chemin à Auvers
        EM:*Bords de l'Oise*
          Paysage, effet du soir.
1865   BM:*Etude*
          Nature morte
        EM:*Falaises d'Houlgate (Calvados)*
          Fleurs
1866   BM:*La Bermondière (Orne)*
          Chaumière de Normandie
        EM:*La Rance, à marée basse*
1867   BM:*Vue prise en aval du pont d'Iéna*
        EM:*Falaises d'Houlgate*
          Portrait de femme; étude
1868   BM:*Ros-Bras (Finistière)*
        EM:*Nature morte; pommes et poires*
          Paysage

Neither Berthe nor Edma submitted work to the Salon of 1869. Berthe's Salon submissions in the 1870s were:

1870   *La Lecture*
          Jeune femme à sa fenetre
1872   *Portrait de Mme E.P.* (pastel)
1873   *Blanche* (pastel)

Berthe's submissions to the 1865 Salon were commented on by Paul Mantz in the *Gazette des Beaux-Arts* in terms which reveal standard assumptions about appropriate subjects for women: 'Since it is not necessary to have had a long training in draughtsmanship in the academy in order to paint a copper pot, a candlestick, and a bunch of radishes, women succeed quite well in this type of domestic painting. Mlle. Berthe Morisot brings to this task really a great deal of frankness with a delicate feeling for light and colour.'

20. Léon Belly was a pupil of Troyon who was awarded a first-class medal at the Salon of 1861. He exhibited *Coucher du soleil à marée basse; côtes de Normandie* at the Salon of 1865. To be hung in the Salon Carré, the central exhibition hall, was a mark of distinction.

    Rosalie Riesener was entered in the Salon catalogue as a pupil of her father Léon. She exhibited *Rame, epagneul anglais* at this Salon. In the following year she showed a portrait of Marcello, Duchess of Colonna.

    Léon Flahaut showed two works at the Salon of 1865, *L'Etang de Saint-Hubert* and *Printemps*.

21. Academic training and popular taste placed importance on finish, *le fini*. Individual brushstrokes were not to be distinguished and surfaces were generally highly varnished.

22. Edouard Manet (1832–83) was one of Morisot's closest friends and colleagues. She modelled for him several times, most notably for *Le Balcon* (1868–9) and *Le Repos* (1870). Although he was associated with the Impressionist group, Manet never exhibited with them, preferring to submit work to the Salon.

23. Cadart was a picture framer and dealer at whose premises Manet and other contemporary artists exhibited.

24. Madame Loubens was the wife of a distinguished headmaster and part of the Manet and Morisot circles. Manet included her in his *Musique aux Tuileries* (1862), and she was also painted by Degas, *Madame Lisle et Madame Loubens*, (c. 1869–72).

25. Zoé Laure de Chatillon, née Delaune (1826–1908) exhibited at the Salon between 1851 and 1867, and was a portraitist, a painter of religious scenes, and of scenes inspired by the Franco-Prussian War.

26. Detrimont was an art dealer, with premises at 33 Rue Laffitte. He offered a variety of services to painters: Courbet, for instance, entrusted the cleaning, framing, and even the varnishing of some of his work to him.

    Berthe and Edma Morisot were not dependent on sales for their livelihood, unlike artists such as Pissarro and Renoir who were continually preoccupied with resolving the dilemma posed her by Madame Morisot between 'art for art's sake' and the necessity to sell. Nevertheless, as the letters suggest, the Morisots did not detach themselves from the commercial aspects of art production and distribution.

27. The play by Victor Hugo.

28. Bougival was a popular bathing place on the Seine, easily reached from Paris by train.

29. Fanny Claus (1846–77) was a professional violinist, a member with her sisters of the Sainte-Cécile quartet. She married the sculptor Pierre Prins, and was a member of the Manet circle, often playing music with Suzanne Manet, an accomplished pianist.
    Le Balcon was shown at the 1869 Salon.

30. Charles Pierre Baudelaire (1821–67) was the renowned poet and art critic.
    Edgar Degas (1834–1917) was one of the most committed supporters of independent group exhibitions. He worked in a variety of media, and is best known for his representations of urban subjects such as the ballet and racecourse scenes.
    Charles Cros (1842–88) was a poet, philosopher and scientist, a pioneer of colour photography, and one of the founders of the cabaret *Le Chat Noir*.
    Emile Zola (1834–1902) was a naturalist novelist and art critic.
    Zacharie Astruc (1835–1907) was a painter, sculptor, poet, critic and one of the earliest collectors of Japanese art in Paris.
    Pierre Puvis de Chavannes (1824–98) first showed at the Salon of 1850. He painted large-scale decorative schemes, often prestigious public commissions. In 1868 he met Morisot, for whom he developed a strong admiration.

31. A novel by Benjamin Constant.

32. Degas exhibited *Portrait de Mme G. . .*, his portrait of Yves Gobillard, Morisot's sister.

33. Victoria Dubourg (1840–1926), painter of floral still lifes, exhibited at the Salon from 1869. She won an honourable mention in 1894 and a medal in 1895. She met her future husband Henri Fantin-Latour while copying Correggio's *Mystic Marriage of St. Catherine* at the Louvre, but their friendship did not begin until some time later. They married in 1876.

34. Stanislas Lépine (1835–92) exhibited at the *Première exposition de Société anonyme des artistes peintres, sculpteurs, graveurs, etc* in 1874, now known as the First Impressionist exhibition, but thereafter only exhibited at the Salon.

Notes

35. Frédéric Bazille (1841–70) studied under Gleyre with Renoir and was also a close friend of Monet and of Manet. He was a member of the group who met at the Café Guerbois. He served in the regiment of Zouaves and was killed at the battle of Beaune-la-Rolande on 28 November 1870.

36. James Tissot (1836–1902) studied in Paris under Lamoth and Flandrin. He left France after the Franco-Prussian War and settled in London, where he became a popular society painter.

   Auguste Toulmouche (1829–90) was a pupil of Gleyre and a genre painter. It was he who directed Monet to Gleyre's atelier.

37. Degas's portrait of Yves Gobillard, painted in 1869, is now in the Metropolitan Museum of Art, New York.

   This refers to Marie Collart (1842–1911), a Belgian painter.

38. Charles Blanc (1813–82) was an art historian and critic. In 1848 he was Director of Fine Arts and in 1859 he founded the *Gazette des Beaux Arts*. In 1870 he was again made Director of Fine Arts, and he held this post for three years.

   Paul-Marc-Joseph Chenevard was a painter who was a pupil of both Ingres and Delacroix.

39. Eva Gonzalès (1849–83) was a painter who exhibited at the Salon from 1870–83. Her work included scenes from modern life, portraits, still lifes, and outdoor scenes. Her first teacher was Charles Chaplin, a fashionable society portraitist. She married the etcher Henri Guérard in 1879 and died in 1883 at the age of 33 after childbirth.

40. Louise Riesener was a painter, the daughter of Léon Riesener and sister of Rosalie. Fantin-Latour painted a portrait of her working in her studio, *Portraits*, or *La Leçon de dessin dans l'atelier*, which was exhibited at the Salon of 1879.

41. These paintings are *Portrait de Madame Pontillon (Jeune femme à sa fenêtre)* and *Vue du petit pont de Lorient*.

42. This is Manet's portrait of Eva Gonzalès, now in the National Gallery, London.

43. Gustave Flaubert's *Madame Bovary* was first published in 1857.

44. The painting referred to is *Deux sœurs sur un canapé*.

45. This portrait is *Portrait de Mme Morisot et sa fille Mme Pontillon*, also called *La Lecture*.

46. Mlle Valentine Carré posed for *La robe rose* and *Jeune fille en robe de bal*. She may also have been the model for Manet's *Au jardin*, 1870.

47. This is *La Lecture* showing the sisters Victoria and Charlotte Dubourg.

Notes

Manet's submissions to the 1870 Salon were *La Leçon de musique* and *Portrait d'Eva Gonzalès*.

Puvis de Chavannes' submissions to the Salon were *Madeleine au désert* and *La Décollation de saint Jean-Baptiste*.

48. The French declared war on the Prussians on 19 July 1870 and were forced to capitulate at Sédan on 1 September. Napoleon III abdicated three days later. Paris was under siege from September until it fell on 28 January 1871. Following this, peace talks began and on 1 March France agreed to surrender the province of Alsace and most of Lorraine and to pay an indemnity of five billion francs. On 8 March 1871, rioters in Montmartre seized and executed the Versailles Generals Lecomte and Thomas commanding the 'Bordeaux Troops'. Adolphe Thiers, head of the executive power, withdrew all forces from Paris and on 26 March a central committee calling itself the Commune seized power in Paris. French troops under MacMahon retook the city during the *semaine sanglante* (21 to 28 May) leaving more than 20,000 people dead.

49. Joseph Cuvelier (d.1870) was a sculptor.

50. Helmuth van Moltke (1800–91) was a German field marshal and Prussian Minister of War.

51. On 27 October 1870 the French troops capitulated at Metz. More than 180,000 men were taken captive.

52. Léon Gambetta (1838–82) was elected to the Assembly as a member for Marseilles in 1869. He proclaimed the Third Republic in September 1870. In Paris for the first part of the siege of 1870, he escaped by balloon to Tours and organised the later stages of the war as Minister of the Interior and War. He resigned when peace was made but from 1879–91 was an important force behind republican governments. He served as Prime Minister for only nine weeks, in 1881.

53. Edma Morisot refers to the government under Adolphe Thiers, who was President of the Republic from 1871–3.

54. Guiseppe Garibaldi (1807–82) fought for the French during the Franco-Prussian War. Garibaldi and his followers were believed to be heretics because of their anti-clerical views.

Jules Favre was minister of Foreign Affairs who declared that it was folly for France to go to war with the Prussians.

General Trochu was the President of the government during the war, with full military powers for the national defence. He misjudged Paris's ability to withstand the Prussian siege, and was blamed by the populace for the city's capitulation.

55. The painter Alexandre Georges Henri Regnault (1843–71) was killed during the defence of Paris on 31 October 1871. He had submitted to the Salons of 1864–70 and was on the brink of a successful career. His *Salomé* (Salon of 1870) was highly praised.

56. The government was now located at Versailles, not Paris. Contrary to Madame Morisot's statement, it was Puvis de Chavannes' brother-in-law, not Puvis himself, who was a member of the assembly.

57. Admiral Saisset attempted to establish a compromise between the communards and the government and to organise municipal elections. He was unsuccessful and retreated to Versailles.

58. The Minister of War was General Cluseret, not Chiseret as given in the text.

59. This could be *Vue du petit pont de Lorient*.

60. General MacMahon's headquarters were at the Trocadéro.

61. The Vêndome Column was destroyed on 16 May. The column had been erected in 1805 in honour of Napoleon Bonaparte's victories, and was a symbol of Bonapartism.

62. Henri Rochefort's journal, *La Lanterne*, had virulently opposed the Second Empire. He had been a member of the government of National Defence and head of the barricades committee during the siege and commune. He and his secretary Mourot had tried to flee Paris, but were captured by the Versailles troops and escorted to Versailles amidst excited crowds. In 1874 he was sentenced to life imprisonment, but he escaped from the penal colony at New Caledonia shortly afterwards.

63. MacMahon and his forces entered Paris at 9 p.m. on 21 May and took the Porte de Passy. Further divisions of the army entered Paris during the night of 21 and morning of 22 May. They took a third of Paris from the communards in a day. Madame Morisot's rejoicing at the entry of the troops indicates that her sympathies were strongly pro-Versailles.

    Vincy is an error. It was General Vinoy who was commander-in-chief of the army of Paris.

64. This should read General Vinoy.

65. The communards had vowed to destroy Paris rather than surrender it. On the night of 23 May and morning of 24 May they set fire to the Tuileries, part of the Louvre, part of the Palais Royal, the Palace of the Legion of Honour, the Prefecture of Police, the Ministry of Finance, the Audit Office, the Council of State, the Gare de Lyon, the Grénier d'Abondance, and the Mairie of the 4th *arrondissement*. Theatres, barracks, and many homes were burned as well.

Notes

66. Within monarchist circles there were conflicting claims for the legitimacy of the Bourbon and Orleans houses. The Comte de Chambord was the posthumous son of the Duc de Berry and was known as *l'enfant du miracle*. He had declared on 12 May in *Le Gaulois* that there could be no order or justice outside of the monarchy of Henri V, which he represented.

67. Pagans was a Spanish guitarist and tenor. He had made his debut at the Opera in *Sémiramide* in 1860, and was a popular favourite in Paris by 1865. Degas depicted him in 1865 in *Paysans chantant et le père de Degas*.

68. Madame Camus, a skilled pianist, was interested in Japanese art. She was a regular visitor to the Manet salon, and was painted twice by Degas between 1869–70.

    Champfleury was the pseudonym of Jules Husson (1828–89). He was a novelist and critic, and had been a supporter of Courbet and spokesperson for the realist movement.

69. The painter Nélie Jacquemart was a pupil of Léon Cogniet. She received medals at the Salons of 1868, 1869, and 1870, and a second class award in 1878.

70. Félix Bracquemond's wife was Marie Quivoron (1840–1916). She was a painter who exhibited at the Impressionist exhibitions of 1879, 1880, and 1886 as Marie Bracquemond. Unlike Morisot, Cassatt, or Gonzalès, who came from cultured, prosperous backgrounds, she was the daughter of a sea captain who died shortly after her birth. Her mother soon remarried, and the family led an unsettled life, moving frequently. She studied in Etampes with a M. Wassor. She met Félix while copying from a Rembrandt. They married in 1869. From the beginning Félix's authoritarianism was apparent. Through him she became acquainted with many of the young artists of the time, and she was profoundly influenced by the Impressionists. Félix disapproved of her new approach to painting, and of her admiration for Monet and Renoir. Her son Pierre reported that Félix was jealous of her ability, and that, worn down by friction at home and discouraged by the lack of interest in her work, she all but stopped painting in 1890. In 1894 Gustave Geffroy described her as one of 'les trois grandes dames' of Impressionism.

71. Morisot, like other painters of her generation, including Cassatt and Manet, travelled to Spain to study the collection of Velazquez and Goya in the Prado.

72. While it was standard academic practice to make rapid sketches in the open air, the Impressionists sought to retain the effect of spontaneity and instantaneity in a finished work (*le tableau*). From this the myth has arisen that their works were always quickly executed on the spot in a casual, uninhibited fashion.

73. Paul Durand-Ruel took over his father's gallery in 1862. He began to acquire a stock of works by the Barbizon school in the 1860s, and in the 1870s, following his meetings with Pissarro and Monet in London during the Franco-Prussian war, expanded his interests to include Manet and the Impressionists.

74. The exhibition was called simply the exhibition of the *Société anonyme des artistes peintres, sculpteurs, graveurs, etc.* It was organised to provide a forum for the display of art outside both the official Salon with its constraining jury system, and the rising commercial dealer system. In all thirty painters participated, and the range of work was greater than is generally acknowledged, covering the range of realist and naturalist practices.

    Rouart's citing of Guichard's hostile comments seems to endorse the standard view that the work on view at this exhibition, subsequently known as the first Impressionist exhibition, was generally misunderstood and hostilely received by critics. However, even those critics who disliked the work showed some understanding of its aims, and there was a substantial degree of support from such critics as Jules Castagnary and Philippe Burty.

    In addition to the works cited by Rouart, Morisot showed *La Lecture* and *Portrait de Mlle M.T.*

    Claude Monet (1840–1926) spent his childhood in Le Havre. He went to Paris in 1859, and met Camille Pissarro at the Atelier Suisse. He met Manet in 1866, but it is not certain when he met Morisot.

    Alfred Sisley (1839–99) met Monet, Renoir and Bazille while he was at the Ecole des Beaux-Arts. He exhibited at the Salon des Refusés in 1863. The date of his meeting Morisot is not known.

    Pierre Auguste Renoir (1841–1919) was a pupil of Gleyre and a friend of Monet, Bazille, and Sisley. It is difficult to determine when he first met Morisot. Their close friendship dates from the 1880s.

    Paul Cézanne (1839–1906) was born in Aix-en-Provence. He worked with Pissarro in Pontoise in the years preceding the first Impressionist exhibition.

    Armand Guillaumin (1841–1927) had met Pissarro at the Atelier Suisse and was a friend of his and of Cézanne.

75. The photographer Gaspard Félix Tournachon was known as Nadar.

76. No painting named *Le Rêve du celibataire* appears in the catalogue of the exhibition. Guichard was almost certainly referring to Cézanne's *Une moderne Olympia.*

77. The art market in Paris was extremely buoyant in the 1870s, with painters like Bouguereau and Breton commanding the highest prices. Durand-Ruel was

buying and selling at profits of 400 per cent and more.

78. Manet's portraits of Morisot were executed between 1869 and 1874. They are: *Le repos* (1870), the half-recumbent pose referred to by Rouart; *Berthe Morisot au bouquet de violettes* (1872); *Portrait de Berthe Morisot au chapeau de deuil* (1874); *Berthe Morisot à l'éventail* (1874, watercolour).

79. Jacques-Emile Blanche described this apartment: 'imagine a bourgeois apartment in which one room is the studio of a young artist; scarcely any *bric-à-brac*, no *objets d'art*, but hanging on the grey Chinese moiré wallpaper some studies and in a place of honour, a landscape by Corot.' (from *Les Ecrits nouveaux*, quoted in M. Angoulvent, *Berthe Morisot*, p. 41.)

80. Morisot's works were sold at the following prices:

Intérieur 56 × 47 cms to Hoschedé   480f.
Chalet au bord de la mer 51 × 61 to Rouart   230f.
Les Papillons 47 × 56 to Duez   245f.
La Lecture 45 × 70 to Daliphort   210f.
Blanche 61 × 51 (pastel) to Thomas   255f.
Plage de Fécamp 38 × 60 to Houssaye   100f.
Sur l'herbe 70 × 90 (pastel) to G. Manet   320f.
Plage des Petites Dalles 22 × 48 to G. Manet   80f.
Sur la plage (watercolour) 48 × 64 to Rouart   60f.
Environs de Paris (watercolour) 48 × 64 to Duez   50f.
Marine (watercolour) 48 × 64 to Hoschedé   45f.
Lisière de bois (watercolour) 48 × 64 to Chesnau   45f.
(Quoted from M. Bodelsen, 'Early Impressionist Sales 1874–94 in the light of some unpublished "procès-verbaux" ', *Burlington Magazine*, June 1968.)

Morisot's works fetched relatively the highest prices at the sale, the average amount received for a work being 100 francs. Her presence at the sale excited some antagonism. Jean Renoir's apocryphal anecdote points to the construction of femininity within which Morisot is to be located. He 'reports' in *Renoir, My Father* (1962, p. 148) that a man called Morisot a *'gourgandine'* (streetwalker) to which Pissarro reacted by punching him in the face, precipitating such a fracas that the police had to be called in.

81. *L'Enfant dans les blés* is now in the Musée d'Orsay, Paris. *Les Blanchisseuses plaine de Gennevilliers*, known as *Un percher de blanchisseuses*, is in the collection of Mr and Mrs Paul Mellon, Upperville, Virginia.

82. Madame Morisot refers to Zola's novel *Le Ventre de Paris*, published by Charpentier in 1873. The painter Claude Lantier was to reappear in the later novel *L'Oeuvre*, published in 1886.

Notes

83. Rodolph Töpffer published *La Presbytère* in 1832. He also wrote an essay on aesthetics, *Reflexions et menus propos d'un peintre genevois* (Paris, 1848), in which he attacked the doctrine of 'art for art's sake'.

84. Gustave Doré (1832–83) was born in Strasbourg and went to Paris in 1847. He contributed to the *Journal pour rire*. In 1868 he founded the Doré Gallery (now the premises of Sotheby's) in Bond Street, London, and he illustrated many aspects of London life.

85. Durand-Ruel opened his London gallery in 1871 in New Bond Street and founded the Society of French Artists. Due to financial difficulties, he was forced to close the gallery during the winter of 1875.

86. Achille Degas was the younger brother of Edgar Degas.

87. According to Bataille and Wildenstein, this refers to *Dans les blés*, Musée d'Orsay, Paris.

88. Marguerite Carré was the sister of Valentine Carré and may have posed for one of the foreground figures in *Vue de Paris des hauteurs de Trocadéro*.

89. Rouart is inaccurate here. The second Impressionist exhibition was held in April 1876 at 11 Rue Lepeletier. On that occasion, twenty artists exhibited.

90. Rouart refers to the critic Albert Wolff (Wolf is incorrect) (1835–91), notorious for his hostile critiques of Impressionism, which often appeared in *Le Figaro*.

91. In all, eighteen artists showed at the third Impressionist exhibition. The critic Paul Mantz wrote in *Le Temps*, 21 April 1877: 'There is but one real Impressionist in this group and that is Mme Berthe Morisot. Her painting has all the frankness of improvisation; it does truly give the idea of an "impression" registered by a sincere eye and rendered again by a hand completely without trickery.'

92. Julie Manet was born on 14 November 1878. She kept a journal from 1893–99 which is a useful source of information on Morisot's circle in the 1890s. In 1899 she married Ernest Rouart, son of Stanislas-Henri Rouart, at the same time as her cousin Jeannie Gobillard married the poet Paul Valéry.

93. She married the etcher Henri Guérard.

94. In all there were eighteen exhibitors at the fifth Impressionist exhibition which opened on 1 April 1880. Neither Monet nor Renoir exhibited, both having elected to return to the Salon. In addition to the works cited by Rouart, Morisot exhibited two landscapes, *Tête de jeune fille*, four watercolours, and a fan. The

painting Rouart identifies as being in the Tate Gallery is in fact in the Musée Fabre, Montpellier.

95. Only thirteen artists participated in this exhibition, which opened on 2 April at 35 Boulevard des Capucines.

96. Morisot refers to Manet's notoriety, which stemmed from the reception of *Le Dejeuner sur l'herbe* at the 1863 Salon des Refusés, and particularly from the scandal provoked by the showing of *Olympia* at the 1865 Salon.

97. Potain was a doctor who attended Manet in his last illness.
   Portier was an art dealer.
   Jean-Baptiste Faure was a celebrated baritone, renowned for his role in Ambroise Thomas' opera *Hamlet*. Manet painted him in this role in 1877. Faure had a large collection of Manet's works.

98. Eugène Pertuiset was a famous hunter, arms merchant, and art collector. Manet's portrait of him appeared in the Salon of 1881.

99. By 1881 two distinct factions had emerged within the Independents' ranks. Morisot was aligned with Pissarro, Guillaumin, Gauguin and Vignon, while Degas, Cassatt, Forain, Raffaëlli, Rouart, Tillot, Vidal and Zandomeneghi were closely associated. Renoir, Monet and Sisley had withdrawn in order to exhibit at the Salon. Disagreements about the role of the independent exhibitions were rife, with Degas defending the right of artists like Raffaëlli to exhibit. Pissarro commented: 'Each year another Impressionist has left and been replaced by nullities and pupils of the école.'
   In 1882 Durand-Ruel organized the exhibition himself, and it opened on 1 March at 251 Rue St-Honoré. Monet and Renoir had work on view, but Degas and Cassatt had withdrawn. Morisot exhibited thirteen works: *A la campagne*; *Blanchisseuse*; *Baby*; *Vue de Saint-Denis*; *Port de Nice* (2); *Vue d'Andrésy* (pastel); *Paysage au pastel* (2); and ex-catalogue, *Bibi et son tonneau*; *Eugène et Bibi*; *Jeune femme cousant dans un jardin*; and possibly *Villa Arnulfi*.

100. Jean-François Millet (1814–75) lived in the Barbizon forest from 1849. He painted scenes of peasants and their labours as well as landscapes and marines.
   Paul Gauguin (1848–1903) was still working as a stockbroker at this time. It was only in 1883 that he was to commit himself to painting full time. He first exhibited with the Independents in 1880.
   Victor Vignon (1847–1909) was a student of Corot. He worked with Pissarro and Cézanne in Pontoise and Auvers c. 1873 and participated in the last four Impressionist exhibitions.
   Gustave Caillebotte (1848–1894) studied under Léon Bonnat at the Ecole des Beaux-Arts. He participated with the Impressionists for the first time at the

Notes

second exhibition in 1876, and subsequently played an important role in the promotion and organization of the exhibitions. His bequest of his collection of Impressionist paintings to the French state precipitated a major disagreement in artistic circles.

101. Gustave Manet was the younger brother of Edouard and Eugène Manet.

102. The Crédit Lyonnais was affected by the crash of the Union Générale Bank in 1882. It lost half of its deposits in a few weeks and the price of its shares dropped substantially. Its founder, Henri Germain, restored the bank to its former status.

103. Claretie was the pseudonym of Jules Arsène Arnaud (1840–1913). He was a novelist, journalist and historian who had been writing about art and literature in the Parisian press since 1860. In his article for *Le Temps*, Claretie commented on the internal dissension within the group: 'Some opportunists found themselves among the rebels. There were squabbles or near squabbles. M. Degas, the painter of dancers, withdrew; Miss Cassatt followed M. Degas; M. Raffaëlli followed Miss Cassatt. These are artists of rare talent whom the Independents will be unable to replace.' Claretie described the participants as 'people with right ideas and wrong colours. They reason well but their vision is faulty. They show the candour of children and the fervour of apostles'. (Quoted from J. Rewald, *The History of Impressionism*, New York [1946] 1973, p. 472.)

104. Stanislas-Henri Rouart (1883–1912) exhibited at the Salon from 1868 to 1872, and at the Impressionist exhibitions of 1874, 1877, 1880, 1881 and 1886. He did not exhibit in 1882 but advanced funds for the rental of the exhibition space. His son Ernest married Morisot's daughter Julie.

105. Mary Cassatt (1844–1926) was an American painter who lived in Paris for most of her adult life and exhibited with the Impressionist group in 1879, 1880, 1881 and 1886. Prior to this, she had studied at the Pennsylvania Academy of Fine Arts from 1861–4, and in Paris at the atelier of Charles Chaplin. She exhibited at the Paris Salon in the late 1860s and early 1870s as Mary Stevenson. She was instrumental in getting Impressionist work seen and sold in America. She and Morisot were friends and admired each other's work. In a letter to Morisot of autumn 1879, Cassatt wrote: 'You will reclaim your place at the exposition with éclat, I am very envious of your talent I assure you . . .' (Quoted in *Cassatt and her Circle, Selected Letters*, ed. Nancy Mowll Mathews, New York 1984, p. 149. Mathews includes five letters written by Cassatt to Morisot in this selection.)

106. No one called Guillaume appears in the catalogue for this exhibition. This must refer to Armand Guillaumin.

Notes

107. Philippe Burty (1830–90) was an art critic for *La Presse*, the *Gazette des Beaux-Arts*, and for Gambetta's newspaper *La Republique Francaise*. In 1878 he published a collection of Delacroix's letters. He collected Japanese prints and *objets-d'art*, and paintings and graphic work by his contemporaries such as Manet and Bracquemond.

108. Théodore Duret (1838–1927) was a journalist and art critic. He published *Les peintures françaises* in 1867, *Histoire des peintres impressionnistes* in 1878 and *Manet and the French Impressionists*, 1910. In the latter he counted Morisot: 'Among the fine painters who have developed sufficient originality and discovered something so striking that it became necessary to refer to them under a newly invented title . . .'

109. Victorien Sardou was a prolific contemporary playwright.

110. Charles Ephrussi (1849–1905) was an art critic, collector, and director and owner of the *Gazette des Beaux-Arts* from 1885.

    Guiseppe de Nittis (1846–84) was a painter who was born in Naples but settled in Paris in 1868. He first showed at the Salon in 1869 and rapidly achieved success in France and England. In 1874 he showed both at the Salon and at the first Impressionist exhibition. He was a close friend of Degas.

    Princesse Mathilde (1820–1904) was the daughter of King Gérôme. She married Anatole Demidoff in 1840.

    Juliette Adam (née Lamber) was one of the foremost political journalists of her time. She wrote an important response to Proudhon's misogynist references to women in his *La Justice dans l'église et dans la revolution*, published in 1858, in her *Idées anti proudhoniennes sur l'amour, la femme et le mariage*, 1858. She renounced her early feminism in the wake of the Franco-Prussian war, becoming wholly committed to Republicanism and patriotic moves to achieve revenge against Germany for the humiliation suffered by France after its defeat.

    Jean-François Raffaëlli (1850–1924) was a pupil of Gérôme and first exhibited at the Salon in 1870. A visit to Brittany in 1876 led him to begin painting realist themes and he sought his subject matter among the working people and outer suburbs of Paris. He exhibited with the Impressionists in 1880 and 1881.

111. Léon Koëlla Leenhoff was the son of Suzanne Leenhoff Manet. He was born in 1852, and after his mother married Manet, was brought up in their household and introduced as Suzanne's younger brother.

112. Eva Gonzalès' father was the novelist Emmanuel Gonzalès and her sister Jeanne was a painter, who married Eva's husband Henri Guérard after Eva's death.

113. Antonin Proust (1832–1905) was a boyhood friend of Manet. He was Minister of the Interior during the siege of Paris and served as Minister of Fine Arts in Gambetta's Cabinet from November 1881 to January 1882.

114. Charles Haviland was a prominent collector of Japanese and contemporary French art. The Haviland family owned potteries at Limoges and at Autueil, where Félix Bracquemond was the artistic director.

115. Jean-Charles Cazin (1841–1901) was Professor of Architecture and later Director of the Ecole des Beaux-Arts at Tours, and conservator of the Tours museum. In 1876 his *Le Chantier* was a sensation at the Salon, and his reputation grew steadily. In 1898 he was commissioned to complete the mural decoration of the Panthéon begun by Puvis de Chavannes. Henry Lerolle was a painter, violinist, and a collector of Impressionist paintings. He was a friend of Degas.

116. John Singer Sargent (1850–1925) was a highly successful American portrait painter who settled in London.

117. In mid-1883 a large Impressionist exhibition was arranged by Durand-Ruel at Dowdeswell's Galleries, 133 New Bond Street, London. The show consisted of 65 works, of which three were by Morisot. Other painters who participated were Boudin, Cassatt, Degas, Manet, Monet, Pissarro, Renoir, and Sisley.

118. Henri de Régnier described the salon/atelier where she worked and received guests: 'A room with beautiful Empire furniture with Manet's large canvas *Le Linge* on the wall . . . In this atmosphere of discreet silence and sober elegance Mallarme found great pleasure.' (*Faces et profils*, Paris 1931, pp. 49–50).

119. A posthumous exhibition of 179 works by Manet was held at the *Ecole des Beaux-Arts* in January 1884. The preface to the catalogue was written by Zola. The sale was at the Hôtel Drouot on 4 and 5 February 1884. 169 works were sold for a total of 116,637 francs.

120. Ernest Ange Duez (1843–96) was a student of Pils, who first achieved success at the Salon of 1874. In the 1880s he began working as a portraitist, but later returned to genre and landscape subjects. He purchased two paintings by Morisot at the 1875 Drouot auction.

121. *La Dame aux éventails (Portrait of Nina de Callias)* (1873–4) was presented to the Musée du Louvre in 1930 by Julie and Ernest Rouart on the occasion of the State purchase of Morisot's *Le Berceau*.

122. Monet was at Bordighera on the Italian Riviera between January and April 1884. This landscape, painted especially for Morisot's salon-studio on the Rue de Villejust, where it eventually replaced Morisot's copy of Boucher's *Vulcan*, is in the Rouart collection.

    The Monet-Morisot correspondence is included in D. Wildenstein, *Claude*

Notes

Monet, biographie et catalogue raisonné, Vol.iii, 1887–1898, Lausanne and Paris 1979.

123. Marie Pau (1845–70) wrote a history of Joan of Arc, published in 1874, in addition to the published diaries. She attended Léon Cogniet's studio, and in 1868 attempted unsuccessfully to open a drawing academy at home.

124. The La Caze collection entered the Louvre in 1869. There were two works by Frans Hals in the collection, *La Bohemienne* and *Portrait de femme*.

125. Stéphane Mallarmé (1844–98) was a symbolist poet and art critic. He met Morisot through his friend Manet, who had painted his portrait in 1876. Morisot and Mallarmé became close friends. Their friendship continued until Morisot's death, when Mallarmé was made a guardian of Julie Manet.

126. The drawings to which Morisot refers are of Aline Charigot, Renoir's future wife, and their son Pierre. Soon after Pierre's birth in March 1885 Renoir began work on a series of maternity images, producing three oil paintings, two sanguine drawings, and several more informal drawings during the next year. It is clear that despite their friendship, Renoir had not explained his relationship with the models to Morisot.

127. Génevière Mallarmé (1864–1919) was the daughter of Stéphane Mallarmé, and a friend of Julie Manet.

128. In all seventeen artists exhibited at the eighth Impressionist exhibition, but the composition of the group had changed. Among the newcomers were Odilon Redon (1840–1916); Emile Schuffenecker (1851–1934); Georges Seurat (1859–91); and Paul Signac (1863–1935).
     Morisot showed eleven paintings: *Jeune fille sur l'herbe*; *Jardin à Bougival*; *Enfants*; *Petite servante*; *Portraits d'enfants*; *Le Lever*; *Paysage à Nice*; *Roses tremières*; *Portrait de Mlle L.*; *Portrait de Mlle P.G.*; *Au bain*. She also showed drawings, watercolours, and fans.

129. Isabelle Lambert posed for two paintings of this year, *Le Bain* and *Le Lever*.

130. This refers to a painting by Jean Louis Forain (1852–1931).

131. Georges Petit was a Parisian art dealer, Durand-Ruel's competitor. He founded the *Exposition internationale* in 1882, in conjunction with de Nittis. From May to July 1886 Monet was exhibiting thirteen works at the fifth *Exposition internationale*, and Renoir had five works on view. The Gallery Georges Petit was on the Rue de Sèze.

132. Jules Barbey d'Aurevilly (1808–89) was a novelist, journalist and critic.

Notes

133. Morisot showed six paintings in the New York exhibition, which was entitled *Works in Oil and Pastel by the Impressionists of Paris: Femme étendant du linge*; *Portrait de Mme X.*; *Port de Nice*; *Plage de Nice*; *Marine*; *Jeune fille à l'ombrelle*. At Georges Petit's she exhibited *Paule Gobillard en robe de bal*; *Intérieur de cottage*; *Fleurs*; a pastel, *Enfant dans un verandah*; and a sculpted bust of Julie Manet. In gratitude for this exhibition, Morisot offered Georges Petit *Le Lever*.

134. Auguste Rodin (1840–1917), the sculptor, was much admired in avant-garde circles, and later acknowledged as one of the most important nineteenth-century sculptors.

135. On 8 May 1887 Pissarro wrote to his son Lucien: 'I went to Asnières . . . still exhausted from the hanging . . . I had all I could stand from that confounded exhibition which smells to heaven of bourgeois values but just the same I wanted the experience of seeing my pictures hanging with those of the leaders and followers of triumphant Impressionism.' In a letter of 14 May he wrote: 'Mme Berthe Morisot has some excellent things . . .', and on 15 May he added: 'Mme Morisot is doing good work, she has neither advanced nor fallen back. She is a fine artist . . . Seurat, Signac, Fénéon, all our young friends like only my works and Mme Morisot's a little.' (Quoted from John Rewald (ed.), *Camille Pissarro: Letters to his son Lucien*, 4th edn., 1980).

136. In 1963 Mme Julie Manet Rouart told Barbara Ehrlich White about Renoir's painting procedure. He used the preparatory drawings to trace the outlines on to the canvas, so that he could transfer the exact silhouette of the drawing. Mme Rouart recalled that Renoir painted her portrait 'bit by bit, one day my head and a little of the background, another day my dress and the cat'. To retard drying while the painting was being executed, he used to leave the canvas in a damp cellar overnight. The painting is still in the Rouart collection. (Quoted from Barbara Ehrlich White, *Renoir, His Life, Art, and Letters*, 1984, p. 175.)

137. John Lewis-Brown (1829–90) was a French painter of horses and battle scenes.

138. The firm of Goupil was founded in 1827 by the then twenty-one year old Adolphe Goupil. By 1864 it was an international network of galleries and he had become the leading art dealer in the world, specializing in Gérôme, Meissonier, and other Salon painters as well as in the work of the Barbizon school. A newly formed gallery at 19 Boulevard Montmartre was known as Goupil – Boussod et Valadon *successeurs*. It showed the work of the Independents and from 1878 was managed by Théo Van Gogh.

139. *Pointillé* refers to the neo-Impressionist technique of applying paint in small dots

or dabs of colour, the theory being that colours would then mix in the viewer's eye. Such 'optical mixing' was deemed to create a brighter, more luminous surface. Pissarro had since 1884 been influenced by Seurat and his colour theories, but he stopped using this technique in 1888, finding it inhibiting.

140. Whistler first delivered the '10 o'Clock Lecture' in February 1885 in Princes Hall, London. It was repeated elsewhere and subsequently published. In Spring 1888 Whistler was taken by Monet to meet Mallarmé, to discuss a French translation. Mallarmé agreed to translate the lecture and the two men subsequently became friends. Morisot met Whistler through Mallarmé. Although she admired his paintings, she found him disagreeable. Whistler and Mallarmé visited Morisot in May 1888, when Whistler saw and admired her work.

141. Morisot showed *La Lecture*; *Etude d'enfant*; *Vue de Tours*; *Jardin*; *Une Baigneuse*; and a watercolour. The exhibition also included work by Sisley, Pissarro, and Renoir. Monet had quarrelled with Durand-Ruel and showed at the Boussod and Valadon Gallery during the same period.

142. Alice Hoschedé was the wife of Ernest Hoschedé. In 1878 she and her six children came to live with the Monets at Vétheuil, after the bankruptcy of her husband, and she continued to live with Monet after the death of his wife Camille. She married Monet in July 1892.

143. Mary Cassatt was immobilized during the summer of 1888, having broken her leg after a fall from a horse.

144. Jacques-Emile Blanche (1861–1942) was a portraitist and prominent society figure. He had had painting lessons from Renoir, was a friend of Manet and of Degas, and painted many of the leading literary figures of his age, among them James Joyce and André Gide.

145. Puvis's pupil Paul Albert Baudoüin (1844–1931) recounted in his memoirs that he and Puvis had been sponsored by the French government to study fresco technique in Italy. Baudoüin fell ill, and Puvis declined to go alone. Baudoüin had come to study under Puvis in 1874 and became his close collaborator c. 1880. His memoirs of Puvis were published in 1935.

146. General Georges Boulanger (1837–91) had served as War Minister in 1886 at which time he was still a committed Republican. By 1888 he had changed position, and with the aid of a group known as the League of Patriots, he began to campaign for revision of the constitution. Towards the end of 1888 he planned to stage a *coup d'état*, but ultimately lacked the resolve to carry this through.

147. Auguste, Comte de Villiers de l'Isle-Adam (1840–89) was a symbolist poet and writer, and a close friend of Mallarmé.

148. In 1889 and 1890 Durand-Ruel held exhibitions of *peintres-graveurs*. *Le societé de peintres-graveurs* was organized by Félix Bracquemond and included Cassatt, Degas, Pissarro, Fantin-Latour, Tissot, Rodin, Redon and others.

149. This could refer to Mary Cassatt and her mother, who were living in Paris at this time. Cassatt's sister Lydia had died in 1882.

150. Monet was showing twenty paintings at Boussod and Valadon, which he refers to as Van Gogh's, in Spring 1889.

151. Morisot, Monet and Sargent undertook to raise 20,000 francs to purchase Manet's *Olympia* from Suzanne Manet and present it to the French nation. They raised 19,415 francs and wrote to Fallières, the Minister of Education and Fine Arts, on 7 February 1890 offering the painting to the State. The painting was accepted by the Musée du Luxembourg, but did not enter the Louvre until 1907.

152. This was an exhibition of 725 Japanese colour woodcuts held in Spring 1890 at the Ecole des Beaux-Arts. The exhibition was important to Pissarro, Cassatt, Morisot and others who had become interested in adding colour to etchings and drypoints with which they were experimenting.

    At this time Cassatt wrote to Morisot: '. . . we could go to see the Japanese prints at the Beaux-Arts. Seriously, you *must not* miss that. You who want to make colour prints you couldn't dream of anything more beautiful. I dream of it and don't think of anything else but colour on copper. Fantin was there the first day I went and was in ecstasy. I saw Tissot there who also is occupied with the problems of making colour prints . . . PS. You *must* see the Japanese – *come as soon as you can*.' (Quoted in Mathews, p. 214).

153. Maurice Joyant had by this time taken over the running of Boussod and Valadon following the death of Théo Van Gogh on 21 January 1891.

154. The diaries of the artist Marie Bashkirtseff (1860–84) were published in Paris in 1890. They have recently been republished with an introduction by Rozsika Parker and Griselda Pollock (London 1985). Bashkirtseff was born in the Ukraine of a wealthy Russian family who moved to Paris in 1870. She studied at the separate women's studio of the Académie Julian (which she depicted in 1880). She considered herself a 'naturalist'. The *Meeting*, to which Morisot refers, represents street urchins painted in a painstaking naturalist mode. It was exhibited at the Salon of 1884.

155. Henri de Régnier (1864–1936) was a poet and writer, and a member of a group which met at the *Revue indépendant*. He contributed regularly to a magazine called *Les Ecrits pour l'art* which proclaimed Mallarmé its master.

    Teodor de Wyzewa (1863–1917), the Polish-born poet and critic, was educated and lived in France. He was an enthusiastic Wagnerian who sought to establish links between Wagner and French literature and painting.

156. In this article, published in the March edition of *L'Art dans les deux mondes*, Wyzewa described Morisot's vision as totally feminine. He was one of the first to proclaim the Impressionist method as particularly suitable for 'the realization of a feminine painting'.

157. 'Young D' could refer either to Charles Durand-Ruel, then aged 25, or to his younger brother Georges.

158. Mallarmé translated Edgar Allan Poe's poem *The Raven* in 1875. It was published in an edition illustrated by Manet.

159. Marcellin Desboutin (1823–1902) was a painter who studied at the Ecole des Beaux-Arts and later worked under Thomas Couture. He was an accomplished graphic artist, who did an etching of Morisot in 1876. Degas used him as a model for *L'Absinthe*, and Manet for *L'Artiste*.

160. Georges Charpentier's publishing house the Bibliothèque Charpentier published the work of the naturalist school, including Zola, Daudet, de Maupaussant and Flaubert. Charpentier collected Impressionist paintings, and in 1879 founded a gallery, *La Vie moderne*, which exhibited works by Manet, Renoir, Monet, etc. He also established a journal of the same name.

    Zola's novel *Au bonheur des dames* had been published in 1883.

161. Jean Richepin (1849–1926) was a writer.

162. This was Morisot's first one-person exhibition. At the exhibition she sold *La Jatte de Lait* to Monet for 1,500 francs; *Dans la verandah* to Ernest Chausson for 3,000 francs; *La Vue du Bois de Boulogne* to Denis Cochon for 700 francs; *Les Faneuses* for 600 francs; *Cygnes* to Gallimard for 1,500 francs. She also sold two watercolours, *Baigneuse* for 250 francs and *Homme et femme assis* for 200 francs; and drawings of a *Petite fille près d'un arbre* and *Petite fille assise* for 200 francs and 150 francs respectively.

    (M.-L. Bataille and G. Wildenstein, *Berthe Morisot: catologue des peintures, etc.*, Paris 1961.)

    Mary Cassatt visited the exhibition and in a letter of 17 June 1892 wrote to Pissarro: 'Mme Manet has her pictures on exhibition now at Boussod and Valadon. A very charming collection.' (Quoted in Mathews, p. 229).

    Gustave Geffroy, incorrectly spelled in Rouart's text, (1855–1926) was a novelist and art critic.

163 Federico Zandomeneghi (1841–1917) was born in Venice and came to Paris in 1874. He exhibited at the fourth, fifth, sixth and eighth Impressionist exhibitions.

164. Paul Durand-Ruel's son Charles died on 18 September 1892.

165. Paul Gallimard was the owner of the Théâtre des Variétés. He had a large collection of Renoir's works.

166. Laërtes was a dog that Mallarmé had given Julie. He is the greyhound depicted in many paintings of the period.

167. The Franco-Russian alliance was originally a proposal made in 1891 for joint consultation in the case of a war crisis. The agreement was extended in December 1893 and January 1894 to a formal secret military convention aimed against the triple alliance powers of Germany, Austro-Hungary and Italy. The rapprochment with Russia was widely popular in France.

168. Jean Forain (1852–1931) painted scenes of contemporary life. He was also a newspaper illustrator and watercolourist.
     Paul-Albert Bartholomé (1848–1907) was a realist painter.

169. At *La Libre esthétique*, Morisot showed *Dans la verandah*; *Bergère couchée*; *Tête de jeune fille*; and *Marine*. Morisot had previously shown in Brussels at the Salon des XX in 1887.

170. The violinist Jules B. Ysaië is described by Julie Manet in her diary as 'large, fat, fairly ugly (but very appealing) . . .'

171. Rouart's date, October 16, is incorrect. Morisot returned to Paris on 17 March and the Duret sale was held on 19 March. She bought the Manet portrait *Berthe Morisot au bouquet de violettes* for 5,100 francs. It was at this sale that Mallarmé purchased *Jeune femme en toilette de bal* on behalf of the state.

172. Renoir did execute a portrait of Morisot and Julie Manet which is now in a private collection in Paris. The pastel study is in the Musée de Petit Palais, Paris.

173. Renoir's oldest son Pierre was born on 23 March 1885 and was then aged nine years.

174. Camille Mauclair succeeded Albert Aurier as art critic for *Mercure de France* in 1893. He was hostile to the new tendencies in art, but enthusiastic about Manet's work.

175. Jean Renoir was born on 15 September 1894. He became a prominent film maker, and wrote a biography of his father entitled *Renoir, my Father*, published in 1962.

176. Julie Manet wrote in her diary: 'We enjoyed *Mariage forcé* by Molière above all . . . *La Joie fait peur* was very well acted by Got who played the manservant. I liked *Il le faut jurer de rien* by Alfred de Musset . . . It was Maman who took me

Notes

to the Français for my sixteenth birthday.' (*Journal de Julie Manet*, 1979, p. 51.)

177. Jeanne Baudot was a pupil of Renoir and a friend of Paule Gobillard, Julie Manet and Jeanne Pontillon. She wrote a book entitled *Renoir, ses amis, ses modèles* (1949). In writing of her own decision to become a painter she points to the problems of the choices open to women in the late nineteenth century. Most women who worked, she wrote, earned little and those who did not were raised entirely for the purpose of marriage. She poses the problem of those who did not marry, saying that they either vegetated or entered a convent. For those, like herself, without a religious vocation, there remained no option but to brave public opinion, open doors, and become a 'pariah'. She became aware of Impressionist painting through the collection of Paul Gallimard and decided to become Renoir's pupil. He agreed to criticize her work from time to time, and suggested that she work in the women's studio at the Académie Julian. Baudot, Paule Gobillard, Julie Manet and Jeanne Pontillon copied together in the Louvre.

178. Jeannie was the daughter of Yves Gobillard.

In connection with this last letter, Julie Manet wrote in her diary: 'Oh my dear Maman, she has left me a letter. This letter is precious and she wrote to Jeanne, take care of Julie. Her last word was "Julie". Oh, how she suffered for me. The night of Friday to Saturday was terrible. Maman said that she wanted to last until morning to see me again . . . Oh, what sadness, I have never contemplated being without Maman.'

Years later, Julie recorded Renoir's reaction to her mother's death: 'Renoir was painting alongside Cézanne when he heard of the death of Maman. He closed his paint box and took the train. I have never forgotten the way he came into my room in the rue Wéber and hugged me. I can still see his white cravat with red polka dots.'

Renoir told the dealer Portier: 'We have just lost a dear friend Berthe Morisot. We are taking her to her last resting place. Friends only, Tuesday morning at 10.00.'

Mallarmé sent telegrams to Octave Mirbeau, de Régnier, Degas and others: 'I am the bearer of very sad news. Our poor friend Mme Eugène Manet, Berthe Morisot is dead . . .' (Quoted in Henri Mondor, *La Vie de Mallarmé*, p. 709).

Pissarro wrote to his son Lucien on 6 March 1895: 'Still in Paris because I want to attend the funeral of our old comrade Berthe Morisot . . . You can hardly conceive how surprised we all were and how moved, too, by the disappearance of this distinguished woman, who had such a splendid feminine talent and who brought honour to our impressionist group which is vanishing – like all things. Poor Madame Morisot, the public hardly knows her!' (Quoted in J. Rewald (ed.) *Camille Pissarro; Letters to his son Lucien*, 1980, p. 262.)

FURTHER READING

Catalogue raisonné

M.L. Bataille and G. Wildenstein, *Berthe Morisot: catalogue des peintures, pastels, aquarelles*, Paris 1961.

Monographs

Kathleen Adler and Tamar Garb, *Berthe Morisot*, Oxford, 1987.
Monique Angoulvent, *Berthe Morisot*, Paris 1933.
A. Fourreau, *Berthe Morisot*, Paris 1925.
Jean Dominique Rey, *Berthe Morisot*, Naefels 1982.

Personal Accounts

Stéphane Mallarmé, *Preface to catalogue of 1896 exhibition*, reprinted in *Divagations*, Paris 1897.
Julie Manet, *Diary of Julie Manet,* Paris 1979.
Paul Valéry, 'Tante Berthe', preface to catalogue of 1926 exhibition; and 'Au sujet de Berthe Morisot', preface to catalogue of 1941 exhibition, both translated in Paul Valéry, *Degas Manet Morisot. The Collected Works of Paul Valéry*, volume twelve New York 1960.

Articles

Janine Bailly-Herzberg, 'Les estampes de Berthe Morisot', *Gazette des Beaux-Arts*, May–June 1979.
Rosamond Bernier, 'Dans la lumière impressionniste', *L'Oeil*, May 1959.
Alain Clairet, ' "Le Cerisier" de Mézy', *L'Oeil*, May 1985.
Claude Roger Marx, 'Les femmes peintres et l'impressionnisme: Berthe Morisot', *Gazette des Beaux-Arts*, 1907.

Studies on Impressionism

Charles S. Moffett *et al, The New Painting: Impressionism 1874–1886*, Oxford 1986.
John Rewald, *The History of Impressionism*, New York [1946] 1973.

Contextual Studies

Tamar Garb, *Women Impressionists*, Oxford, 1986.
Griselda Pollock and Rozsika Parker, *Old Mistresses: Women, Art and Ideology*, London and Henley 1981.
Ann Sutherland Harris and Linda Nochlin, *Women Artists 1550–1950*, Los Angeles 1978
Charlotte Yeldham, *Women Artists in Nineteenth Century England and France*, London and New York 1984.

INDEX

Abbema, Louise 4
Académie Julian 213, 233, 236
Adam, Juliette (nee Lamber) 228
Adolphe 32
Amsterdam 144
Apprin 183
Argenteuil 183
L'art dans des deux mondes 179
Astruc, Zacharie 31, 88, 89, 149, 188, 218
Atelier Suisse 214, 223
Auguste, Comte de Villiers de l'Isle-Adam 165, 172, 173, 232
Auray 208
Aurier, Albert 235
Aurevilly, Jules Barbey d' 147, 230

Bartholomé, Paul-Albert 204, 212, 235
Bashkirtseff, Marie 177, 233
Baudelaire, Charles Pierre 31, 218
Baudot, Jeanne 210, 236
Baudoüin, Albert 162, 232
Bayonne 85, 87
Bazille, Frederic 2, 37, 61, 219, 223
Belgium 144, 172
Belle-Isle 146
Belly, Léon 24, 217
Bernhardt, Sarah 215
Berry, Duc de 222
Bertaux, Mme Léon 213
Bertin 214
Beuzeval-Houlgate 20, 21, 25, 116
Biard, Mme 156
Blanc, Charles 39, 219
Blanche, Jacques-Emile 224, 232
Boisbaudran, Horace Lecoq de 214
Bonheur, Rosa 4
Bonheur des Dames 188
Bonnat, Léon 226
Bonnières, de 148
Bordighera 138, 229
Bosc 31
Botticelli, Sandro 164

Boudin 229
Bougival 29, 116, 119–21, 130, 132, 134, 139, 218
Boulanger, General George 163, 166, 232
Bourges 16
Bracquemond, Felix 19, 37, 85, 111, 213, 214, 222, 229, 233
Bracquemond, Marie (*see* Quivoron, Marie)
Breslau, Louise 4
Brittany 205–7
Brussels 205
Buenos Aires 116
Burty, Philippe 126, 223, 228
Busset, Mlle Bourbon 90
Busson, Charles 21, 22, 215

Cadart, Alfred 27, 217
Caen 18
Caillebotte, Gustave 2, 114, 120, 188, 226
Callart 38
Calmette 171
Cambrai 95, 96, 109, 110
Campbell 93
Camus 81, 222
Canat, Sophie 132, 164, 197
Carré, Marguerite 109, 115, 225
Carré, Valentine 51, 52, 219, 225
Carry-Lerouet 210
Carolus-Duran (Charles Auguste Durant) 23, 26, 28, 29, 35, 37, 134, 188, 215
Cassatt, Mary 1, 6, 9, 125–7, 133, 144, 156, 166, 174, 181, 194, 222, 226, 227, 229, 232, 233, 234
Castagnary, Jules 223
La Caze Collection 230
Cazin, Jean-Charles 133, 229
Cézanne, Paul 91, 214, 223, 236
Chabrier, Emmanuel 31
Chambord, Comte de 90, 222
Champfleury (Jules Husson) 81, 221

Index

Chaplin, Charles 219, 227
Charigot, Aline (*later* Renoir) 230
Le Charivari 99, 214
Charpentier, Georges 188, 234
Chartres 200
Chatillon, Zóe Laure de (*neé* Delaune) 26, 29, 217
Chenevard, Paul-Marc-Joseph 39, 219
Cherbourg 74, 75, 82
Chiseret, General 65
Chocarne, Geoffrey-Alphonse 18, 213
Le Chou 20
Cimiez 159
Claire 93
Claretie (Jules Arsene Arnaud) 123, 227
Claudine 109
Claus, Fanny 30, 34, 82, 218
Cluseret, General 221
Cogniet, Léon 222, 230
Collart, Marie 219
Collège Saint-Louis de Gonzague 22
Collona, Duchess Castiglione 21, 97, 115, 117, 214
Les comptes fantastiques d'Haussman 23
Conneau 127
Constant, Benjamin 218
Constantinople 96, 98
Le corbeau 181
Corentin 39
Corot, Jean-Baptiste-Camille 6, 23, 214, 215
Correggio 92, 218
Cour des Comptes 15, 22, 23, 73
Cour-la-Reine 20, 21
Courbet, Gustave 163, 214, 217
Courbevoie 65
Cowes 8, 101, 102, 104, 105
Creuse 168
Croizette, Pauline-Marie-Charlotte 215
Cros, Charles 31, 218
Cuvelier, Joseph 56, 220

Dally 63, 65
Darwin, Charles 90
Daubigny, Charles François 214
Daumier, Honoré 20, 214
Degas, Achille 106, 110, 225
Degas, Edgar 2, 9, 31–3, 36–43, 45, 51, 52, 56, 62, 76, 81, 84, 91, 95, 110, 114, 118, 120, 123, 126, 127, 133, 135, 143, 144, 146, 148–56, 163, 165, 166, 181, 182, 188, 191, 194, 204, 205, 209, 212, 218, 226, 227, 229, 233, 236
De Ganay Collection 110
Dejouy, Jules 149, 156, 181, 196, 205
Delacroix, Eugène 20, 213, 228
Delaroche, Paul 44, 45, 46, 56
Derrida 3
Desboutin, Marcellin 181, 234
Deschamps 106
Detrimont 217
Devoy, Jules 146
Dewhurst, Wynford 1
Donop de Monchy Collection 100, 110
Doré, Gustave 104, 225
Douarnenez 25
Drouot, Hotel 99, 100, 136
Dubourg, Victoria 36, 51, 214, 218, 220
Ducasse 24
Dudley Gallery 109
Duez, Ernest Ange 135, 229
Durand, Charles *see* Carolus-Duran
Durand-Ruel, Paul 89, 93, 106, 120, 123, 147, 152, 153, 165, 179, 180, 186, 205, 223, 225, 226, 229, 230, 233, 234, 235
Duret, Théodore 6, 124, 126, 228
Duret auction 205

Ecole de Beaux-Arts 10, 135, 136, 174, 229
English contemporary taste in art 102
Ephrussi, Charles 127, 228
Exposition universelle 170, 215

Index

Fantin-Latour, Henri-Jean-
Théodore 19, 24, 26, 30, 36, 37–9,
45, 49, 51, 82, 88, 90, 100, 118, 133,
135, 149, 214, 218, 219, 233
Faure, Jean-Baptiste 61, 118, 123,
127, 136, 226
Favre, Jules 220
Fécamp 25, 93
Ferry, Charles 22, 23
Ferry, Jules 22, 23, 27, 29, 72, 140,
215
Figaro 9, 111, 121, 171, 172
Flahaut, Léon 24, 217
Flaubert, Gustave 219
Florence 118
Fontainebleau 182, 203
Forain, Jean Louis 204, 226, 230, 235
Franco-Prussian War 53, 220, 223,
228
Franco-Russian Alliance 204
Free Aesthetics Exhibition 205
Fulmann 121, 125

Gainsborough, Thomas 105, 154
Gallimard, Paul 235
Gambetta, Léon 60, 90, 98, 220
Gare Saint-Lazare 205, 207, 208
Gargenville 195, 196
Garibaldi, Guiseppe 61, 220
Gauguin, Paul 118, 120, 125, 127,
226
Geffroy, Gustave 191, 234
Gennevilliers 100, 108–10
Genoa 118
Gérôme 228, 231
Giverny 138, 146, 147, 152–4, 166,
172, 175, 204
Gleyre 219
Gobelin tapestries 120
Gobillard, Jeannie 213, 225, 236
Gobillard, Paul 213
Gobillard, Paule 213, 236
Gobillard, Yves 16–19, 25, 38, 41, 46,
51, 53, 60, 62, 64, 82, 84, 85, 95, 96,
109, 115, 142, 144, 161, 196, 197,
199, 218, 219, 235

Gonzalès, Emmanuel 228
Gonzalès, Eva 1, 40, 43–5, 49, 51, 81,
84, 94, 115, 131, 132, 219, 220, 222,
228
Gonzalès, Jeanne 228
Goodwood 104
Goupil, Adolphe 152–4, 231
Goya 88, 222
Greenwich 154
Grenoble 97
Guérard, Henri 219, 225, 228
Guichard, Joseph-Benoît 19, 92, 213,
214, 223
Guillaumin, Armand 91, 223, 226,
227
Guillemet, Jean Baptiste Antoine 20,
30, 34, 37, 73, 214

Hals, Frans 144, 230
Hamerton, P.G. 215
Haviland, Charles 229
Haviland, Eva 199, 201
Heymonet 71
Hogarth, William 105
Holland 144
Holliot 94
Honfleur 195, 196, 208
Hoschedé, Alice 158, 161, 232
Hubbard, Gustave-Adolphe 191
Hubbard, Mme 205
Hugo, Victor 218
Hyères 28

Impartial, L' 142
Impressionist exhibitions 91, 100,
110, 111, 114, 115, 116, 118–26, 134,
147, 153, 154, 214, 223, 225
Indépendents 2, 125
Ingres 145
Isle of Wight 8
Italy 117

Jacquemart, Nélie 35, 82, 222
Jersey 146
Joyant, Maurice 174, 191, 194, 233

Index

Kaempfen 171
Kensington 154
Kew 154

Labarre, Mme 125
Laertes 202, 203, 206, 235
Lajeunesse, the brothers 16
Lambert, Isabelle 145
Lamoureux concerts 204
Las Cas Gallery 144
Lecomte, General 220
Leenhoff, Léon Koella 142, 228
Legrand, M. 114
Lépine, Stanislas 37, 218
Léouzon-Leduc, Mme see Riesener,
    Louise
Lerolle, Henry 133, 209, 229
Lewis-Brown, John 151, 156, 157,
    165, 231
Lille, Mme 36
Limoges 18, 200
Limousin 199–201, 203, 204
London 104–6, 154
Lorient 38, 41, 43, 45, 48, 52
Loubens, Mme 26, 36, 76, 217
Louvre 19, 30, 36, 73, 92, 137, 179
Luxembourg Museum 7, 171

MacMahon, Marshall 220, 221
Madame Bovary 44
Madrid 88, 89
Mallarmé, Geneviève 147, 156, 157,
    181, 185, 199, 206, 230
Mallarmé, Stephane 10, 144, 146–56,
    160, 161, 164, 168, 169, 172–81, 184,
    188, 189, 191, 194–6, 201–5, 209,
    210, 229, 230, 232, 234, 235, 236
Manet, Mme Auguste 30, 31, 40,
    131–3, 136, 137, 140
Manet, Clément 100
Manet, Edouard 6, 8, 9, 26, 28, 30,
    33–5, 36, 37, 40–52, 57, 61, 73, 74,
    76, 81, 82, 84, 85, 89, 92, 95, 99, 109,
    111, 117, 126, 130, 131, 132, 134,
    135–7, 138, 141, 147, 149, 170–2,
    179, 205, 214, 217, 224, 226
Manet, Eugène 9, 31, 54, 74, 76, 93,
    97, 98, 100, 101, 107, 172, 173, 189
Manet, Gustave 31, 119, 120, 122,
    133, 137, 140, 141, 227
Manet, Julie (Bibi) 6, 115–17, 118–
    24, 127, 133, 137, 142, 143, 148, 153,
    160, 161, 166, 176, 179, 180, 184,
    194, 196, 197, 202–7, 209, 210, 225,
    227, 230, 235
Manet, Suzanne 31, 81, 89, 131, 204,
    218, 228, 233
Mantz, Paul 217, 225
Marcello see Colonna, Duchess
    Castiglione
Marras 173
Martigues 199, 210
Massé, Maître 196
Mathilde, Princess 228
Mauclair, Camille 235
Maurecourt 89, 92, 100, 106, 109, 184
Mayniel, Marie-Caroline 16
Médécin Malgré Lui 145
Mesnil 184, 194–6
Mézy 173–6, 180–6
Michallon 214
Micromegas 95
Millet, Aimé 21, 55, 120, 215
Millet, Jean-François 226
Mirande 88
Mirbeau, Octave 236
Modernism 1, 3, 4
Moliere 145
Moltke, M. de 57, 220
Monaco 127
Monet, Claude 2, 8, 9, 91, 118, 120,
    124, 133–5, 138, 140, 141, 144–7,
    151, 153, 161, 165–8, 170, 172, 174,
    175, 177, 182, 191, 203, 204, 212,
    214, 222, 223, 226, 229, 232, 233
Monet Collection 110
Monte Carlo 117
Moore, George 6, 7
Moret 203

Morisot, Berthe
biography
birth   16
lessons under Père Chocarne   18
lessons under Guichard   19
family life (1864)   22
working at the Louvre   30
meeting with Edouard Manet   30, 31
separation from Edma   32, 33
health in 1869   34, 35
inability to paint (1869)   38
health in 1870–1   57, 58
reactions to the 1871 war   60
first interest in Eugène Manet   76
courtship and marriage   93, 95, 96
birth of her daughter   115
feelings at Edouard Manet's
    death   131, 132
the fancy dress ball   142, 143
Thursday dinners   146, 149, 172, 173,
    179, 188
illness 1890   179
negotiations to buy chateau   182–5
emotions on husband's death   189
move to smaller Paris flat   197
last illness and death   209, 210

exhibitions
first picture at the 1865 Salon   23, 24
pictures entered at 2nd Impressionist
    exhibition   110
pictures exhibited at 3rd Impressionist
    show   114
exhibition in New York   147
exhibition at Joyant's Gallery   191,
    194

opinions
of war   54
of Manet's portrait of Eva
    Gonzalès   49
of the 1870 Salon   51
of the 1869 Salon   35

miscellaneous
melancholy   67
description of mother and
    grandmother   16

Corot's influence   23

visits
Bougival   130
Brittany   205–7
Brussels   205
Cherbourg   67, 82
Cimiez   159
Gennevilliers   100
Holland and Belgium   144
Isle of Wight   101–5
Italy   117, 118
Jersey   146
London   105–7
Madrid   89
Mézy   173, 180
Normandy   170
Nice   118–30
Pyrenees   19, 20
Saint-Jean-de-Luz   85, 88

works
A la compagne   226
L'Amazone   114
Au Bain   230
Au Bal   110
Au Jardin   116
L'Avenue du bois sous la neige   116
Baby   226
Une baigneuse   232, 234
Le bateau à vapeur   110
Le berceau   92, 229
Bergère couchée   235
Le bermondière (Orne)   216
Bibi et son tonneau   226
Blanche   216, 224
Blanchisseuses   120, 121, 124, 226
*Les blanchisseuses plaine de
    Gennevilliers* (known as *Un pecher
    de blanchisseuses*)   100, 110, 224
Cachecache   92
Chalet au bord de la mer   224
Cerisier   183
Chantier   110
Chasse aux papillons   99
Chaudron   24
Cygnes   234

Index

La dame aux perroquets 126, 127
Dans la verandah 234, 235
La dejeuner sur l'herbe 110
Edma 1869 43
Edma 1864 46, 48
Edma 1871 84
L'enfant dans les blés 224, 225
L'enfant des blés 100
Enfant dans un verandah 231
Enfants 230
Environs de Paris 224
Eté 116
Etude d'enfant 232
Eugène et Bibi 226
Falaise du desert 25
Les faneuses 234
Femme 24
Femme a sa toilette 116
Femme dans un jardin 134
Femme étendant du linge 134, 231
Fleurs 231
Hiver 116
Homme et femme assis 234
Ile de Wight 110
Interieur 224
Interieur de cottage 231
Italienne 26
Jardin à Bougival 230
Jardin 232
La jatte de lait 234
Jeune femme à sa toilette 114
*Jeune femme cousant dans un
    jardin* 226
Jeune femme en toilette de bal 205,
    235
Jeune fille sur l'herbe 230
Jeune fille à l'ombrelle 231
La lac du Bois de Boulogne 116
La lecture (also called *Portrait of Mme
    Morisot et sa fille Mme
    Pontillon*) 216, 223, 224, 232
Le lever 110, 230, 231
Lisiere de bois 224
Marie 121–4, 126
Marine 224, 235
Les papillons 224

Paule Gobillard en robe de bal 231
Paysage à Nice 230
Petite fille pres d'un arbe
    (drawing) 234
Petite fille assise (drawing) 234
Petite servante 230
Plage de Fécamp 110, 224
Plage de Nice 231
Plage des petites dalles 224
Port de Nice 226, 231
Portrait de Mlle L. 230
Portrait de Mille M.T. 223
Portrait of Mille P.G. 230
Portrait of Mme E.P. (pastel) 216
*Portrait of Mme Morisot et sa fille Mme
    Pontillon* (also called *La
    lecture*) 216, 219
*Portrait of Mme Pontillon (jeaune fille a
    sa fenetre)* 216, 219
Portrait of Mme X 231
La Psyche 14
Ros-Bras (Finistière) 216
Roses tremières 230
Souvenir des bords de l'Oise 216
Sur la plage 224
Sur l'herbe 224
La terrasse 114
Tête de jeune fille 114, 225, 235
La toilette 110
La verandah 192
Vieux chemin à Auvers 216
Villa Arnulfi 226
Vue d'Andrésy 226
*Vue de Paris des hauters de
    Trocadéro* 225
Vue de Saint-Denis 226
Vue de Tours 232
La vue de Bois de Boulogne 234
Vue de Solent 110
Vue du petit pont de Lorient 219, 221
Vue prise en aval de pont d'Iéna 216
West Cowes 110

Morisot, Edma (*later* Pontillon) 8, 10,
    16, 19, 20, 21, 23, 24, 25, 26, 28, 31,
    32, 33, 39, 46, 52, 63, 84, 94–6, 97,

Index

128, 131, 132, 134, 136, 139, 154, 159, 164, 179, 204, 212, 213, 220
Morisot, Edme-Tiburce 15, 16, 22, 91
Morisot, Marie-Cornélie 16, 24, 28, 29, 41, 49, 51, 55, 62, 63, 71, 72, 75, 76, 80, 83, 95, 96, 98, 100, 101, 106, 107, 113, 213, 218, 221
Morisot, Tiburce 16–20, 22, 23, 27, 40, 46, 48, 52, 54, 58, 60, 64, 65, 67, 70–4, 81, 84, 96, 97, 101, 109, 117, 127, 128, 131, 134, 213
Morisot, Yves (*later* Gobillard)
Morize 123, 125, 126

Nadar (Gaspard Félix Tournachon) 223
Nadar Gallery 91, 92
Nantes 209
National Gallery, London 105
New York 147
Nice 117–19, 127, 128, 140, 159, 160, 168
Nittis, Guiseppe de 228
Nivard 120, 121, 123
Nochlin, Linda 2
Noirmoutiers 195
Noisy 25
Normandy 20, 200

Odette 127
Ollivier, Emile 144, 149
Oudinot, Achille François 20–22, 24, 25, 37–9, 67, 74, 214

Pagans 222
Pages 151, 181
Paris 18, 20, 34, 35, 61, 62, 63, 66, 71–3, 118, 119, 121, 126, 128, 138, 140, 141, 144, 146, 149, 152–4, 159, 160, 162, 163, 166, 169, 173, 182, 184–6, 192, 195, 197, 200, 202, 209
Pasie 119–121, 124–5
Passy 66, 70, 72, 74, 80–2, 84, 87, 95, 96, 114, 132, 142, 180
Pau, Marie 139, 230

Personnaz Collection 100
Pertuiset, Eugene 118, 226
Petit, Georges 146, 147, 152, 230
Pils 229
Pinguet 208
Pisa 118
Pissarro, Camille 2, 8, 9, 23, 91, 118, 120–2, 124, 127, 152, 179, 214, 215, 217, 223, 226, 229, 231, 232, 233, 236
Poe, Edgar Allen 2, 3, 4
pointillé 231
Pontillon, Adolphe 31, 32, 34, 45, 55, 58, 128, 131, 137, 213
Pontillon, Blanche 213
Pontillon, Edma *see* Morisot, Edma
Pontillon, Gabriel 212
Pontillon, Jeanne 213, 236
Pontillon, Jeannot 139
Pornic 195
Portier 118–21, 126, 226, 236
Portieux 205, 206
Potain 118, 226
Poussin 109
Presbytère, Le 101
Prins, Pierre 218
Proust 171, 172
Proust, Antonin 133, 228
Punch 94
Puvis de Chavnnes, Pierre 9, 31, 33, 35–41, 45, 48–54, 62, 64, 67–70, 76, 80, 83, 85, 89, 90, 100, 108, 113, 114, 133, 135, 141–5, 149, 161, 171, 180, 192, 218, 220, 221, 232

Quimperlé 27, 40
Quivoron, Marie (*later* Bracquemond) 1, 214, 222

Raffaëlli, Jean-François 127, 226, 227, 228
Rafinesque 58
Raphael (Raffaello Sanzio) 22
Ratti, Villa 161, 168
Redon, Odilon 145, 230, 233
Régnault, Alexandre Georges Henri 61, 213

Index

Regnier, Henri de 179, 229, 233, 236
Rembrandt van Rijn 144
Rennes 18
Renoir, Pierre-Auguste 8, 9, 91, 99,
114, 118, 120, 123, 127, 133, 144–54,
160–5, 172, 176, 177, 182, 185, 189–
97, 204–12, 214, 217, 222, 223, 226,
229, 236
Renoir, Jean 184, 235
Renoir, Mme 182, 183, 205
Renoir, Pierre 182, 183, 206, 230, 235
Revue Independente 147, 149
Reynolds, Joshua 154
Rewald, John 1, 2
Rey, Joan Dominique 6
Richelieu, Cardinal 94
Richepin Jean 188, 234
Riesener, Léon 20, 21, 37, 39, 57, 63,
69, 75, 214, 219
Riesener, Louise 24, 43, 219
Riesener, Rosalie 25, 30, 217, 219
Riesener, Mme 135
Rochefort, Henri 70, 221
Rodin 147, 231, 233
Rosbras 27, 29, 39
Rose et Colas 209
Rossignol 196
Rotterdam 144
Rouart, Denis 4, 5, 6, 8, 9, 10, 223
Rouart, Ernest 225, 227, 229
Rouart, Henri 118, 123
Rouart, Julie 229, 231
Rouart, Stanislas-Henri 225, 226, 227
Rubens, Peter Paul 30, 144, 213
Rueil 130
Ryde 102, 105

Saint-Charnas 199
Saint-Germain 64, 66
Saint Jean-de-Luz 85–8
St. Paul's Cathedral, London 105
Saisset, Admiral 65, 221
Salle des Panoramas 119
Salon, the Paris 5, 8, 10, 23, 35, 38,
40, 43, 51, 84, 100, 108, 111, 115,
180, 181, 214, 215, 216, 223, 227

Salon Carré 24
Salon des Femmes 8, 10
Santemarina Collection 116
Sardou, Victorien 127, 228
Sargent, John Singer 134, 229, 233
Schuffenecker, Emile 230
Seurat, Georges 145, 230, 232
Signac, Paul 145, 230
Signoret 204
Sisley, Alfred 8, 91, 99, 118, 120,
123, 124, 133, 145, 203, 223, 226, 229
Société des Amis des Arts 32
Stanley, Dean 105
Stevens, Alfred-Emile-Léopold 23,
31, 33, 36, 38, 39, 43, 56, 84, 87, 108,
135, 215
Stevens, Mme 23, 40

Tante Aurore 209
Tasia, M. de 24
Tate Gallery, London 116
Le Temps 22, 63
Thames 105, 106, 154
Théâtre Français 209
Thiers, Adolphe 54, 63, 71, 90, 98,
220
Thomas, General 220
Thomas, Marie Cornélie *see* Morisot,
Marie Cornélie
Thomas, Octave 23, 97
Tillot 226
Tissot, James 82, 105, 106, 154, 219,
233
Toledo 89
Töpffer, Rodolph 101, 225
Toulmouche, Auguste 219
Touraine 148, 197
Trocadéro 67
Trochu 61, 220
Troyan 217
Turner, Joseph Mallord William 105,
121

Union des Femmes Artistes 10

Vaissières 148, 149

Index

Valadon, Suzanne 6
Valenciennes 16
Valéry, Paul 8, 213, 225
Valvins 156, 160, 168, 169, 176, 180–2, 195, 196, 201–3, 206, 207
Van Gogh, Theo 168, 231, 233
Vassé 172, 197
Valasquez, Diego Rodriguez de Silva 88, 222
Venice 117, 118
La Verité 81
Versailles 64, 69, 70, 72
Veronese 213
Vidal 226
Vignon, Victor 120, 125, 226
Ville d'Avray 19
Vinoy, General 72, 221
Viollet-le-Duc 215
Voltaire 95

Wales, Prince of 94
War and Peace 189
Wassor 222
Whistler, James Abbot McNeill 105, 154, 160, 182, 232
Wilkie 105
Windsor 154
Wolff, Albert 225
Wyzewa, Téodore de 7, 179, 191, 192, 233

Ysaïe, Jules B. 205, 235

Zandomenghi, Frederico 195, 226, 234
Zola, Emile 31, 36, 101, 188, 213, 218, 224, 229, 234